SCANDINAVIA AT THE POLLS

LEARNING RESOURCES CENTER

MONTGOMERY COUNTY COMMUNITY COLLEGE

Cognitio Ad Futurum

1964

BLUE BELL, PENNSYLVANIA

SCANDINAVIA AT THE POLLS

Recent political trends in Denmark, Norway, and Sweden

Edited by Karl H. Cerny

American Enterprise Institute for Public Policy Research
Washington, D.C.

AEI Studies 143

Library of Congress Cataloging in Publication Data
Main entry under title:

Scandinavia at the polls.

(AEI studies ; 143)
"This study is based on a conference which was held
on February 10 and 11, 1975, in Washington, D.C.;
sponsored by AEI in association with the Graduate School
of Georgetown University."
Includes index.
1. Scandinavia—Politics and government—Addresses,
essays, lectures. 2. Scandinavia—Social conditions—
Addresses, essays, lectures. 3. Scandinavia—Economic
conditions—Addresses, essays, lectures. I. Cerny,
Karl H. II. American Enterprise Institute for Public
Policy Research. III. Series: American Enterprise
Institute for Public Policy Research. AEI studies ;
143.
√ JN7042.S26   329'.023'4808   77-1343
ISBN 0-8447-3240-0

Printed in the United States of America

CONTENTS

Preface

PART ONE: PARTIES AND ELECTIONS   1

1   **Recent Trends in Danish Voting Behavior**   *Ole Borre*   3

     Development of the Danish Party System, 1955–75   4
     Social Bases of Danish Voting Behavior   14
     Ideology and Domestic Issues   21
     Foreign Policy: The EEC Issue   27
     Alienation and Involvement   30

2   **Electoral Trends and Foreign Politics in Norway: The 1973 *Storting* Election and the EEC Issue**   39
     Henry Valen and *Willy Martinussen*

     The Upheaval of 1973   39
     Trends in Electoral Behavior   45
     The Issues of the 1973 Election   54
     Some Concluding Remarks   70

3   **Recent Electoral Trends in Sweden**   *Bo Särlvik*   73

     The Electoral Stalemate in 1973   73
     Party Strategies under Minority Government   79
     Uncertainty and Stability in the Party System   81
     The Social Bases of the Parties   90
     The Voters' Views   97
     A Scandinavian Trend?   111
     Postscript: The 1976 Election   115

**PART TWO: SOCIAL DISCONTENT AND
THE MASS MEDIA**   **131**

**4 The Changing Basis of Radical Socialism in
Scandinavia** *Daniel Tarschys*   **133**

   Exit the Old Guard 135
   Enter the New Left 138
   1968 and Beyond 141
   The New Profile of the Scandinavian Left 145
   The Impact of Radical Socialism 148
   The Future of Radical Socialism in Scandinavia 152

**5 On Welfare, Happiness, and Discontent in the
Scandinavian Countries** *Erik Allardt*   **155**

   Patterns of Alienation 156
   Satisfaction and Happiness 161
   Dissatisfaction 162
   Summary and Discussion 174
   Methodological Note 177

**6 The Political Role of Mass Communication in
Scandinavia** *Steen Sauerberg and Niels Thomsen*   **181**

   The Changing Structure of Political Communications
      in Scandinavia 182
   The Danish General Election of 1973 208
   Concluding Remarks 215

**PART THREE: BUSINESS AND LABOR IN THE
WELFARE STATE**   **217**

**7 Economic Development in Denmark, Norway, and
Sweden** *C. G. Uhr*   **219**

   Before the War, 1919–45 220
   The Postwar Decades 223
   The Welfare Impact of Structural Change in the
      Scandinavian Economies 237
   Concluding Comments 247

8 **The Changing Role of Private Enterprise in Sweden** *Göran Ohlin* **249**

Socialization of Income, Not Production   249
Beyond the Welfare State   253
Old Business and New   259
A New Industrial Society?   262

9 **Current Problems of Scandinavian Trade Unionism** *Walter Galenson* **267**

The Setting   267
Wages and Taxes   274
Collective Bargaining   283
Non-Wage Issues   286
Conclusions   295

Contributors **297**

Index **299**

PREFACE

Scandinavia at the Polls: Recent Political Trends in Denmark, Norway, and Sweden is another volume in the AEI series of studies of national elections in selected democratic countries. Volumes have already been published on the two 1974 British parliamentary elections, the 1974 French presidential election, the 1974 Canadian general election, and the 1974 Japanese House of Councillors election. In progress are studies of the 1975 Australian national election, the 1975 British referendum, and the 1976 elections in Italy, the Federal Republic of Germany, and Japan. Also launched are studies of the projected 1977 elections in Spain and Israel.

The present study does not attempt to discuss all of Scandinavia. Parliamentary elections happened to be called in 1973 in Denmark, Norway, and Sweden. Because these three elections occurred in the same year, and because their outcomes shared certain unusual features, they seemed to form a natural group for purposes of analysis. It should also be noted that the approach adopted here is slightly different from that used in earlier AEI election studies. First, this study is based on a conference which was held on February 10 and 11 1975, in Washington, D.C., sponsored by AEI in association with the Graduate School of Georgetown University. These essays are revised versions of papers that were originally presented at the conference. They incorporate suggestions made by conference participants as well as the reactions of the writers to issues raised in the conference discussions.

A second difference between this and earlier AEI election studies is that this one includes more extensive analysis of social and economic developments. The present study does not explicitly describe and analyze the institutional framework of the 1973 Scandinavian elections nor trace the course of the several political party campaigns. Rather, it analyzes the 1973 election outcomes—as well as concomitant socioeconomic developments—with a view to determining whether the political party systems of Denmark, Norway, and Sweden are undergoing significant long-term change. In addition, it examines the extent to which the 1973 election outcomes can be related to the development of the welfare state in the three Scandinavian countries.

The most striking outcome of the 1973 elections in Denmark, Norway, and Sweden was the electoral decline of the Social Democratic parties. For decades—in Sweden, for example, since 1932—these parties had in varying degrees been the dominant parties within their respective political party and governmental systems. Under their leadership, Scandinavian politics had come to be characterized by stability, gradual change, pragmatism, and consensual decision making. Under their leadership, too, the major features of the Scandinavian welfare states were fashioned; some initial steps were taken in the 1930s and much more extensive reforms enacted throughout the post-World War II period. Against this background the electoral outcomes of 1973 suggested a repudiation of Social Democratic leadership. In Denmark the Social Democrats declined from 37.3 percent of the popular vote in the previous 1971 elections to 25.7 percent in 1973, and in Norway from 46.5 percent in 1969 to 35.2 percent in 1973. In Sweden the decline was admittedly more modest—from 45.3 percent in 1970 to 43.6 percent in 1973—but it was unprecedented in that it followed upon a 4.8 percentage-point loss registered in the 1970 elections and thus raised the possibility of a long-term erosion of socialist support among the Swedish electorate.

The 1973 election outcomes were striking in other ways. The world press focused, for example, on the surprising success of new antitax parties in Denmark and Norway. But the far left also improved its position, especially in Norway where a newly organized league of left-wing groups, the Socialist Election Alliance, secured 11.2 percent of the popular vote as compared with a combined total of 4.5 percent for individual left-wing parties in 1969. In all three countries there were significant shifts of electoral support among established nonsocialist parties. In Denmark, the Conservatives dropped from 16.7 percent in 1971 to 9.1 percent in 1973. In Norway and Sweden it was especially the historic Liberal parties that suffered reverses: in Sweden, the People's party declined from 16.2 percent in 1970 to 9.4 percent in 1973; in Norway, the Liberal party (*Venstre*) split and the two factions together polled 6.9 percent of the vote in 1973, a drop from the 9.4 percent won by the old *Venstre* in

1969. Conversely, other established nonsocialist parties significantly strengthened their positions. In Norway, the Christian People's party increased its support from 9.4 percent in 1969 to 12.3 percent in 1973; in Sweden, the Center party (the old Agrarian party under a new name) moved from 19.9 percent in 1970 to 25.1 percent in 1973.

Overall, the 1973 Scandinavian elections were characterized by unusual electoral instability. The extent of electoral shifts ranged from massive in Denmark to moderate in Sweden, but in all three countries the shifts were substantial enough to seriously raise the question of whether the party systems were reaching a turning point and whether the familiar features of Scandinavian politics were undergoing change. Observers were quick to point out the potential significance of the new antitax parties in Denmark and Norway: the high taxes against which so many Danish and Norwegian voters protested were largely a consequence of the generous welfare and social security programs enacted during the post-World War II period. Was the taxpayers' revolt a clue to more wide-ranging political changes attributable to the impact of welfare-state policies? Was electoral instability a consequence of the voters' reassessing their commitment to the goals of the welfare state or becoming aware of new issues and thereby reexamining their political party allegiances?

The three Scandinavian countries provide an excellent context for the comparative examination of these questions. Denmark, Norway, and Sweden have more in common than most advanced industrial democracies. Although there are differences of degree among them, they largely lack serious religious, ethnic, and linguistic divisions. They rank among the countries with the highest standards of living. Their parliamentary monarchies have been remarkably stable and their multiparty systems, dominated by Social Democratic parties, share quite similar features. Through democratic means they have developed welfare systems that are more extensive than that in the United States and compare favorably with those in Western Europe. Clearly, these countries lend themselves especially well to a comparative examination of the relationship between political party changes and developments within their welfare-state systems. With other variables being kept to a minimum, it is possible to focus on the nexus between politics and socioeconomics in a modern industrialized context. And, with due allowance for the unique aspects of every political system, it is possible to draw from the Scandinavian experience lessons useful to other advanced industrial societies.

These considerations guided the selection of topics and the organization of the present study. Eleven Scandinavian and American experts have contributed essays that analyze the significance of the 1973 elections from a variety of perspectives. In Part I, Ole Borre, Henry Valen in collaboration with Willy Martinussen, and Bo Särlvik describe the scope of changes that have taken place in the party systems of Denmark, Norway, and Sweden, respectively. Each seeks to isolate the major variables that help explain the election outcomes. In Part II, the focus shifts from predominantly electoral studies to an examination of selected facets of social discontent and the structure and role of the media. Daniel Tarschys discusses the changing basis and impact of extremist movements to the left of the Social Democrats. Erik Allardt reports on the findings of a 1972 comparative survey of the relationship between welfare, happiness, and discontent in Scandinavian societies. Steen Sauerberg and Niels Thomsen describe both the changing structure of the mass media and their role in a context of unusual electoral instability. Finally, in Part III, the focus moves to the economic context of contemporary Scandinavian society. Carl G. Uhr provides an overview of the scope and structural consequences of recent economic developments. Against this background Göran Ohlin and Walter Galenson review and assess the changing roles of private enterprise and trade unionism respectively.

Amidst the wealth of detail and commentary in the individual essays, some important general findings deserve to be emphasized. First of all, the authors of Part I make it clear that, despite appearances, the stability of the Swedish political party system was not seriously threatened by the 1973 election. In Sweden the more moderate electoral shift did not work to the advantage of the minor parties or spur the creation of new ones. Furthermore, although the Social Democratic party suffered its second consecutive loss of popular votes, the increase of strength for the Center party was in keeping with a familiar pattern of shifting strength among established nonsocialist parties. In Denmark and Norway, on the other hand, the party systems faced a much more serious threat, different in nature and intensity from that in Sweden. New and minor parties gained significant strength in 1973 and the Social Democratic parties suffered unprecedented losses. In Denmark the fragmentation of the party system was severe, and the relationship between significant levels of distrust and alienation among the electorate and significant shifts in voter allegiances to new and smaller parties was clearer than in Norway. This divergence between Denmark at one end of a continuum, Sweden at the other end, and Norway somewhere in between will frequently be noted in the several essays.

A second noteworthy finding confirmed by all of the essays in

Part I is that sociological variables, such as social class, age, and education, have limited utility in explaining the voting changes of the 1973 elections. It may well be that, as Allardt suggests, the middle class—both old and new—constitutes an "unstable and strategic group" in Scandinavian politics. Nevertheless, a more adequate explanation of the 1973 elections is provided by an examination of the specific campaign issues that were perceived to be important by the voters. Some of these issues, such as taxation, social welfare benefits, and regional development, have an obvious relationship with the broader issue of the welfare state and its policies. Yet each of the authors in Part I urges caution in assessing the importance of this connection. For one thing, issues quite unrelated with the welfare state could be much more important. Valen and Martinussen conclude, for example, that the European Economic Community issue was clearly the dominant issue in the Norwegian election. Yet even where issues that could logically be linked to the broader issue of the welfare state had demonstrable importance, voters did not necessarily perceive the logical connection.

Särlvik notes, for example, that the antitax sentiments of Swedish respondents in 1973 went hand in hand with highly favorable reactions to the Social Democrats' achievements in social welfare. Moreover, the same mix of negative and positive judgments was registered in the 1968 election when the Social Democratic party received an absolute majority of the vote. In the case of Denmark, Borre suggests that the apparently more conservative views of Danish respondents on welfare-state issues in 1973 have to be placed in perspective. He demonstrates that significant numbers of Danish respondents—including Social Democratic respondents—have regularly supported conservative positions in test surveys of ideological opinion. Borre's own hypothesis is that in the past the electorate supported the Social Democratic party out of a sense of party identification and trust in the party leadership. In 1973, when the rewards of the welfare state did not seem to match the tax burdens, voters became disillusioned with Social Democratic leaders. They were especially susceptible to the appeals of leaders of new parties who did not appear to be the "class enemies" of the old established nonsocialist parties.

The impact of welfare-state issues on the 1973 Scandinavian election campaigns would appear therefore to have been quite mixed. Nevertheless, a third general finding of the essays in this study is that the continuing development of the Scandinavian welfare systems most definitely points toward changes in the politics of these countries. The nature of these changes is best illustrated in Part III. As Uhr indicates, there are limits to the additional benefits to be derived from continued expansion of welfare programs. At a certain point—and Uhr suggests that the Scandinavian countries have reached that point—the expansion of welfare programs begins to conflict seriously with the achievement of other social and political values. It thereby opens the way for an intensification of political conflict. The combination of inflation, cyclical fluctuation, and high tax rates necessary to support rapidly mounting public sector expenditures for welfare programs triggers a whole series of new, as well as old, forms of conflict between business and labor, between skilled and unskilled labor, between the productive labor force and the unproductive labor force.

As the essays of Ohlin and Galenson demonstrate very effectively, the response of Scandinavian leaders to the problems posed by the expansion of welfare programs has led to significant changes in the structure of economic decision making. Collective bargaining is no longer reserved to business and labor; the state must necessarily be an active partner because of the impact of its inflation, taxation, and subsidy policies. Again, the state has been called on to give legislative effect to the demands of the trade unions for greater industrial and economic democracy. The result is a degree of active state intervention in the details of the economy that heretofore had never been part of the Scandinavian political pattern. This result is all the more important in the light of Tarschys's essay in Part II. He suggests that the New Left's chief role in contemporary Scandinavian society is to influence "the building of the agenda," that is, the social perception of important political problems. In doing this, the New Left has, as Tarschys shows, helped raise the ideological temperature of Scandinavian politics. Will this departure from pragmatism, combined with the much greater degree of active state intervention in the economy, cause an "overloading" of the decision-making structure? Or will Scandinavian political and economic leaders be able to adjust to the new circumstances?

It is questions such as these—and not answers—that emerge from a consideration of the continuing development of the welfare state in the three Scandinavian countries. Their recent history clearly points to political change. But the fourth general finding in these essays is that there is nothing inevitable about the direction and impact of such change on Scandinavian political parties in particular or on the Scandinavian political systems in general. Unquestionably, Scandinavian leaders are being faced with unusual challenges. It is nevertheless they who must adjust and who have to make the policy decisions; there is no necessary logic to the politics of the welfare state. Sauerberg and Thomsen devote a large part of their essay in Part II to noting the correlation between types of recent public policy decisions responding to changes in the structure of the communication media and types of party systems and electoral stability. Equally interesting are some of the conclusions in Allardt's essay. Noting that increases in the standard of living do not necessarily lead to greater satisfaction or dissatisfaction, he suggests that the consequences of the welfare state are not quite as all-encompassing as they have been presented as being by friends and foes. He also demonstrates that an important dimension of expressed dissatisfaction in a welfare state is a function not of underlying social and economic variables but rather of a political variable, namely the political parties to which the electorate is attracted.

On balance the authors of this study are extremely cautious in their assessment of the prospects for far-reaching change in the three Scandinavian political systems. In part they are wary of making predictions based on the outcomes of one or two elections. But more important, they point in different ways to political developments in each society that suggest the potential ability of these systems to adjust effectively to the new challenges of the welfare state without having to undergo far-reaching systemic change. In January 1975, Denmark had a sequel to the parliamentary election of 1973. As Borre carefully notes, the 1975 election, despite many resemblances to the previous election, showed signs of a "recovery"—recovery from the unusual level of distrust and instability witnessed in the 1973 election. Should this recovery continue, Borre suggests that the alarming rise of new and minor parties is likely to be contained. The older and more traditional parties will have the opportunity to regain their dominance.

In September 1976, Sweden had its sequel to the parliamentary election of 1973. The electoral decline of the Social Democrats that began in 1970 and continued in 1973 persisted in 1976—albeit to a lesser degree. This time, however, the Social Democrats were unable to remain in power. For the first time in forty-four years, the established nonsocialist parties, campaigning as a combined opposition bloc against the Social Democrats, gained a parliamentary majority and proceeded to form a coalition cabinet. Unquestionably this outcome marks a significant shift to the right in the Swedish government. The shift has nevertheless not been accompanied by the sharp rise of new or minor parties and the weakening of established parties that occurred in Denmark and Norway in 1973. Just as Sweden lacked these developments in 1973, so too it lacked them in 1976. And it is noteworthy that Särlvik does not anticipate them in the immediate future. In the postscript to his essay on electoral trends in Sweden, Särlvik suggests that the likely consequences of the 1976 election for the Swedish political party system can be reduced to four main alternative scenarios. Whatever the party alignment in each scenario, the party system that Särlvik foresees will be composed of the traditional established parties. At most, moreover, welfare policies will be modified; they will not be reversed.

Developments in Denmark and Sweden since 1973 appear to suggest the potential ability of their political systems to respond, in admittedly uneven fashion, to the challenges of the welfare state. Whether such signs exist in Norway and whether they will increase will be revealed by the forthcoming 1977 Norwegian elections as well as subsequent elections in the three Scandinavian countries.

Karl H. Cerny

PART ONE
PARTIES AND ELECTIONS

1

RECENT TRENDS IN DANISH VOTING BEHAVIOR

Ole Borre

Denmark's image as a society whose citizens were well contented with their welfare state changed almost overnight when the returns of the general election of December 4, 1973, became known. In that election the number of parliamentary parties doubled, leaping from five to ten, with more than one-third of the electorate supporting the insurgent parties. The new antitax Progress party emerged as the second-largest party in the system. Though some observers spoke of a right swing and others of a protest election, it was generally agreed that the welfare politics associated primarily with the Social Democratic party had suffered a dramatic setback, at least temporarily. Hence the election came to signify a backlash against welfare socialism that might have parallels later in other mature industrial societies.

We hope in this paper to trace some of the causes of the 1973 election and of recent voting behavior generally in Denmark, benefiting from survey data that cover the preceding election of September 1971 as well as the recent election of January 1975.[1] The intro-

Editor's Note: The names of the Danish political parties are translated in this volume as follows: *Venstresocialisterne*, Left Socialist party; *Danmarks Kommunistiske Parti*, Communist party; *Socialistisk Folkeparti*, Socialist People's party; *Socialdemokratiet*, Social Democratic party; *Danmarks Retsforbund*, Justice (or Single-Tax) party; *Liberalt Centrum*, Liberal Center party; *Radikale Venstre*, Radical Liberal party; *Centrumdemokraterne*, Center Democratic party; *Kristeligt Folkeparti*, Christian People's party; *Venstre*, Agrarian Liberal party; *Konservative Folkeparti*, Conservative party; *De Uafhaengige*, Independent party; *Fremskridtspartiet*, Progress party.

[1] The analysis presented in this paper is based on surveys directed by members of the Institute of Political Science, University of Århus, the Institute of Social and Political Science, University of Copenhagen, and the Institute of Contemporary History, University of Copenhagen, and financed by the Danish National Science Foundation. The first wave of a panel survey was conducted

3

ductory section sketches the development of the Danish party system since the mid-1950s, without going into a close analysis of related socioeconomic developments. Succeeding sections relate voting behavior for the period 1971–75 to survey information on (1) the social bases of the most important political cleavages, (2) ideology and domestic concerns, (3) foreign policy issues, with particular emphasis on the question of Danish membership in the European Community, and (4) indicators of political involvement and alienation. The relative prominence of these electoral forces varies from one election to another; because they are studied topically here, several breaches in chronology will be encountered, and at some points it may be helpful to refer to the introductory section to avoid confusion.

Development of the Danish Party System, 1955–75

During the second half of the 1950s, the four parties which had dominated Danish politics since the beginning of the century still commanded close to 90 percent of the vote.[2] (See Table 1–1.) In this four-party system, the main adversaries were the Social Democratic party, which based its strength on the working class, and the Agrarian Liberal and Conservative parties, which drew their main support from the farmers and the urban middle class respectively. The fourth party was the Radical Liberal party, which received support from such diverse sources as the smallholders and the urban intelligentsia, and which usually supported the Social Democratic party, thereby tipping the majority to this side at most elections. Of the minor parties, the Justice party (or Single-Tax party) and the Communist party had parliamentary traditions dating from around 1930, but the four-party monopoly on participation in governments was broken only in

in August 1971, just before the 1971 election campaign. The second wave was conducted in October, after the election. Interviews were conducted with the same panel of 1,302 respondents on both occasions; this amounts to 62 percent of the respondents originally selected. The sample is somewhat biased in favor of rural areas and against the suburbs of Copenhagen, but it shows no serious distortion with respect to age, sex, occupation, or partisan distribution. A random subsample of the 1,302 respondents was interviewed in a third wave just after the election in December 1973 and yielded 533 interviews. Finally, some fifty questions were included in a Gallup survey of about 1,200 new respondents conducted just after the election of January 1975.

[2] Two recent studies of long-term political development in Denmark are Erik Damgaard's "Stability and Change in the Danish Party System over Half a Century," and Palle Svensson's "Support for the Danish Social Democratic Party 1924-39, Growth and Response," both in *Scandinavian Political Studies*, vol. 9 (1974), pp. 103-46.

Table 1-1
RESULTS OF DANISH NATIONAL ELECTIONS, 1953–75

	1953	1957	1960	1964	1966	1968	1971	1973	1975
Results by Party (in percentages of votes cast)									
Left Socialist party						2.0	1.6	1.5	2.1
Communist party	4.3	3.1	1.1	1.2	0.8	1.0	1.4	3.6	4.2
Socialist People's party			6.1	5.8	10.9	6.1	9.1	6.0	4.9
Social Democratic party	41.3	39.4	42.1	41.9	38.2	34.2	37.3	25.7	30.0
Subtotal, socialist parties	(45.6)	(42.5)	(49.3)	(48.9)	(49.9)	(43.3)	(49.4)	(36.8)	(41.2)
Justice (Single-Tax) party	3.5	5.3	2.2	1.3	0.7	0.7	1.7	2.9	1.8
Liberal Center party						1.3			
Radical Liberal party	7.8	7.8	5.8	5.3	7.3	15.0	14.4	11.2	7.1
Center Democratic party								7.8	2.2
Christian People's party							2.0	4.0	5.3
Agrarian Liberal party	23.1	25.1	21.1	20.8	19.3	18.6	15.6	12.3	23.3
Conservative party	16.8	16.6	17.9	20.1	18.7	20.4	16.7	9.1	5.5
Independent party	2.7	2.3	3.3	2.5	1.6	0.5			
Progress party								15.9	13.6
Subtotal, nonsocialist parties	(53.9)	(57.1)	(50.3)	(49.9)	(50.1)	(56.5)	(50.4)	(63.2)	(58.8)
Remaining small parties	0.5	0.4		1.2		0.2	0.2		
Total	100.0	100.0	100.0	100.0	100.0	100.0	100.0	100.0	100.0
Voter Turnout (in percentages of electorate)	80.6	83.7	85.8	85.5	88.6	89.3	87.2	89.0	88.2

Source: Danmarks Statistik, *Statistiske Meddelelser: Folketingsvalget den (valgdato)* [Statistical information series: the *Folketing* election of (election date)], Copenhagen, various years.

5

1957–60, when the support of the Justice party was enlisted to ensure a continuation of the Social Democratic-Radical Liberal coalition government.

A more permanent rearrangement of the party system, however, came about in 1960 with the appearance of the Socialist People's party, led by the former leader of the Communist party. The leftist current favoring the Socialist People's party seems to have derived strength from several developments such as the anticipated end of the cold war, rising prosperity, the spread of television, and of course the failure of the Social Democratic and Communist parties to accommodate the new leftist movement. The virtual eradication of the centrist Justice party in the 1960 election and the simultaneous, though short-lived, success of a right-wing party, the Independents, increased the polarization of the party system. The division between the socialist and nonsocialist or "bourgeois" parties became more straightforward as a five-party constellation replaced the four-party system.[3]

Though the Radical Liberals remained in coalition with the Social Democrats in 1960–64 and provided outside support for a Social Democratic minority government in 1964–66, it was evident that this center-left alliance rested on an increasingly delicate voter base. In the spring of 1966 the Socialist People's party made heavy inroads in the municipal elections, profiting in particular from its opposition to an agreement on housing endorsed by the four parties, which entailed considerable rent increases. The general election half a year later showed, however, that the menace on the left flank of the Social Democratic party had become permanent. Even though the dominant issue was a purely administrative income tax reform, on which the Social Democratic leadership found the opposition divided, the Socialist People's party managed to double its voting strength, and the socialist parties for the first time obtained a slim majority in the *Folketing*. Though Denmark in this respect lagged almost a generation behind Sweden and Norway, it is worth noting that in the Danish

---

[3] On postwar legislative behavior, see Mogens N. Pedersen, "Consensus and Conflict in the Danish Folketing 1945-65," *Scandinavian Political Studies*, vol. 2, (1967), pp. 143-66; Mogens N. Pedersen, Erik Damgaard, and P. Nannestad Olsen, "Party Distances in the Danish Folketing 1945-68," *Scandinavian Political Studies*, vol. 6 (1971), pp. 87-106; Erik Damgaard, "The Parliamentary Basis of Danish Governments: The Patterns of Coalition Formation," *Scandinavian Political Studies*, vol. 4 (1969), pp. 30-57; Erik Damgaard, "Party Coalitions in Danish Law-Making 1953-70," *European Journal of Political Research*, vol. 1 (1973), pp. 35-66; and Erik Damgaard and Jerrold G. Rusk, "Cleavage Structures and Representational Linkages: A Longitudinal Analysis of Danish Legislative Behavior," in Ian Budge and Ivor Crewe, eds., *Party Identification and Beyond* (New York: Wiley, 1976), pp. 163-88.

case the left wing was a supporting partner of the Social Democratic party and thus was recognized as a strong factor in government decision making.

After the 1966 election the Radical Liberal party, finding itself robbed of influence over the Social Democratic government, joined the Agrarian Liberal and Conservative forces in opposing what they dubbed the red cabinet. In the course of 1967, a split developed within the Socialist People's party. Its left wing opposed the party's yielding to Social Democratic policies such as the introduction of a value-added tax. Following the British devaluation in November 1967, the Social Democrats wanted to counter the anticipated inflationary development with a proposal to suspend the wage increases that were due in January; to protest this proposal, a splinter group within the Socialist People's party helped vote the government down. This group appeared at the ensuing election in January 1968 under the name of Left Socialists.

The socialist parties took a heavy beating in the 1968 election, and the Radical Liberal party, which had campaigned for a centrist course opposing "extremism," triumphed. Together with the Agrarian Liberals and the Conservatives, the Radical Liberals formed a three-party government, a constellation which naturally tended to vindicate the new two-bloc situation. The bourgeois majority government, however, did not conspicuously alter the expansion of welfare services associated with past Social Democratic dominance. In particular, it was noted that the rise in income taxes continued or even accelerated.

This government remained in office until a few months before the maximum term of four years had expired. The succeeding election campaign was devoid of major issues except for the question of Denmark's entry into the European Community (EEC). On this question the Socialist People's party took a clear negative stand and the Agrarian Liberal party an equally clear positive stand, while the Social Democratic and Radical Liberal parties, in particular, were inclined to defer the debate until the referendum planned for 1972. To a large extent, then, the campaign dealt with the question of who should run the country, a Social Democratic government under Jens Otto Krag or the bourgeois coalition which had been headed by the Radical Liberal Hilmar Baunsgaard. The public's verdict in the 1971 election produced a deadlock in the *Folketing*, and only with the support of candidates from the Faroes and Greenland was Krag able to muster a slight majority.

During the next year no attempt was made to overturn the Social Democratic minority government, probably because of the repercussions this would have had on the EEC debate preceding the referendum on October 2, 1972. The leadership of the four old parties all favored Danish entry into the EEC, but significant minorities in the Radical Liberal party and especially in the Social Democratic party opposed entry. The public was much more divided, and the opposition gained strength until a few weeks before the referendum. In these last weeks, however, the pendulum swung decisively in favor of Danish membership, in spite of Norway's decision not to join on September 24–25. The result of the Danish referendum was 63 to 37 percent in favor, with a voting turnout of 90 percent. Together with England and Eire, Denmark entered the EEC at the beginning of 1973.

The day after the EEC referendum Krag handed over the reins of government and of the Social Democratic party to a former leader of the workingmen's trade union, Anker Jørgensen. The distinction between the socialist and nonsocialist blocs was, if anything, more marked than ever, and new reforms came more clearly into focus, notably "economic democracy" by which funds would gradually be built up to allow employees decisive influence in private firms. A proposal for wage compensation for illness, for even a single day's absence, was carried by Social Democratic and People's Socialist votes. In the early months of 1973, however, attention shifted from these divisive issues toward the more general problems of the rising cost of living and the apparently built-in tendency of the government's budget to increase. The resulting squeeze on the living standards of most households (except those profiting from the guaranteed EEC prices on farm products) led to consumer boycotts.

Two-bloc politics came under fire, especially when the rating of the new Progress party, led by the successful tax lawyer Mogens Glistrup, rapidly rose to 25 percent in the polls. Glistrup had earlier made the headlines when, in a televised discussion with the Conservative minister of finance in the bourgeois three-party government of 1968–71, he had demonstrated the loopholes of the income tax system. Now, as he turned his ideas into a political movement, the scope of his criticism was broadened to include the bureaucracy, the academic class, and the established two-bloc party system. Apparently the public decided that his criticisms were not countered effectively, and during the summer and fall of 1973 a general instability was noted in the polls as people reacted against the established parties.

With the balance between the two sides in the *Folketing* as delicate as it was, the Social Democratic government might fall almost by accident. The election was triggered when Erhard Jacobsen, a prominent Social Democrat known for his opposition to his party's collaboration with the Socialist People's party and, in particular, to the rising taxes on one-family houses, failed to appear in the *Folketing* at a crucial roll call. During the three-week election campaign in November 1973, Jacobsen organized his own party, the Center Democrats, for which the polls forecast a big success. Simultaneously three minor parties increased their support in the polls well above the 2 percent of the vote that is the requirement for representation under the proportional representation system. These were the Communist and the Single-Tax parties, both of which had lost their parliamentary footholds in 1960, and the Christian People's party, a party opposed to secularized politics which had appeared in 1971, but which had not crossed the 2 percent threshold that year.

In terms of net change as well as gross turnover between parties, the 1973 election constitutes a high point in political instability.[4] Our panel data suggest that of those eligible to vote and actually voting in both 1971 and 1973, 40 percent voted for different parties. This figure is composed of 27 percent switching from the "conventional" parties (the four old parties plus the Socialist People's party) to the "unconventional" parties (new or minor parties); 9 percent switching among conventional parties, but within the same bloc (socialist or bourgeois); 3 percent switching from one of these blocs to the other; and 1 percent following other voting patterns.

The new or previously unrepresented nonsocialist parties received almost half their votes from the three older bourgeois parties, but also a substantial proportion from the Social Democratic party and even some from the left-wing parties. These in turn conquered some Social Democratic votes, whereas the exchange of votes between the Social Democratic party and the three older bourgeois parties was negligible.

The election of December 1973 presented the parties with a chaotic and unfamiliar *Folketing* and left them without a recipe for forming majority coalitions. Though both of the conventional party blocs had been damaged by the influx of new parties, it was clear above all that the Social Democrats' effort to extend the welfare state had been thwarted. It was natural that the initiative should shift to the bourgeois side, and, as leader of the old party that had fared best in the election, the Agrarian Liberal Poul Hartling was commissioned to lead the negotiations for a new government. After some negotia-

---

[4] The 1973 election is reviewed in Ole Borre, "Denmark's Protest Election of December 1973," in *Scandinavian Political Studies*, vol. 9 (1974), pp. 197-204.

tions for a broadly based government, he announced his intention of forming an Agrarian Liberal government on the slim base of 12 percent of the votes or seats.

During the 100 days when a new government is customarily free from serious challenge by the opposition, Hartling took the initiative to form ad hoc coalitions to carry through one wave of bills after another. In February 1974 a state subsidy to employers (to prevent extra wage costs' being added to prices) and a compulsory savings act were passed with the assistance of the Social Democrats, the Christian People's party, and the Center Democrats. In May measures to protect the balance of trade were passed in the form of taxes on automobiles and other durable consumer goods, together with some changes in the taxes on fixed property; besides the Agrarian Liberals, the Progress party, Conservatives, Center Democrats, Christian People's party, and on some points the Radical Liberals joined forces to support these measures. In June a package of bills and agreements on future housing policy was passed with the aid of the Social Democrats, the Radical Liberals, the Conservatives, the Center Democrats, and the Christian People's party. In September a reduction of the income tax by 7 billion kroner was passed by a new coalition, which also agreed to curb governmental expenses by the same amount (though its members disagreed somewhat on *which* expenses!); this time the Radical Liberals, the Conservatives, the Center Democrats, the Christian People's party, and the Single-Taxers joined the Agrarian Liberals, but the coalition was saved only by last-minute defections from the Progress party.

This pattern of coalition formation shows that the Center Democrats and the Christian People's party functioned as close allies, and the Conservatives and Radical Liberals as relatively close allies, of the Agrarian Liberals. From the left, the Social Democrats offered occasional support; from the right, the Progress party occasionally joined forces with the coalition group, though its support was less welcome and, during the formation of the May coalition, led to violent protests from the socialists (a number of political strikes followed in the wake of this so-called black compromise). The two parties to the left of the Social Democrats, namely the Socialist People's party and the Communists, were never seriously considered as coalition partners. Of the remaining parties, the Left Socialists (not represented in parliament during this election period) would be expected to align with the left-wing group, while the Single-Taxers (not represented in parliament after the 1975 election) took stands that suggested a highly erratic centrist course.

The agility of Poul Hartling in staging these successive coalitions was undoubtedly a key factor in raising Agrarian Liberal support in the opinion polls from 12 percent to upwards of 20 percent in the course of 1974. In December the Agrarian Liberal government launched a comprehensive plan, including a wage freeze, in order to counter the dramatic increase in unemployment to over 10 percent. The allegedly cool reception of this plan by the *Folketing* was given by Prime Minister Hartling as his reason for announcing the January election. The significance of his party's standing in the polls seemed clear, however, and the prime minister declared that he was hoping for a "handshake" with the voters. The election campaign, alternating with Christmas and New Year broadcasts on television and radio, revolved around the aggravated economic situation and prospective governmental constellations.

The outcome of the 1975 election (see Table 1–1) suggests a tendency to rally around the Social Democratic and the Agrarian Liberal parties, which were seen as the major alternatives for government. Given the political polls of the previous months, the major surprises of the election were, however, the sustained strength of the Progress party, which had suffered from internal conflicts as late as during the selection of candidates for election, and the relatively poor showing of the Communists in the face of widespread unemployment. The voter turnout was, as usual, high, around 88 percent.

The decreasing support for Conservatives, Radical Liberals, and Center Democrats illustrates a characteristic of Danish politics: that the role of supporting party is risky. All three parties vented some bitterness against the prime minister's party during the campaign, and in a close roll call one week after the reassembly of the *Folketing*, Hartling was forced to resign. Successive attempts to form a majority government ran aground, despite the unprecedented appointment of the *Folketing* chairman, Karl Skytte, as "royal investigator" of the possibilities. Specifically, it proved impossible to reconcile Agrarian Liberal and Social Democratic solutions to the economic problems because of (1) Social Democratic demands for rapid measures to increase employment, (2) Agrarian Liberal insistence on stable wages, and (3) the distance between these two parties with regard to the amount by which the government budget would be reduced.

The solution to the government crisis then hinged on which of these parties could form a government—possibly with the inclusion of minor parties—that would not be immediately defeated in the *Folketing*. Poul Hartling's efforts failed when the leader of the Progress party, Mogens Glistrup, refused to accept a government composed of the September coalition parties under Hartling. Finally, five weeks after the election the Social Democratic leader Anker Jørgensen (prime minister in 1972–73) formed a pure Social Democratic minority government that was not opposed by the Radical Liberals and therefore might be expected to survive the reconvention of the *Folketing*.

Because, as we shall see later, the level of political distrust and partisan instability exhibited at the 1973 election probably is unparalleled in the modern histories of Western democracies, no prediction is safe concerning the further development of the Danish party system. Tentatively, however, it can be suggested that a recovery is under way, accompanied by the emergence of a new party structure.

On the ashes of the 1973 debacle, four party blocs seem to be rising: (1) the left wing, (2) the Social Democrats, (3) the center-right group dominated by the Agrarian Liberals, and finally (4) the Progress party. Considering the relative size of these four blocs (see Table 1–1), the power to govern would normally be expected to reside with the center-right group, provided these parties can resist the temptation to compete among themselves for votes. Except for the Agrarian Liberals, however, the parties in this group encounter problems of visibility because of their very similar legislative behavior. It is perhaps significant that the Christian People's party, with its clear stand on moral and religious issues, appears to be the one with the largest capacity for resisting erosion of strength.

A similar struggle for visibility is of course proceeding on the left wing, but with less significant implications for the government power because the net effect is fairly predictable: in the first place, the combined strength of the left wing has proved relatively constant, varying only between 9 and 12 percent in the five elections since 1966; and in the second place, none of the three parties in question can leave their shared niche in the party system to interfere with center politics without being seriously damaged by the other two. The Social Democratic government, sizing up the situation at the opening session in the *Folketing*, declared that its proposals would take into account the fact that a bourgeois majority prevailed.

More generally, the major political problem at the present time appears to be whether the fragile crystallization of the party system into these four groups will be reinforced or whether the party system has entered a longer period of flux. If the latter is true, it is unlikely that any long-range solution to Denmark's economic problems can be implemented for some time.

Table 1–2

MUTUAL EVALUATION OF THE MAJOR DANISH PARTIES AND PARTY GROUPS ON THE "SYMPATHY THERMOMETER," JANUARY 1975

	Mean Evaluation of				
Evaluation by Voters of	Left-wing parties	Social Democratic party	Minor center-right parties	Agrarian Liberal party	Progress party
Left-wing parties (People's Socialist, Communist, Left Socialist)		39°	−29°	−34°	−50°
Social Democratic party	−18°		−6°	−1°	−43°
Minor center–right parties (Radical Liberal, Conservative, Center Democratic, Christian People's)	−66°	12°		58°	−7°
Agrarian Liberal party	−73°	5°	29°		19°
Progress party	−55°	7°	16°	34°	

Note: Respondents were shown a picture of a thermometer ranging from +100° through −100° and were asked to score each party. Parties that they liked very much were to be scored +100° and parties that they disliked strongly, −100°. Parties that they neither liked nor disliked were to be scored 0°. The evaluations given here for groups of parties (left-wing and minor center/right) are simple averages of the evaluations of the separate parties. Evaluations by respondents supporting these groups, however, have been weighted according to the number of respondents voting for each party.
Source: See footnote 1.

A variety of voter sympathies and antagonisms may reinforce or obstruct this development (see Table 1–2). Left-wing voters are on the average quite sympathetic toward the Social Democratic party but antagonistic toward bourgeois parties, in particular the Progress party. Social Democratic voters seem fairly indifferent toward the center-right parties, somewhat antagonistic toward the left-wing, and much more so toward the Progress party. Voters of the four minor center-right parties seem very much attracted to the Agrarian Liberal party and generally prefer the Social Democratic party to the Progress party. Agrarian Liberal voters have the opposite ranking, which is interesting because Agrarian Liberal leadership has been very reluctant to accept the Progress party as a companion in coalitions. Finally,

Progress party voters on the average have positive feelings not only toward the Agrarian Liberal party and the minor center-right parties, but also toward the Social Democratic party (in contrast with the feelings that flow the opposite way), and they are not quite as resentful of the left-wing parties as are voters of other bourgeois parties. Thus, in *making evaluations*, Progress party voters seem to be in a more centrist position than when *being evaluated*. For the overall matrix presented in Table 1–2, however, the order of the party groups from left to right indicated by the table is the most descriptive. If we assign the values 1 through 5 to the five party groups in the order of the table (left wing = 1, . . ., Progress party = 5), the distances between these party groups will vary between 1 and 4. The correlation between the distance and the table entry (N = 20) is then $r = -0.73$. This is a numerically larger correlation than those resulting from other orderings of the party groups, such as an ordering having the Progress party in a more centrist position.

Social Bases of Danish Voting Behavior

In view of the transformation of the Danish party system that has taken place during the period 1971–75, an account of party preferences within distinct sectors of the population at any single point in time can no more convey the overall reality of voting behavior in recent years than a snapshot can capture the course of a saloon brawl. Nevertheless, we shall begin by presenting a "snapshot" of party preferences dating from the first half of 1974 and proceed to give what little evidence we have concerning the long-term development of voting patterns determined by class and other simple indicators of the basic social cleavage.[5]

Table 1–3 combines data from ten surveys made by the AIM polling bureau during the period December 1973–May 1974. The parties have been grouped into five blocs which are similar to those presented in Table 1–2, except that the Justice party has been included in the group of minor center-right parties. Section (1) shows the distribution of party preferences within separate occupational categories. The stronghold of the left-wing parties is the students and other persons outside the occupational categories. The Social Democratic party is overrepresented among pensioners as well as among skilled and unskilled workers. The minor center-right parties are more

[5] A larger study of structural and ideological cleavages is being prepared by Ingemar Glans, Institute of Political Science, University of Århus, under the working title, *Ideological Cleavages in Denmark and Norway* (forthcoming, 1976).

14

Table 1-3
PARTY PREFERENCE BY OCCUPATION, AGE, AND EDUCATIONAL LEVEL, 1974

	Party						
	Left wing	Social Demo-crats	Minor center-right (in percentages)	Agrarian Liberals	Progres-sives	Total	N
(1) Occupational Group							
Self-employed in urban industry	5	10	36	22	27	100	(520)
Self-employed farmers	1	2	24	61	12	100	(298)
Higher-salaried employees	11	15	39	23	12	100	(526)
Lower-salaried employees	14	30	33	12	11	100	(1,020)
Skilled workers	19	42	19	7	13	100	(819)
Unskilled workers	15	55	13	5	12	100	(673)
Pensioners (elderly or disabled)	4	45	27	19	5	100	(1,161)
Students, other unoccupied	42	19	22	12	5	100	(275)
(2) Age Group							
20–24 years	37	18	22	9	14	100	(589)
25–29 years	23	24	27	10	16	100	(640)
30–39 years	12	29	27	19	13	100	(924)
40–49 years	9	35	28	16	12	100	(860)
50–64 years	6	38	27	18	11	100	(1,273)
65 years and over	3	42	27	22	6	100	(963)
(3) Educational Level							
Primary, 7–9 years	9	41	23	16	11	100	(3,407)
Secondary, 9–12 years	14	19	36	16	15	100	(1,266)
Higher, 12+ years	29	13	29	20	9	100	(643)
All Respondents	13	33	27	16	11	100	(5,361)

Source: *Vaelgernes Veje* [The voters' ways] (Copenhagen: Børsen, 1974); computed from several tables in the book.

15

evenly represented across the occupations, but their strongest standing is within the urban middle classes. The Agrarian Liberal party commands a large majority of the farmers and is overrepresented also in the upper sections of the urban middle classes. The Progress party has a strong standing among the self-employed in urban occupations, where it is the largest single party, and a weak standing among pensioners and students, while its strength oscillates around the mean for the rest of the categories; thus, it is the second strongest single party among both skilled and unskilled workers.

Comparing the information in Tables 1–2 and 1–3, section (1), we observe that the occupational categories have aligned themselves with the students on the left wing and the self-employed on the right wing. Between the remaining and numerically much larger categories the cleavages are more shaded, with the lower white-collar category in an intermediate position between the working class and upper middle class categories.

Section (2) shows that generational differences are another vital basis of political cleavage. The variation in left-wing support from the youngest voters to the oldest is especially impressive. At the opposite end of the political spectrum, the Progress party also has a comparatively strong standing among the young, though the age variation of its supporters is far less pronounced. Conversely, Social Democratic support increases consistently with the respondents' age, and the Agrarian Liberal party is markedly stronger among respondents over thirty than among the younger generation. Finally, the minor center-right parties as a group are almost equally supported by all age groups except the youngest, where these parties have a weaker standing. Of the individual parties in this grouping, however, the Radical Liberals and the Center Democrats are somewhat stronger among the younger respondents than among older ones, whereas the reverse is true of the Conservative and Christian People's parties.

Section (3) breaks down the respondents by level of education and shows a considerable variation in the strength of each of the party blocs. Contrary to what has been observed in most other countries, the left wing is definitely much stronger among persons with higher education than it is among those with primary school education only. Of the three left-wing parties, only the Communist party is approximately equally strong at all three levels of education. The Social Democratic party has a weak standing among those with more than primary education. The Progress party and the minor center-right parties receive their strongest support among respondents with secondary education. Again, the individual minor parties differ somewhat: the Radical Liberals fare best among those with higher education, while the Christian People's party falls off slightly as the level of education increases. The Agrarian Liberals, finally, receive slightly more support among those with higher education than among the other two groups. Unfortunately, the data cannot be cross-classified by age and education to disclose to what extent the higher level of education in the younger generation influences the differences observed in section (3).

The differential pattern of partisanship associated, according to these figures, with generational differences and with the spread of secondary and higher education raises some intriguing questions which we can only answer tentatively. During the fifty years between 1920 and 1970, Danish politics gave an impression of stability, both in terms of aggregate voting behavior and in terms of the legislative behavior of the various parties. The most plausible way of accounting for this stability would be to assign great importance to the transmission of partisanship from one generation to the next. Such transmission would undoubtedly be reinforced by the predictability of the behavior of the parties in the legislative process. But the generational transmission of partisanship would be expected to entail a blurring of occupational differences in party support to the extent that social mobility tended to throw children into different occupations from their parents. Since the tendency to vote by occupation, age group, and level of education revealed by Table 1–3 is rather marked, we need to know how much the phenomenon of generational transmission—and the degree of social mobility—have changed during recent decades.

A considerable degree of social mobility can be inferred merely from the change in the aggregate occupational distribution between 1950 and 1970 shown in Table 1–4. The number of farmers has been reduced by half, and the relative number of the self-employed in urban industries has decreased markedly, so that the proportion of voters with profit-seeking occupations has dropped from around 30 percent to around 20 percent over these twenty years. Furthermore, the proportion of blue-collar workers began to decrease around 1960, while the white-collar categories expanded rapidly. These categories, as we saw in Table 1–3, Section (1), divide among the various parties without a particular preference for any one party. Consequently, one would expect the various white-collar categories to contain a high proportion of marginal voters and to furnish the most important battleground for the election campaign.

To what extent are these structural changes accompanied by

Table 1–4

OCCUPATIONAL DISTRIBUTION OF THE INDUSTRIALLY
ACTIVE IN DENMARK, 1950–70

(in percentages)

Occupation	1950	1960	1970
Self-employed farmers	15.8	11.0	7.9
Self-employed in business	13.3	12.6	11.1
Salaried employees	22.6	28.1	36.4
Workers	48.3	48.3	44.6
Total	100.0	100.0	100.0

Source: Danmarks Statistik, *Statistisk Årbog* [Statistical yearbook] *1955*, Table 13; *Statistisk Årbog 1965*, Table 19; and *Statistisk Årbog 1975*, Table 16.

social mobility, a weakening of parental norms of political orientation, and the maintenance or the emergence of occupational, educational, and age standards of partisanship? Unfortunately our data do not reach back into the past, but we have applied to our 1971 data a crude socialist/nonsocialist dichotomy, manual and non-manual occupational categories, and a breakdown of the respondents into three age groups in order to provide at least a tentative, suggestive analysis of these questions.

In Table 1–5, column (1) shows the extent to which respondents employed in manual occupations voted socialist and those employed in non-manual occupations voted nonsocialist and thus can be taken to indicate the extent of class voting among respondents; column (2) indicates, by similar means, the extent of class voting among respondents' fathers; column (3) shows the extent to which respondents and their fathers both voted either socialist or nonsocialist and thus indicates the degree to which political orientation was transmitted from father to son; and column (4) shows the extent to which sons remained in the same occupational category—manual or non-manual— as their fathers, thus giving some indication of the degree to which social mobility between the generations was absent.

The low coefficients in column (4) imply a great degree of generational social mobility in Danish society. This is true not only of the youngest respondents but equally of the middle-aged, whereas the degree of social mobility is slightly lower for those over fifty. Looking at the other columns of Table 1–5, we find the respondent's vote to be somewhat more closely correlated with the respondent's father's vote [column (3)] than with respondent's occupational class [column (1)]

Table 1-5

CORRELATION BETWEEN VOTES AND OCCUPATIONS
OF RESPONDENTS AND THEIR FATHERS,
BY AGE OF RESPONDENT, 1971 NATIONAL ELECTION

Age of Respondent	Correlation (phi) between			
	(1) Respondent's occupation and respondent's vote	(2) Father's occupation and father's vote	(3) Respondent's vote and father's vote	(4) Father's occupation and respondent's occupation
21–29 years	0.33	0.44	0.56	0.23
30–49 years	0.51	0.74	0.54	0.23
50 years or more	0.47	0.51	0.49	0.28

Note: Votes have been classified as either socialist or nonsocialist. Occupations have been classified as either manual or non-manual. They are considered correlated when a socialist vote coresponds with a manual occupation, a nonsocialist vote with a non-manual occupation.

Source: See footnote 1.

within each age group, but especially in the youngest age group. The low tendency toward class voting in the young generation (0.33) is due to the inclination of middle-class youth to vote socialist; working-class youth do not exhibit a complementary inclination to vote for bourgeois parties. In fact, working-class youth vote socialist to the same extent as other age groups in the working classes, namely by 76 percent, while the socialist vote among middle-class youth is as high as 44 percent, compared with roughly 25 percent in older middle-class categories. These tendencies are exactly the opposite of those predicted by the "embourgeoisement" hypothesis.

Looking at class voting coefficients for the parents of our respondents [column (2)], we might hope to trace this process back one generation further. These figures, however, depend on the capacity of our respondents to recall which party their fathers voted for. Thus, in the first place, the female population of the previous generation is excluded; in the second place, fathers with several children are over-represented, while childless males are excluded; and in the third place, approximately one-quarter of the respondents were unable to recall which party their fathers had voted for. This last factor in particular might well have resulted in incorrectly high estimates since it is psychologically plausible that the respondent might have been less able to recall his father's party preference if it had been contrary to his own.

Nonetheless, it can at least be said that the figures in column (3) do not support the hypothesis of a weakening of parent-child transmission. Columns (1) and (2) suggest strongly that class voting reached a peak among the fathers of those who are now in their thirties and forties, that is, in the generations entering the electorate between 1910 and 1930. This was the period of rapid industrialization and of the formation of the party system, during which the Social Democratic party become dominant. Before that period, the cleavage between the middle class and the working class was at least blurred by another cleavage, that which separated the urban population from the agrarian and defined the support bases of the Conservative and the Agrarian Liberal parties.

These data are certainly not conclusive, but they do convey an impression of a secular decline in the extent of class voting from the early years of the party system until the present. It is interesting, however, that this decline is due to the unilateral erosion of bourgeois support within the middle classes. This trend has more than offset the simultaneous expansion of the middle-class occupations, and the net result over the long term up till 1971 has been the strengthening of the socialist parties. In the youngest generation, which entered the electorate after 1960, both of these tendencies have accelerated. The young have shown signs of "bypassing" the Social Democratic party in favor of parties further to the left.

It is tempting to view the 1973 election as a reversal of this trend. Did the middle class finally (as the 1968 election suggested) stand up and be counted in an all-out effort against "creeping socialism"? If this were true we would expect defections from the socialist camp in 1973 to have been especially heavy among middle-class voters. Our panel data from the 1973 election show that among respondents with working-class occupations, the socialist parties suffered a setback of fourteen percentage points (from 74.5 to 60.5 percent), whereas among respondents with middle-class occupations the socialists' support dropped by nine points (from 29.5 to 20.5 percent). Thus the socialist parties obviously suffered a heavy defeat within their own target group as well as in the middle class. Indeed, the correlation between social class and partisanship decreased from 0.44 in 1971 to 0.38 in 1973. The data for 1974 in section (1) of Table 1-3 produce an even lower class-vote correlation: if the first four occupational categories are taken as middle class and the next two as working class, while the remaining categories are discarded in this context, the correlation between social class and socialist-bourgeois party preference is no higher than 0.36. Hence it follows that the 1973 debacle occurred in the middle of a trend toward depolarization of the class struggle, at least so far as our crude indicators are concerned. It seems, therefore, that a simplified class analysis of this sort is inadequate as an explanation of the recent upheavals in Danish voting behavior. Let us turn to a study of issues and ideological orientations for a more comprehensive understanding of the disarray in the party system.

Ideology and Domestic Issues

Voting research has accumulated evidence of a growing trend toward "issue voting" during the 1960s. Though most of the evidence comes from electoral behavior in the United States, some of the factors that are frequently cited as responsible for this trend are common to many industrial societies: the economic upswing, the expansion of higher education, the spread of communications facilities (especially television), and the greater differentiation of international issues which has blurred the dichotomy between democracy and communism. Unfortunately no survey data exist before 1971 by which the extent of issue voting in the Danish electorate might have been assessed. But there can hardly be any doubt that the television coverage of the election campaigns in 1960, 1966, and 1968 made a large proportion of the public aware of issue cleavages among the parties. For the elections of 1971 and 1973, our surveys provide more definite clues as to which issues seemed most important to the electorate. Before the election campaign of 1971, social problems, housing, and general economic conditions were foremost in the public's mind. The election campaign increased the concern about economic conditions and brought the EEC issue forward, while social problems and housing moved somewhat to the background. At the same time, the proportion of survey respondents who regarded some problem as "important" increased from 79 percent before the 1971 election to 88 percent after that election.

During the 1973 campaign economic conditions were again in focus, according to survey data, but this time taxes and public expenses were considered the most pressing issues, along with wages and business incomes. The budgets of the nation, the government, and the household were all at the center of attention. Interest in social problems and housing had decreased further, but there was some dissatisfaction with the quality of politicians and the government.

In its determination of which issues are important, the electorate is naturally influenced greatly by the parties in the course of the campaign. Danish election campaigns, which in recent times have been centered around TV presentations and debates during the last couple of weeks before the election (equal time is allotted to all contestant parties), probably offer the greatest possible opportunity for political leaders to reach the nation. In surveys conducted after the elections of 1971 and 1973, respondents were asked to recollect which issues in particular had been brought up by the major parties. The results confirmed that in 1971 the EEC issue was foremost for the Agrarian Liberal and the Socialist People's parties, whereas general economic problems were associated with the other three major parties. Other issues were in the background including the social and housing issues that had occupied the attention of the public before the campaign got under way. A check of the recollections of these respondents against what was actually said on radio and television during the campaign does not leave much room for the assumption that the data are distorted by selective perception.[6]

During the 1973 election campaign, the two new major contestants, the Progress party and the Center Democrats, each brought up a set of issues that it succeeded in associating with itself in the minds of the great majority of voters. The campaign of the Center Democrats was perceived to be heavily centered around housing, that of the Progress party was perceived by some to be focused on decreasing or even abolishing income taxes, by others on attacking the "old style" politicians of the five established parties.

The issues perceived by the electorate as the key ones are naturally those we expect to have swung votes at the two elections. But the impact even of top-ranking issues can easily be overrated if we do not control for a more general ideological factor. Danish political debate tends to revolve around a set of perennial issues dealing with economic problems and their social implications. In housing, for example, the economic advantages of house owners and apartment dwellers are usually at stake, while considerations of health and quality of life tend to slide into the background, when the major parties struggle for votes. As we shall see in the next section, even the EEC issue, despite its rather obvious implications for national independence and other symbolic values, was widely perceived in pragmatic economic terms. This tendency of single issues to spring

---

[6] Karen Siune and Ole Borre, "Setting the Agenda for a Danish Election," *Journal of Communication*, vol. 25 (1975), pp. 65-73.

from, and to revive, the socioeconomic issue complex makes it necessary to investigate these general orientations first.

Table 1–6 presents eight ideological statements, of which the first four are worded so as to appeal to socialists and the last four to conservatives. The extent of agreement with these statements varies widely according to the respondent's party affiliation, with supporters of the Socialist People's party on one end of the spectrum and either Conservatives or Agrarian Liberals on the other. But with respect to the *level* of agreement, it is interesting to observe that even socialist supporters tend to agree with conservative statements, whereas the reverse is not true. At any rate, the dissident socialists are usually confined to the Socialist People's party on these items, whereas the Social Democratic voters agree to conservative statements almost to the same extent as the sample of the electorate as a whole. Of the three bourgeois parties, the Radical Liberals in most cases take a moderately conservative view, while the Agrarian Liberals and the Conservatives alternate in taking the more conservative viewpoint. The Conservatives appear to be more negative toward socialistic statements, whereas the Agrarian Liberals tend to agree more emphatically with the idea of protecting private property.

The broad acceptance of basic capitalistic institutions such as free competition and private property may come as a surprise to those who think of Denmark as a socialist society. One hypothesis that is tempting in view of the collapse of the old party system in 1973 is that the slight socialist majority in the electorate has been held together mainly by means of party identification and trust in political leadership rather than by socialist beliefs. When the rewards of the welfare state no longer were perceived as keeping pace with the increasing tax burden of average citizens, the pragmatic rank and file of the Social Democratic party became highly vulnerable to attacks from the new parties, whose leaders had not been identified as "class enemies" by the socialists as the leaders of the traditional bourgeois parties had been long since.

We shall look into party identification and political trust later. Here we must dwell on a question which appeared in the 1971 survey. As we noted in the introduction, the 1971 campaign was to a great extent focused on "who should run the country," Krag and his Social Democrats or Baunsgaard and his bourgeois coalition. When asked, "Thinking of your own economic situation, from which of the two governments would you personally benefit the most, or wouldn't there be any difference?" 36 percent of the respondents named the Social Democratic government, and 23 percent named the bourgeois govern-

Table 1-6

AGREEMENT WITH IDEOLOGICAL STATEMENTS, BY PARTY PREFERENCE, 1971

(in percentages of respondents)

Ideological Statement	Party Preference						All Respondents
	Socialist People's	Social Democratic	Radical Liberal	Agrarian Liberal	Conserva- tive		
In politics one ought to strive to give everybody the same opportunities and the same treatment, regardless of his education and occupation.	68	67	39	50	25		55
The government has too little control over private investments.	77	71	48	38	30		57
High incomes should be taxed more heavily than they are today.	83	67	46	37	26		52
One must prevent people from getting rich merely by inheritance.	48	28	21	16	15		24
It is important to preserve free competition.	81	93	98	97	97		93
Highly educated people have a right to high incomes.	40	60	67	65	77		62
The government interferes too much with private property.	57	72	68	82	73		72
Those who save should not be punished by property taxes.	76	82	82	88	84		83

Source: See footnote 1.

ment, while another 36 percent thought there would be no difference and the remaining 5 percent did not know. Thus, on a utility-oriented question, the Social Democratic government clearly had the upper hand. In 1973 this question was not asked because the election campaign made it clear that these governmental alternatives were no longer relevant.

The three-way responses to the above question were entered in a regression analysis of the 1971 vote along with specific issues such as (1) eliminating the tax advantages of one-family house owners, (2) reducing the income tax at the cost of increased indirect taxation, and (3) installing a credit board to control private investments. The utility question alone explained 45 percent of the dichotomous party choice (socialist versus bourgeois), and each of the three issues cited added significantly to the prediction of the vote. Interestingly, socialist voters were more likely than bourgeois voters to advocate an income tax cut financed by indirect taxes, contrary to the ideology of the two partisan sides. Altogether these four variables explained 51 percent of the vote. When occupation (working class or middle class) and the index of conservative ideology (see Table 1–6) were brought into the regression analysis, they contributed only another 5 percent to the variance reduction between them in spite of their strong correlation with the dichotomous voting choice ($r = 0.44$ in each case).

Turning to the 1973 election, the highly salient issue of tax reduction and the curbing of governmental expenses does not relate directly to party switching, according to our data. Rather, as we shall see later, most of our evidence concerning government spending suggests a cross-partisan concern which operated so as to lower the prestige of the old parties. When separating those respondents to whom this issue was highly salient from those who were less concerned with it, we found similar proportions switching toward the new or minor parties. And contrary to much rationalization about the differential interests of socialist and bourgeois sympathizers, the "salient" respondents tended to be more socialist than the "not salient" respondents, though the difference is not large. It is quite possible, of course, that other ways of questioning would have elicited a causal connection between opposition to income taxes and switching to the new parties, in particular the Progress party.

The search for proximate causes of the 1973 socialist versus bourgeois vote, paralleling the regression analysis for 1971, yielded the following domestic issues: (1) economic democracy ($r = 0.27$), separating voters who thought the employers should keep the right to make the important decisions in private firms from voters who argued that a development toward employees' co-ownership was desirable; (2) the control of welfare costs (r = 0.20), on which we pitted those who thought that we should be more on our guard as to who was supported against those who held that social support in almost every case went to people who needed it; and (3) tolerance of deviant behavior (r = 0.14), based on censorship of extreme views on television and the radio and on the policy with respect to "Freetown Christiania," a barracks area in Copenhagen which had been occupied by countercultural groups. The correlation of the socialist vote with respondents' occupational class and with the index of conservative ideology was somewhat lower (r = 0.38 and 0.32, respectively) than in 1971, but the combined explanatory power of the five variables amounted to a variance reduction of 52 percent, or similar to the one found for the 1971 election.

It will emerge from the findings in this section that the question of a "right swing" in 1973 is not easy to answer. In what sense are we to speak of a right swing? In the first place, in relatively broad and abstract ideological terms, such as those of Table 1–6, the electorate did not move to the right in any systematic way. Some of these statements were repeated in the 1973 survey; and while a few, such as the quest for equality (item 1), revealed a slightly more conservative mood in the electorate, others shifted in the opposite direction. A lot more people, for example, thought in 1973 that "High incomes should be taxed more strongly than they are today" (item 3), no doubt alerted by the problem of tax evasion so ingeniously exploited by Glistrup. This brings us to the second point. At the level of specific, concrete issues, a set of new concerns and grievances emerged in 1973 and affected the vote, as witnessed by the two regression analyses just discussed. That the beliefs which the public supported in 1973 were more rightist than the quite different beliefs it supported in 1971 seems to be a largely subjective judgment.

In the third place, voters in all parties generally agreed not only in their desire to cut income taxes, but also in their assessment of the value of specific government expenditures. Presented with a list of thirteen budget items, practically none of the respondents wanted to cut back on old-age pensions, medical care, or the police. Few wanted to curb expenditures on schools, support to large families, or rent support for low-income groups. Instead, the popular targets for reduction were defense, salaries of public employees, support for students in higher education, and road and bridge building, in that order. With little variation, this ranking was chosen by supporters of different parties. The bourgeois-socialist cleavage notwithstanding, those at the far bourgeois end of the party spectrum are not iconoclasts bent on attacking the basic welfare institutions. This, however, still leaves room for disagreement as to how, and by whom, the welfare state is to be managed.

Foreign Policy: The EEC Issue

Denmark's relationship with the European community has been the overriding foreign policy issue in recent Danish history. Foreign policy concerns usually seem to attract much more attention from historians and politicians than from the voting public, but as we have seen, the EEC issue came into the foreground of voter perceptions during the 1971 election campaign, only to vanish again in 1973 after Denmark's membership in the community had become a fact.

Danish policy toward the EEC and the public debate surrounding it have been extensively investigated elsewhere.[7] Here we shall chiefly be concerned with tracing the relationship between party preferences and attitudes toward EEC membership at the level of the individual voter. Since the Danish electorate decided to support entry into the EEC in the period between the elections of 1971 and 1973, our panel survey which spans these two elections gives us an opportunity to study the voters' motivations.

One of the most conspicuous facts about the voters' stand on the EEC issue is its close correlation with the main partisan cleavage between socialist and bourgeois parties and with the left-right ideological cleavage. Even though Social Democratic voters were strongly divided on the issue, and the nonsocialist Justice party opposed membership in the EEC, all published evidence shows voter stands on EEC membership to be strongly correlated with socialist-bourgeois partisanship, often with coefficients exceeding .5. Their correlations with leading indicators of left-right ideological attitudes such as some

---

[7] Peter Hansen, "Die Formulierung der dänischen Europapolitik" [The formulation of Danish European policy], *Oesterreichische Zeitschrift für Aussenpolitik* [Austrian journal for foreign policy], vol. 13 (1973), pp. 1-31; Peter Hansen, "Denmark and European Integration," *Cooperation and Conflict*, vol. 4 (1969), pp. 13-46; Nikolaj Petersen and Jørgen Elklit, "Denmark Enters the European Communities," *Scandinavian Political Studies*, vol. 8 (1973), pp. 193-213; Nikolaj Petersen, "Federalist and Anti-Integrationist Attitudes in the Danish Common Market Referendum," Hans Jørgen Nielsen, "Attitudes Toward EC in Denmark 1971-75," and Henry Valen, Jørgen Elklit, and Ole Tonsgaard, "Economic Conflicts and Orientations Toward Europe in Denmark and Norway," papers presented at the ECPR Joint Sessions of Workshops, London, April 7-12, 1975, as yet unpublished.

of those listed in Table 1–6 approach the same magnitude. Among other foreign policy issues, only the question of Denmark's NATO membership has had similar properties, and this issue has been dormant in recent years. Since attitudes toward NATO membership and attitudes toward EEC membership are closely connected, one can consider the reluctance to participate in larger Western alliances a comparatively well-integrated aspect of socialist thinking.

The maneuvering of the major parties in the course of 1971 demonstrated clearly that the EEC issue was to a large extent being cast in left-right terms. The Conservatives and Agrarian Liberals supported entry wholeheartedly, the Radical Liberals offered lukewarm and cautious support while tending to sweep the issue under the rug, and the Socialist People's party opposed EEC membership vehemently. In May 1971 the Social Democrats, anticipating electoral losses to the Socialist People's party at the approaching election if the EEC issue were to dominate the campaign, requested that EEC membership be decided upon at a referendum some time in 1972, and the bourgeois coalition agreed to this suggestion. During the election campaign in September 1971, the Social Democratic and Radical Liberal parties permitted individual candidates to oppose membership and in a number of constituencies ran candidates who disagreed with one another on this issue. But as we have seen, these attempts to cool down the issue for the time being failed when the People's Socialists and the Agrarian Liberals based a large part of their campaigns on it.

Already before the election campaign in September 1971, supporters and opponents of Danish membership in the EEC differed sharply in their partisan preferences. Among the opponents of membership, 78 percent voted socialist: among the supporters, only 31 percent.[8] To what extent was this difference aggravated during the campaign by the influence of party preferences, and, conversely, to what extent did attitudes toward the EEC issue cause changes in party preference during the campaign?

This question can be answered with some confidence since our survey data record EEC attitudes as well as party preferences for both August and October 1971. By grouping the parties into five categories according to their degree of support for Danish member-

---

[8] The item used in the survey was, "We should under no circumstances join the EEC." The response categories were "Agree completely," "Agree partly," "Neither agree nor disagree," "Disagree partially," and "Disagree completely." The first two categories are here considered as identifying opponents, and the last two, supporters. For source, see footnote 1.

ship in the EEC,[9] one discovers that before the election campaign there was already a fair correlation between the stand of the respondent and that of his party on the EEC ($r = 0.38$ in August 1971). During the election campaign in a number of cases the respondent changed his stand on the EEC to align it with that of his party; this is shown by the significant partial correlation between the stand of the respondent after the election and the stand of his party before the election, controlling for the party's stand before the election ($r = 0.25$). But in very few cases did the respondent switch to a party that took a stand more like his own on the EEC issue; this is shown by the negligible partial correlation between the stand of the respondent before the election campaign and that of his party after the election, controlling for party preference before the campaign ($r = 0.06$).

Thus the election campaign in September 1971 served to mobilize public interest in the EEC issue and caused the voters to form opinions in line with their partisan attachments, with the notable exception that Social Democratic voters continued to stand divided on the question of Danish membership. Revisiting our respondents two years later, we found that the EEC issue was no longer a major controversial topic, even though a large swing could be registered in the direction of more negative attitudes toward EEC membership. Of the respondents who reported their vote at the referendum, 65 percent recalled having voted "Yes," but only 50 percent would now vote "Yes" "if another EEC referendum were held tomorrow." [10]

We have not succeeded in tracing specific partisan changes between 1971 and 1973 to changes in attitudes toward EEC membership, yet indirectly the EEC debate may well have set the stage for the reshuffling of the party system revealed in December 1973. Frustration may have arisen first among the overruled opponents of EEC membership and later, when the expected gains from membership failed to materialize, among EEC supporters as well. The most likely target for protesting voters would in this case seem to have been the political establishment as a whole. Despite the partisan alignment of opinion on EEC membership, the issue was generally recognized by both sides as being somehow bigger than existing partisan cleavages and invited many voters to reconsider, or consider for the first

---

[9] In the following analysis, the five-way responses to the item cited in footnote 8 were correlated with the stand of the party preferred by the respondent. Party preference ranged from strongly supporting parties to opposing parties: (5) Agrarian Liberal party, (4) Conservative party, (3) Radical Liberal and Christian People's parties, (2) Social Democratic party, and (1) Socialist People's, Communist, Left Socialist, and Justice parties. For source, see footnote 1.

[10] See footnote 1.

time, the functioning of the political order. We shall include an investigation of this possibility in the next section.

Alienation and Involvement

In the course of 1972–73 the quality of Danish political leadership became a major issue. Complaints over the lack of control and coordination of government expenses and policies were heard from many quarters of the population. The notion of a confidence gap between politicians and the public was the leitmotif in this debate, which worked to lower the prestige of politicians in general.

The general nature of this issue explains, at least in part, why the conventional bourgeois parties were unable to turn the dissatisfaction with Social Democratic policy to their own advantage in the election of December 1973. A study of the changing pattern of sympathy with the parties in 1971–73 and its attitudinal correlates suggests that the voters, having no credible alternatives within the established party system, were attracted to new or minor parties with widely differing policy proposals. The resulting disarray of the party system can be seen in a model of the "party space," constructed in such a way that intercorrelations between the respondents' sympathies with the different parties are depicted as distances in space between points representing these parties. This party space shows, besides the usual left-right dimension, the existence of a cross-cutting dimension on which the new and minor parties were pitted against the five established parties. This second dimension was clearly related to scorings on an index of political distrust composed of four attitudinal items (see Table 1–9).[11]

Table 1–7 furnishes rather striking evidence on the connection between feelings of distrust in government and the inclination to switch toward the "unconventional" parties in the 1973 election. By accumulating the five-way responses to four items indicating distrust in government, or what is sometimes called political cynicism, we classified respondents into those with high trust and those with low trust in government. Looking separately at party identifiers and non-identifiers, we observe a clear propensity for the distrustful to switch toward the new or minor parties with greater frequency than the trustful. Party identifiers (defined as those usually considering themselves adherents of one party or another) were far less inclined to

---

[11] Jerrold G. Rusk and Ole Borre, "The Changing Party Space in Danish Voter Perceptions, 1971-73," *European Journal of Political Research*, vol. 2 (1974), pp. 329-61.

Table 1–7

PARTY SWITCHING 1971–73, BY DEGREE OF RESPONDENTS'
PARTY IDENTIFICATION AND TRUST IN GOVERNMENT

(in percentages of respondents)

	Voting Behavior, 1971–73			
	Voted for same party	Switched between old parties	Switched to new or minor parties	N
Party Identifiers, 1971				
High trust in government, 1973	84	8	8	(101)
Low trust in government, 1973	74	6	20	(112)
Non-identifiers, 1971				
High trust in government, 1973	48	20	32	(97)
Low trust in government, 1973	39	14	47	(114)

Source: See footnote 1.

switch parties than non-identifiers, although no distinction is made between different types of party switching. Feelings of political distrust, on the other hand, did not lead to switching among the five established parties: judging from the second column of the table, there was, if anything, a tendency among the trustful to be *less* stable than the distrustful within the conventional party system. Incidentally, as we observe from the right-hand column displaying the number of respondents in each category, party identification and political distrust operated independently of one another.

Hence a combination of low trust in government and weak party loyalty was characteristic of voters who supported the insurgent parties in 1973. With respect to the low involvement in politics and low level of political information often associated with unstable voters and with supporters of populist movements, our data again differentiate between the two types of party switchers. Table 1–8 shows the correlations between conventional and unconventional party switching, on the one hand, and various general political attitudes and behavioral indicators on the other hand. The tendency, though not very pronounced, is for the conventional switchers to be low with respect to feelings of personal political efficacy, mass media exposure, and political discussion at the personal level. The unconventional

Table 1–8

CORRELATION BETWEEN INDICATORS OF POLITICAL
INVOLVEMENT AND PARTY SWITCHING, 1971–73

(in correlation coefficients)

Indicator of Political Involvement	Type of Party Switching	
	Between old parties	From old to new parties
1971, Level of		
Party identification	−0.20	−0.18
Trust in government	0.05	−0.11
Political efficacy	−0.17	0.01
Exposure to mass media	−0.11	−0.05
Participation in political discussion	−0.08	0.11
1973, Level of		
Party identification	−0.29	−0.33
Trust in government	0.04	−0.21
Political efficacy	−0.06	0.01
Exposure to mass media	−0.05	0.01
Participation in political discussion	0.00	0.08

Note: Strength of *party identification* was rated from 1 to 4: 4, adheres strongly to one party; 3, adheres to one party, but not strongly; 2, does not adhere to any party, but feels closest to one party; and 1, does not feel closest to any party. *Trust in government,* rated from 4 to 20, was calculated from respondents' five-way ratings of statements 11 to 14 in Table 1-9. *Political efficacy,* rated from 3 to 15, was calculated from respondents' five-way ratings of the following statements: "Sometimes politics is so complicated that a person like me really doesn't know what is going on," "I know so little about politics that I really should not vote," and a third statement, which was different for the two rounds. *Exposure to mass media* was based on responses to the questions, "Did you follow the election campaign on TV, radio, or both?" and "During the campaign did you often, sometimes, or not at all read about politics in the newspapers?" ("often" here counted 1, "sometimes" ½). *Participation in political discussion* was based on responses to items 3 to 5 in Table 1-9. *Switching between old parties* included only respondents who voted Social Democratic, People's Socialist, Radical Liberal, Conservative, or Agrarian Liberal both in 1971 and 1973, and was assigned 0 if they voted for different parties, 1 if they voted for the same party twice. *Switching from old to new parties* was assigned 0 if the respondent voted for one of the above five parties both in 1971 and 1973, 1 if the respondent voted for one of the above five parties in 1971 and for one of the remaining parties in 1973.

party switchers, however, rate about average for most indicators of involvement and as regards political discussion, above average. It is worth noting that the degree of political discussion in the 1971 campaign is a better predictor of subsequent switching to the new or minor parties than is the degree of discussion in 1973.

On the whole, those switching toward the new or minor parties in 1973 did not conform to the accustomed image of the floating voter. Indeed, some of them exhibited the characteristics of demonstrators and protest voters. The movement of aggregate indicators of political involvement, partisan stability, and distrust in government also tends to support the interpretation of the 1973 election as having been above all a protest election from which the polity seems to be recovering slowly at the present time. The development of these indicators for the period 1971–75 is summarized in Table 1–9.

As shown in rows (1) to (6) of Table 1–9, the level of voter involvement as revealed by five indicators was much higher in December 1973 than in either September 1971 or January 1975, even though voter turnout varied only slightly over the three elections (87 percent in 1971, 89 percent in 1973, and 88 percent in 1975). Rows (7) to (10) display three indicators of party stability. The level of party identification dropped markedly from 1971 to 1973 but recovered this drop by half between 1973 and 1975.[12] A parallel development is revealed by the two indicators tapping the decision process [rows (8) and (9)]: by 1975 party choice had become somewhat more stable than it was in December 1973, when it reached its lowest point. The five indicators in rows (11) to (15) all confirm an ominous propensity for political distrust to increase from 1971 to 1973. During the latter period the indications were less consistent, but overall [row (16)] there was a slight decrease in political distrust from 1973 to 1975. The last item [row (15)], an indicator not of distrust but of sympathy for an authoritarian solution to the crisis, was included in this section of Table 1–9 because of its general scope and its fairly high correlation with the distrust index composed of the other four items.

Some of the campaign issues discussed earlier, especially the EEC and the government budget, are so broad that the dissatisfaction they entail may be expected to promote negative attitudes toward the political system as a whole. If so, stands on such issues should be

---

[12] For an assessment of the party identification concept relative to Danish voting behavior, see Ole Borre and Daniel Katz, "Party Identification and Its Motivational Base in a Multiparty System: A Study of the Danish General Election of 1971," *Scandinavian Political Studies*, vol. 8 (1973), pp. 69-111.

Table 1-9

INDICATORS OF POLITICAL INVOLVEMENT, STABILITY OF
PARTY CHOICE, AND DISTRUST IN GOVERNMENT, 1971–75

(in percentages of respondents)

Indicator	Date of Survey		
	Oct. 1971	Dec. 1973	Jan. 1975
Political Involvement			
Percentage of respondents who			
(1) are "very much" or "somewhat" interested in politics	60	73	63
(2) "often" read about politics in the newspapers during the election campaign	46	59	50
(3) discussed politics during the campaign with close family	60	63	63
(4) discussed politics during the campaign with friends	54	68	52
(5) discussed politics during the campaign with colleagues at work	42	48	39
(6) Simple average of rows 1 to 5	(52)	(62)	(53)
Stability of Party Choice			
Percentage of respondents who			
(7) usually consider themselves adherents of one party or another	57	48	52
(8) decided on party before campaign	86	69	78
(9) did not consider voting for another party	78	65	73
(10) Simple average of rows 7 to 9	(74)	(61)	(68)
Distrust in Government			
Percentage of respondents who			
(11) agree that "politicians care too little about what the voters think"	72	78	76
(12) agree that "the politicians are too generous with the taxpayers' money"	80	91	84
(13) disagree that "in general one may trust our political leaders to make the best decisions for the country"	26	38	45
(14) agree that "people who want to get to the top in politics have to give up most of their principles"	57	67	67
(15) agree that "it would be sensible to have a strong man seize power in a situation of economic crisis"	47	56	45
(16) Simple average of rows 11 to 15	(56)	(66)	(63)

Source: See footnote 1.

correlated with either the degree of political distrust or the increase in political distrust.

The political distrust items represent a set of beliefs that are fairly coherent internally as well as relatively stable over time. The correlation between the scale scores of individual voters on these items in 1971 and in 1973 is .50. But the separate distrust items are quite differently related to stands on current issues. The complaint that politicians waste the taxpayers' money, for example, feeds on what Miller has termed the "cynicism of the right." [13] This opinion is correlated with the belief that "too many get social welfare without really needing it." The belief that politicians have to give up their principles in order to get to the top, on the other hand, is associated with the "cynicism of the left," correlated with opposition to NATO and the EEC and with a desire for investment control. The consequence of this pattern of relationships is typically that one finds political distrust to be rising on both sides of an issue, although nourished by different grievances.

The EEC issue is a particularly interesting example since it was plausible that the heated campaign on a question that was recognized by everybody as being somehow bigger than the usual partisan skirmishes might have severe repercussions on the party system at the ensuing election. Before and during the campaign, the opponents of the EEC would be expected to show signs of frustration in their uphill struggle against the establishment. Later when the economic situation deteriorated in the year following Danish entry into the EEC, one might have expected the EEC supporters to react against the politicians in their disappointment.

By and large, our data conform to these expectations. Agreement with the statement that "politicians care too little about the voters' opinions" [row (11) in Table 1–9] in the 1971 survey was somewhat more common among EEC opponents (80 percent) than among EEC supporters (63 percent). From 1971 to 1973, agreement with this statement rose considerably among EEC supporters (to 73 percent) but hardly at all among EEC opponents (81 percent). The average of four distrust items [rows (11) to (14) in Table 1–9] shows an increase of thirteen percentage points for supporters of the EEC as against only eight percentage points among opponents of the EEC from 1971 to 1973, thereby narrowing the lead of the opponents over the supporters with respect to political distrust almost by half. It might be agreed that the largest potential for an increase

13 Arthur H. Miller, "Political Issues and Trust in Government: 1964-1970," *American Political Science Review*, vol. 68 (1974), pp. 951-72.

in political distrust existed among the supporters of the EEC, who started from a lower point. But the fact remains that the rise in political distrust which we observe between 1971 and 1973 occurred to a great extent within the camp of electors supporting Denmark's membership in the EEC.

The link between stands on issues and generalized distrust in government is, however, usually much less clear than the link between distrust in government and preference for the new or minor parties at the 1973 election. This is probably due to a certain tendency of a single distrusting belief to color a voter's entire view of political leadership if other negative opinions about politicians are communicated to him in his primary environment or in the mass media, whatever the specific foundation of these opinions. A reinforcing process of this sort may work much too rapidly to be analyzed adequately by means of interviews within intervals of one or two years.

The sudden emergence of the Progress party in the opinion polls of February–April 1973 is highly significant in this respect. All our evidence points toward a close association between sympathy with the Progress party and indicators of distrust, an association which is found again in our latest survey of January 1975. Here 68 percent of the Progress party voters agreed strongly with the statement, "Politicians generally care too little about what the voters think," compared with 50 percent among other voters; the corresponding figures for the statement, "Politicians are too generous with the taxpayers' money," were 83 percent among Progress party voters and 61 percent among other voters; and on the statement, "In general we may trust our political leaders to make the right decisions for the country," 39 percent of the Progress party voters disagreed strongly as against 20 percent of other voters. Finally, the idea that "It would be sensible to have a strong man seize power in a situation of economic crisis" was strongly endorsed by 47 percent of Progress party supporters, compared with 27 percent of other voters. Thus, the Progress party still represents discontent with the political leadership in addition to representing a right-wing location in the new party system.

It is obvious that we are not in a position—even after the 1975 election—to predict what will happen to the Danish party system in the years ahead. The fact that the shifting in votes at the 1973 election was disproportionately larger than the drop in the level of party identification would warrant suggests that much of the preference for the insurgent parties was viewed by their supporters as short-term and tentative. The fact that the second dimension appearing in the voter perceptions of 1973 was not founded on any conspicuous social cleavage line, such as religious, cultural, or regional identity, made it plausible to believe that the basic ideological left-right cleavage would regain its dominance; the working order which the parties gradually have established since then, and which seems largely to coincide with voter perceptions, raises the expectation that partisan stability will increase in the future. Much, however, depends on the politicians' capacity for controlling economic development and, in particular, the state budget. The political trust of the Danish electorate has recovered slightly during the last year, but it is still alarmingly low, thereby giving encouragement to a party which, while it does not compare with parties of the authoritarian right from a previous epoch, certainly is outside the tradition of Danish politics.

2

ELECTORAL TRENDS AND FOREIGN POLITICS IN NORWAY: The 1973 *Storting* Election and the EEC Issue

Henry Valen
Willy Martinussen

Denmark, Norway, and Sweden all experienced dramatic elections in the autumn of 1973. In all three countries the extreme left gained ground at the expense of the moderate socialists, and in Denmark a situation of great instability ensued. In Sweden and Norway the moderate socialists maintained enough strength to form viable minority governments. But, while in Sweden the traditional Scandinavian two-plus-three party system—a socialist and a Communist party on the left and three "bourgeois" parties on the right—survived, in Norway the tendency toward fragmentation that had been discernible in the party structure since the early 1960s increased.

The Upheaval of 1973

The Labor party had dominated Norwegian politics since the Second World War. At the *Storting* election of September 1973 it received a severe blow. Labor, which had polled 46.5 percent of the vote in 1969, dropped to 35.2 percent in 1973. The splits on the left deepened, meanwhile, and new parties divided the right. Electoral changes of this magnitude had not occurred in Norway since around 1930. In

Editor's Note: The names of the Norwegian political parties have been translated in this volume as follows: *Arbeidernes Kommunistparti*, Marxist-Leninist party; *Norges Kommunistiske Parti*, Communist party; *Sosialistisk Folkeparti*, Socialist People's party; *Sosialistisk Valgallianse*, Socialist Election Alliance; *Arbeiderpartiet*, Labor party; *Venstre*, Liberal party; *Det Nye Folkepartiet*, New People's party; *Kristelig Folkeparti*, Christian People's party; *Senterpartiet*, Center (Agrarian) party; *Høyre*, Conservative party; *Anders Langes Parti*, Anders Lange's party.

1973 they revealed major changes that had been taking place in Norwegian politics.[1]

The long period of Labor dominance was first broken at the election of 1961, and two rounds of controversy over the question of Norway's entry into the European Common Market (EEC) deepened the split on the left. The issue was brought to a climax in the referendum in September 1972, in which membership in the EEC was rejected by 53 percent of the voters.[2]

The EEC dispute continued to dominate Norwegian politics after the referendum. The minority Labor government resigned and a "mini" coalition of "No" parties took over. During the period between the EEC referendum and the September 1973 election, several changes occurred in the party system. On the left wing there was a merger as well as a split. The "No" front of the Labor party split off and formed a group of its own, the Workers' Information Committee, which then moved into a loose merger with the Communists and the Socialist People's party, known as the Socialist Election Alliance. In the center of the party system, the most spectacular development was the split of the old *Venstre*, the Liberal party. During the EEC dispute the Liberals had been severely divided on the parliamentary level. (Nine Liberal members voted "Yes," four voted "No".) Shortly after the referendum, the "Yes" faction broke away and formed the New People's party. The greatest surprise, however, came from the right wing of the political spectrum. The defeat of the European cause had triggered widespread resentment within the Conservative party, and a high proportion of the voters on the right had been frustrated by the failure of the nonsocialist government of 1965–71 to bring about reductions in the level of taxation. This made it possible for Anders Lange, an old conservative who had been an active leader in the antiparty Patriot League of the 1930s, to rally support for a party of his own, the Anders Lange's party, whose platform involved opposition to taxes and to public expenditure. Politicians at first tended to treat the new party as a joke, but on election day in 1973 it polled a surprising number of votes.

The emergence of antitax parties in Denmark and Norway, the great electoral changes, and the defeat of the moderate socialist parties might well suggest that the elections of 1973 signaled a major shift in public opinion concerning the policies of the Scan-

---

[1] For a more detailed account of the 1973 election, see H. Valen and S. Rokkan, "Norway: The Election to the *Storting* in September 1973," *Scandinavian Political Studies*, vol. 9 (1974), pp. 205-18.

[2] See H. Valen, "Norway: 'No' to EEC," *Scandinavian Political Studies*, vol. 8 (1973), pp. 214-26.

dinavian welfare states. Economic planning and the development of social welfare programs have been keystones in the platforms of the moderate socialists, who have held a dominant position in all Scandinavian countries in recent decades. Of course, many of these policies have been accepted in principle if not always in detail by other parties as well. Nevertheless, in the area of economic policies the moderate socialists in Norway have had to compete with two blocs of parties: (1) the parties to the left—Communists and the Socialist People's party (in 1973 the Socialist Election Alliance), and (2) the bourgeois or nonsocialist parties—Conservatives, Liberals, the Christian People's party, and the Center party (Agrarians). The left-socialist parties demand stronger measures than Labor in terms of economic planning and state ownership. Although the nonsocialist parties present separate platforms, they have more in common with each other than with Labor. Thus, Labor is more in favor of state control and less in favor of private initiative than the nonsocialists. The hypothesis that the election results of 1973 reflected growing distrust of the welfare society certainly deserves to be investigated. And for this purpose the Norwegian parties will be grouped into three major categories in the subsequent analysis: left-socialists, Labor, and nonsocialists. However, it is our contention that the major factors influencing the 1973 election outcome emerged from the special circumstances of that election, particularly the EEC dispute.

As Table 2–1 indicates, the election of 1973 contrasted sharply with previous elections in postwar Norway. During the period 1945–61, the distribution of the vote was remarkably stable from one election to another. Increased volatility was evident at the elections of 1965 and 1969, yet no party suffered a loss or gain of more than 3.7 percentage points at either election. The changes that occurred in 1973 were different both in character and magnitude. Briefly, the election of 1973 had the following results:

(1) The Labor party suffered a severe setback.

(2) The left-wing Socialist Election Alliance obtained 11 percent of the total vote, an increase of about seven percentage points for the participating parties over their showing in 1969.[3]

(3) The socialist parties, which had consistently won a majority of the votes throughout the postwar period, declined to 47 per-

---

[3] In March 1975 the Socialist Election Alliance was transformed into the Socialist Left party (*Socialistisk Venstreparti*). The constituent parties have not been dissolved, however, and it remains to be seen whether there can be unity among the rather disparate members of this organization.

Table 2–1

RESULTS OF NORWEGIAN NATIONAL ELECTIONS, 1945–73

	1945	1949	1953	1957	1961	1965	1969	1973
Results by Party (in percentages of votes cast)[a]								
Marxist-Leninist party[b]								.4
Communist party	11.9	5.8	5.1	3.4	2.9	1.4	1.0	
Socialist People's party					2.4	6.0	3.5	
Socialist Election Alliance[b]								11.2
Labor party	41.0	45.7	46.7	48.3	46.8	43.1	46.5	35.3
Subtotal, socialist parties	52.9	51.5	51.8	51.7	52.1	50.5	51.0	46.9
Liberal party	13.8	13.4	10.0	9.7	8.9	10.4	9.4	
Liberal party[b]								3.5
New People's party[b]								3.4
Christian People's party	7.9	8.4	10.5	10.2	9.6	8.1	9.4	12.3
Center (Agrarian) party[c]	8.1	8.1	9.0	9.3	9.3	9.9	10.5	11.0
Conservative	17.0	17.7	18.8	18.9	20.0	21.1	19.6	17.4
Anders Lange's party[b]								5.0
Other	.3	.7	d	.2	.1	d	d	.5
Subtotal, nonsocialist parties	47.1	48.3	48.3	48.3	47.9	49.5	48.9	53.1
Total	100.0	100.0	100.0	100.0	100.0	100.0	100.0	100.0
Voter Turnout (in percentages of the electorate)	76.4	82.0	79.3	78.3	79.1	85.4	83.8	80.2

a All votes for joint lists have been distributed among the parties in proportion to earlier results on separate lists.
b New in 1973.
c The name of this party changed from Agrarian to Center in 1959.
d Less than .05 percent.
Source: Public Electoral Statistics, published by Central Bureau of Statistics of Norway, Oslo.

Table 2–2
TRANSITION MATRIX OF VOTES FOR MAJOR PARTY GROUPINGS, 1969–73
(in percentages of respondents)

	1973			
1969	Left-socialist	Labor	Non-socialist	Total, 1969
Left-socialist	2.8	.2	.3	3.3
Labor	6.2	*38.0*	4.0	48.2
Nonsocialist	.8	2.1	*45.6*	48.5
Total, 1973	9.8	40.3	49.9	100.0
				(N=973)

Source: See footnote 4.

cent. In parliament, however, Labor and the left-wing Socialist Election Alliance jointly obtained 78 out of 155 seats. Labor subsequently formed a minority government.

(4) Among the nonsocialist parties, both the Liberals (that is, the Liberals and the New People's party jointly) and the Conservatives declined by more than two percentage points, while the Agrarian Center and particularly the Christian People's party increased their shares of the vote.

(5) The Lange antitax party obtained 5 percent of the vote and four seats in the new *Storting*.

A transition matrix for changes of votes between 1969 and 1973 is presented in Table 2–2.[4] The italicized figures along the diagonal indicate stability of choice between the 1969 and 1973 elections.[5] Altogether, 86.4 percent of the sample supported the

[4] Our data are largely drawn from a panel study based upon a nationwide probability sample which was interviewed at three successive elections: 1965, 1969, and 1973. This material is supplemented by data from a nationwide voter survey in 1957. All of these surveys are parts of a larger program of electoral research undertaken jointly by the Institute for Social Research in Oslo and the University of Bergen. On this program see H. Valen and S. Rokkan, "The Norwegian Program of Electoral Research," *Scandinavian Political Studies*, vol. 2 (1967), pp. 296-305; H. Valen and W. Martinussen, *Velgere og politiske frontlinjer* [Voters and political frontlines] (Oslo: Gyldendal, 1972).

[5] In this study we will focus largely upon shifts in the active electorate, that is, people who indicated a preference for some specific party at both elections. It

same major party group in 1969 and in 1973. The figures that are not italicized indicate shifts in party preference. Thus, .2 percent of the sample shifted from left-socialist to Labor and 6.2 percent from Labor to left-socialist.

Most of the shifts occurred between the left-socialists and Labor or between Labor and some nonsocialist party. Very few votes moved back and forth between the two extreme groups, although a few more did so in 1973 than at previous elections. Six percent of our respondents shifted from Labor to the Socialist Election Alliance, but almost none moved in the other direction. The shifts between Labor and the bourgeois parties were more evenly balanced, but Labor still suffered a net loss to the nonsocialists of approximately two percentage points.[6]

In order to analyze the nature and significance of the changes revealed by the 1973 election, this paper will focus upon two major questions: (1) To what extent do *recent changes* fit in with more *long-term trends* in the electorate? Since the end of the nineteenth century, Norway has changed from an agricultural to a highly industrialized economy, and economic development has accelerated since World War II. Trends in electoral behavior will be explored for the period 1957–73 to determine the relationship between Norway's far-reaching socioeconomic transformation and the electoral changes of 1973. (2) To what extent and in what ways do recent electoral changes relate to the specific issues and circumstances of the 1973 election? In this connection it will be essential to study Norwegian attitudes toward the European Economic Community, the issue that dominated Norwegian politics during most of the interval between the elections of 1969 and 1973.[7]

---

should be noted, however, that nonvoting has definitely contributed to the results. Thus the Labor party, the Agrarian Center party, and to a lesser extent the Conservative party lost support owing to the fact that a number of their former voters abstained in 1973. Conversely, Anders Lange's party and the Christian People's party drew disproportionate strength from groups who had not voted in 1969.

[6] The proportion of the electorate who shifted parties in 1973 was very high as compared with other years. After the election this tendency to greater volatility in the electorate has been demonstrated again and again by opinion polls. Of course, this phenomenon is not exclusive to Norway. Professor Borre discusses the same phenomenon in his chapter on "Recent Trends in Danish Voting Behavior" in this volume. Although the topic is unquestionably important, this paper will not attempt to examine the phenomenon of volatility or the relationship between volatility and increasing alienation from the politics and political institutions of modern Norwegian society.

[7] See Valen and Rokkan, "The Election to the *Storting*," and Valen, "Norway: 'No'."

Table 2-3

SHIFTS IN VOTING FOR MAJOR PARTY GROUPINGS,
1969–73, BY OCCUPATION

(in percentages of respondents)

1969	1973				
	Left-socialist	Labor	Non-socialist	Total	N
Manual workers					
Left-socialist	73	9	18	100	(22)
Labor	12	80	8	100	(316)
Nonsocialist	5	5	90	100	(129)
Salaried employees, professionals, and self-employed					
Left-socialist					(12)[a]
Labor	16	72	12	100	(145)
Nonsocialist	7	5	88	100	(247)
Farmers, fishermen					
Left-socialist					(1)[a]
Labor	0	70	30	100	(23)
Nonsocialist	1	1	98	100	(28)

[a] Too few cases for computation of percentages.
Source: See footnote 4.

Trends in Electoral Behavior

Since this analysis of the relationship between long-term socio-economic changes and electoral change has to be limited, we shall only consider three background variables: occupation, education, and age. Several previous analyses have demonstrated that these variables are indeed crucial for explaining political behavior as well as political change in Norway.[8] First we will focus on the period 1969–73; thereafter we will turn to the longer period, 1957–73.

Electoral Changes from 1969 to 1973. Table 2–3 shows the shifts in voting between 1969 and 1973 for three occupational categories.

[8] See, for example, H. Valen and S. Rokkan, "Norway: Conflict Structure and Mass Politics in a European Periphery," in R. Rose, ed., *Electoral Behavior* (New York: The Free Press, 1974), pp. 315-70; Valen and Martinussen, *Velgere og politiske*, pp. 231-360; and W. Martinussen, *The Distant Democracy* (London: John Wiley & Sons, forthcoming in 1977).

It indicates that the Labor party most successfully maintained its support among manual workers. Only two out of ten workers who voted Labor in 1969 switched to some other party in 1973, while the corresponding figure for farmers and fishermen and for middle-class groups was three out of ten. Furthermore, Labor gained more votes among workers than among other occupational groups. As for the direction of change away from Labor, it was rather similar for manual workers and people in middle-class occupations: in both categories a majority of the defectors moved to the left. Among farmers and fishermen, on the other hand, all defectors from Labor moved to bourgeois parties. (Specifically, they moved to the Christian People's party and the Agrarian Center party in the ratio of two to one.)

Practically all of the farmers and fishermen who voted for some nonsocialist party in 1969 remained loyal to this group of parties in 1973. Nine out of ten of the respondents in the other occupational groups who voted nonsocialist also indicated stability, and the few defectors split about evenly between Labor and the Socialist Election Alliance. A further inspection of the data indicates that several shifts occurred among the bourgeois parties, largely to the benefit of the Christian People's party. This party gained most of its new votes among farmers and fishermen: its share of their votes increased by nine percentage points as compared to two and three percentage points gained from workers and the middle class respectively.

Table 2–4 breaks down the shifts in voting between 1969 and 1973 according to level of education. It shows that the stability of choice of respondents who voted nonsocialist in 1969 was high and practically identical for all educational levels. Among respondents who supported Labor in 1969, a rather strong and regular tendency is revealed by the table: the higher the education, the more likely former Labor voters were to shift allegiance. The proportion of defectors from Labor to the Socialist Election Alliance increases strongly with increasing education. A similar tendency is evident for defections from Labor to the right, but in this case the differences according to level of education are so tiny that they are hardly significant statistically. The fact that the Labor party maintained its position best among people with low education is consistent with the tendency for manual workers to be relatively loyal to their party.

The broad occupational categories applied in Table 2–3 are likely to conceal substantial variations in level of education within each category, and we may ask: how do defections from Labor relate to education within specific occupations? Our data permit us to conclude that among both manual workers and people in middle-

46

Table 2–4

SHIFTS IN VOTING FOR MAJOR PARTY GROUPINGS, 1969–73, BY LEVEL OF EDUCATION

(in percentages of respondents)

	1973				
1969	Left-socialist	Labor	Non-socialist	**Total**	**N**
Elementary education					
Left-socialist					(10)ᵃ
Labor	9	82	9	100	(241)
Nonsocialist	2	4	94	100	(115)
Secondary education					
Left-socialist	75	12	13	100	(16)
Labor	16	74	10	100	(205)
Nonsocialist	2	4	94	100	(245)
Higher education					
Left-socialist					(7)ᵃ
Labor	19	68	13	100	(31)
Nonsocialist	1	3	96	100	(128)

ᵃ Too few cases for computation of percentages.

Note: Education has been classified as "elementary" (less than seven and one-half years of schooling), "secondary" (elementary education plus up to three and one-half years), or "higher."

Source: See footnote 4.

class occupations there is a clear tendency for defections from Labor to increase with increasing education. For people with only elementary education, the proportion of loyal Laborites is approximately the same in both groups, but otherwise the patterns differ. Manual workers with some further education are more likely than corresponding middle-class groups to remain Laborites. Furthermore, the patterns of defections are different for the different occupational classes. Among manual workers, defections both to the left and to the right increase with increasing education. Among the middle class the proportion moving to the right is approximately the same for all educational levels, but the proportion shifting from Labor to the Socialist Election Alliance is positively correlated with education: the percentage increases steadily as the level of education rises.

Since the level of education in Norway has risen greatly in recent years, and since people in the younger age brackets tend to be more highly educated than older ones, we may ask to what extent the observed relationship between education and electoral changes is due to age differences among voters. After all, the younger people are, the more likely they are to shift party. This tendency, which is evident for voters of both Labor and nonsocialist parties, is consistent with a general finding in electoral research: as people get older they tend to develop longstanding party loyalties that remain unaffected by shifting electoral winds.[9] As for the direction of party change among different age groups, our data indicate that young and middle-aged Laborites tended to move to the Socialist Election Alliance, while older ones were more inclined to prefer some bourgeois party. Defectors from bourgeois parties in the youngest age bracket were almost equally attracted by the Socialist Election Alliance and by Labor, while older ones largely went to Labor.

Given this relationship between age and voting, we may return to the question of how age interacts with education in determining electoral changes. Table 2–5 indicates that for the Labor party both age and education were related to changes in electoral support between 1969 and 1973. For the bourgeois parties education had practically no impact, although the behavior of respondents in the youngest age bracket differed somewhat from that of older ones. The raw figures in the right-hand column of the table illustrate the growth of education in recent decades. Because of the requirement of nine years of compulsory schooling introduced around 1965, the youngest age bracket contains a negligible number of respondents with only elementary education. Thus, only the two older age brackets are useful for evaluating the significance of education. In considering the impact of age we shall have to compare figures for the different age brackets separately for people with low and high education.

The main tendencies indicated in Table 2–5 can be summarized as follows:

> (1) For people over fifty, education seems to have no impact upon electoral changes. The patterns of change are almost identical for respondents with low and high education, and this tendency is consistent for both Labor and bourgeois voters.
>
> (2) For people under fifty, education did contribute to electoral changes. For respondents under fifty who voted Labor in 1969,

---

[9] See D. Butler and D. E. Stokes, *Political Change in Britain* (London: Macmillan, 1969), pp. 44-64; and Valen and Martinussen, *Velgere og politiske*, pp. 296-98. For the impact and development of party identification, see particularly A. Campbell, P. E. Converse, D. E. Stokes, W. E. Miller, *The American Voter*, abridged edition (New York: Wiley, 1964), pp. 67-96.

Table 2–5

SHIFTS IN VOTING FOR MAJOR PARTY GROUPINGS,
1969–73, BY AGE AND EDUCATION
(in percentages of respondents)

1969 Party, Age, and Education	1973			Total	N
	Left-socialist	Labor	Non-socialist		
Labor					
24–30					
Low					(6) a
High	21	65	14	100	(71)
31–50					
Low	12	83	5	100	(92)
High	17	74	9	100	(114)
Over 50					
Low	7	83	10	100	(143)
High	8	82	10	100	(51)
Nonsocialist					
24–30					
Low					(9) a
High	7	8	85	100	(72)
31–50					
Low	2	7	91	100	(42)
High		3	97	100	(145)
Over 50					
Low	1	3	96	100	(65)
High	1	3	96	100	(156)

a Too few cases for computation of percentages.

Note: The few respondents who voted for some left-socialist party in 1969 have been excluded. Education has been classified as either "low" (up to seven and one-half years) or "high" (more than seven and one-half years).

Source: See footnote 4.

the tendency to shift party four years later was far greater among those with a high level of education than among those with only seven years of schooling. For the corresponding age groups of bourgeois voters, there is a slight tendency in the opposite direction: the inclination to shift toward the socialists was a little greater for people with low education than for those with secondary education or more.

(3) The age of voters whose party preference shifted varies more among people with high than with low education. This tendency is particularly strong for 1969 Laborites: for respondents with high education, the proportion who remained loyal to Labor increases regularly from 65 percent in the youngest age bracket to 82 percent in the oldest one; for Laborites with low education, we observe no variation in stability of party preference according to age. For bourgeois voters, stability increases with increasing age for people with both low and high education, although in the latter group the differences are less sharp and less regular than for Laborites.

(4) The tendency for younger voters to be more inclined than older ones to move to the far left (Socialist Election Alliance) is consistent for people with both low and high education. This trend, of course, is far more pronounced for Laborites than for bourgeois voters.

The data presented so far indicate that changes in voting between 1969 and 1973 are indeed related to our three background variables, occupation, education, and age, although the tendencies differ substantially between people who supported Labor in 1969 and those who voted for some bourgeois party. Labor maintained its position best among its older supporters, regardless of social background, and among younger voters of low social status and low education. The tendency to move from Labor to the Socialist Election Alliance was strongest for younger voters and for people with higher education, while older Laborites were more inclined to move to bourgeois parties. The nonsocialist parties as a group strengthened their position most among farmers and fishermen and among middle-aged and older people in other occupational groups. Changes in the vote for nonsocialist parties do not seem to be related to variations in education.

Electoral Changes from 1957 to 1973. In studying the distribution of the vote for the period 1957–73 with regard to our three main background variables, occupation, education, and age, we can apply occupational categories more detailed than those used in the preceding analysis. It will be recalled that the Labor party, which lost the election of 1965, improved its position considerably in 1969, and was again severely defeated in 1973. These short-term changes are clearly reflected within all occupational groups. In addition, some long-term tendencies are revealed in Table 2–6.

Table 2–6

OCCUPATION AND PARTY PREFERENCE, 1957–73

(in percentages)

Occupation	Party Preference			Total
	Left-socialist	Labor	Non-socialist	
Workers				
1957	2	75	23	100
1965	8	69	23	100
1969	6	69	25	100
1973	14	55	31	100
Lower-salaried employees				
1957	2	51	47	100
1965	8	46	46	100
1969	5	49	46	100
1973	12	34	54	100
Higher-salaried employees				
1957	0	34	66	100
1965	3	24	73	100
1969	2	26	72	100
1973	7	28	65	100
Farmers, fishermen				
1957	0	32	68	100
1965	1	23	76	100
1969	1	18	81	100
1973	1	12	87	100
Self-employed, professional				
1957	0	30	70	100
1965	3	22	75	100
1969	1	30	69	100
1973	5	22	73	100

Source: See footnote 4.

(1) Smallholders and fishermen (who have traditionally been one of the cornerstones of Labor's electoral support) tend to move away from the socialist parties to the benefit of the bourgeois parties, particularly the Agrarians. The trend is consistent from one election to another: the proportion of farmers

and fishermen voting Labor declined from 32 percent in 1957 to 12 percent in 1973.

To some extent this tendency reflects geographical and social mobility. A sizable proportion of the rural population has moved into urban areas and urban occupations. Apparently the under-dogs of the rural community are most inclined to change residence and occupation, shifting from farming and fishing to the secondary and tertiary branches of the economy;[10] precisely these groups have been most inclined to vote Labor. But the downward trend of Labor support among this group is not only due to a diminishing vote potential; it is also a result of a direct move away from Labor within the stable rural population. This tendency, which was clearly evident in a panel analysis of changes between 1965 and 1969, is consistent with the trend we have found for 1969–73 (Table 2–3).[11]

(2) A shift away from Labor is evident for the working-class population. Most of Labor's losses went to the leftist parties, particularly in 1973. But bourgeois parties, especially the Agrarians and the Christians, have improved their working-class support since 1969. A further inspection of the data suggests that the decline of Labor support has been particularly strong among workers who come from rural backgrounds. Again, we may conclude that the changes in the working-class vote we have found for 1969–73 are consistent with a trend that was already present early in the 1960s.

(3) Labor's support from people in middle-class occupations dropped between 1957 and 1965. Since then the tendencies have been less clear. Among lower-salaried employees, all Labor losses went to the leftist parties until 1973, when the bourgeois parties also enjoyed a sharp increase in their support. Apparently, a majority of the higher-salaried employees who defected from Labor after 1957 went to the bourgeois parties, particularly the Conservatives and the Liberals. But in 1973 both Labor and the left-socialists improved their position at the expense of the

---

[10] In the period 1959-69 about 26 percent of all farm holdings in Norway were abandoned as separate holdings. Fifty-three percent of the discontinued holdings were of less than twenty decares each, and as many as 89 percent of them were less than fifty decares, that is, small holdings even in a Norwegian context. *Statistisk Årbok 1975* [Statistical yearbook 1975] (Oslo: Central Bureau of Statistics, 1976), tables 101 and 103.

[11] For the analysis of 1965-69, see Valen and Martinussen, *Velgere og politiske*, pp. 287-88.

bourgeois parties. Among professionals and the self-employed, great fluctuations in party support are evident from one election to another. The data suggest that this group has been particularly sensitive to short-term electoral forces. The diverse voting patterns of various middle-class groups cannot be related in a meaningful way to short-term changes between 1969 and 1973. A closer inspection of the data suggests, however, that since around 1965 middle-class people from rural backgrounds have tended to shift toward the bourgeois parties.

The relationship between electoral changes and level of education does not reveal any consistent long-term trend. On all educational levels, the changes are, by and large, consistent with the changes in the electorate as a whole. Finally, with respect to the relationship between electoral changes and age, the evidence supports our observation that older people tend to be highly stable in their party preferences from one election to another, while younger voters are far more prone to shift. Of course, if a given party suffers a decline at several elections among young voters, it may expect a subsequent long-term decline in the older age brackets. Our evidence does not by itself suggest any consistent generational trend. However, it should be noted that the substantial number of voters who have shifted their support back and forth between Labor and the leftist parties since the beginning of the 1960s have largely been younger people.

Overall, the data presented in this section seem to provide sufficient basis for a tentative conclusion: the defeat of the Labor party in 1973 can only to a limited degree be accounted for by long-term trends. We have seen that the strong tendency in 1973 for farmers and fishermen to move from Labor to bourgeois parties is consistent with a trend that can be traced back to 1957. At recent elections a similar trend seems to have been at work among people in urban occupations but with backgrounds in farming or fishery. Furthermore, the data suggest that the tendency in 1973 for younger Laborites with some higher education to move to the left is consistent with a trend that dates back to the 1960s.

What is interesting, however, is that most of the tendencies observed in 1973 do not fit in with long-term trends. One might, for example, have expected to discover a tendency for people in middle-class occupations to move to bourgeois parties. This did happen to some extent, but not consistently. Lower-salaried employees suddenly flocked toward bourgeois parties in 1973, although their level of support for the right had remained almost constant since 1957.

The support of higher-salaried employees for bourgeois parties rose in the middle 1960s, but dropped sharply in 1973. Finally, professionals and the self-employed have moved erratically. Their support for bourgeois parties dropped in 1969, but then increased in 1973, as did their support for the left-socialist parties.

In short, the election of 1973 cannot be explained satisfactorily in terms of trend analysis of such sociological variables as occupation, education, and age. Even a long-term analysis of these trends must be supplemented by a study of the specific issues and circumstances of the 1973 election.

The Issues of the 1973 Election

Three issues dominated the election campaign in Norway in 1973: women's right of self-determination in the matter of abortion, the level and forms of taxation and tax reductions, and the social and political consequences of the EEC referendum. When asked which single issue had created the most intensive debate among the political parties in the campaign, 77 percent of the respondents (26, 25, and 26 percent respectively) mentioned these three issues, while 20 percent gave no opinion and only 3 percent mentioned other issues. The fact that one out of four respondents perceived taxation as a salient issue supports the hypothesis that the election revealed distrust in welfare policies. However, the abortion and the EEC issues, which are rated as equally important in the perceptions of the respondents, bear no direct relationship to the problems of the welfare state.

There is a clear relationship between the voter's perception of the most important issue in the 1973 election campaign and his vote preference. (The data are presented in Table 2–7.) Traditional Christians and defenders of restrictive moral values, who tend to support the Christian People's party and both offshoots of the old Liberal party (the Liberal and New People's parties), more often than other voters perceived abortion as the most important issue in the campaign. Supporters of right-wing parties and the extreme left were most inclined to see taxation questions as dominating the campaign. Voters of all parties assigned considerable importance to the EEC issue, with one notable exception: supporters of Anders Lange's party gave most of their attention to taxation policies.

On the basis of the evidence in Table 2–7, one would expect the issues of abortion, taxation, and the EEC to have affected the party preferences of the electorate in 1973. We shall first explore the relationship between party preference in 1973 and opinion on abortion

Table 2–7

PERCEPTION OF MOST IMPORTANT ISSUE, BY PARTY, 1973 CAMPAIGN

(in percentages of respondents)

	Most Important Issue						
Party	Abortion	Taxes	EEC	Other	No opinion	Total	N
Socialist Election Alliance	18	38	26	8	10	100	(105)
Labor party	25	29	25	2	19	100	(410)
Liberal party	37	16	26	3	18	100	(38)
New People's party	32	34	20	3	11	100	(35)
Christian party	47	7	25	5	16	100	(139)
Center party	24	19	31	2	24	100	(166)
Conservative party	19	35	28	3	15	100	(148)
Anders Lange's party	22	44	9	9	16	100	(32)
Nonvoters	21	19	22	4	34	100	(122)
All respondents	26	25	26	3	20	100	(1,225)

Note: Interview question—"When looking back on the election campaign this year, which single political issue do you think created most dispute among the political parties?"

Source: See footnote 4.

and taxation. Then shifts in party preference between 1969 and 1973 will be related to the voter's stand on these two domestic issues. Later we will take up the impact of foreign policy issues for party preferences.

Domestic Issues and Vote Preference. Two interview questions were asked concerning taxation policies, one designed to reveal the voters' attitudes toward the present level of taxation in Norway, the other to indicate which income groups they thought should benefit from a possible tax reduction.[12] About 70 percent of all respondents

[12] On the level of taxation, respondents were offered a choice among the following response alternatives: (1) public services are too many and taxes too high, (2) public funds can be used in other ways and taxes lowered, (3) a high tax level is necessary, but public funds can be used in other ways, or (4) high taxes are necessary to solve the many public problems. On the question about who

held that taxes could be reduced under given circumstances. More than half of the survey sample was of the opinion that if tax reductions were enacted they should benefit the lower income brackets, while almost 40 percent thought tax reductions should be evenly distributed.

When opinions on these two questions are related to party preference in 1973, two somewhat different patterns are evident. Supporters of Anders Lange's party come out much more clearly than other voters in favor of a reduction in taxes, as one might have expected. Voters supporting either the Liberal or the New People's party as well as supporters of the Christian People's party were most prepared to accept a high level of taxation.

The picture is different when opinions on who should benefit from tax reductions are considered. Here the traditional left-right cleavage is activated. About 70 percent of the socialist voters hold that low-income groups should benefit from tax reductions, and so do some 50 percent of voters supporting parties at the center of the party system (that is, Christians, Liberals, the New People's party, and the Center party), while fewer than one-third of the Conservatives are of this opinion. The proportion preferring tax reductions for people in higher-income groups, which is only 4 percent for the total sample, is 15 percent for voters of Anders Lange's party.

Predictably, the abortion issue divides voters according to their party position along the moral-religious conflict dimension, which has traditionally been of great significance in Norwegian politics.[13] Only 37 percent of all respondents subscribe to the most restrictive views, that abortion should never be allowed or should be allowed only when a woman's health or life is in danger, but more than 80 percent of Christian People's party voters and 50 percent of Center party voters hold such views. Twenty-six percent of the respondents hold the view that a woman must have the right to self-determination in the matter of abortion. Supporters of socialist and conservative parties were most inclined to hold this position. Thirty-four percent of all respondents hold the view that abortion should be allowed when

should benefit from possible future tax reductions, three response alternatives were offered: (1) reductions should benefit people with high incomes, (2) reductions should benefit people with low incomes, or (3) reductions should be evenly distributed.

[13] On this question the respondents were offered four response alternatives: (1) abortion should never be allowed, (2) abortion should be allowed only when a woman's life or health is in danger, (3) abortion should be allowed also for non-medical reasons, and (4) abortion should be decided by the woman herself. Concerning the moral and religious conflict dimension, see Valen and Rokkan, "Norway: Conflict Structure."

personal circumstances make it difficult for a woman to bring up a child; two-thirds of those who support the New People's party are among this group, along with considerable numbers of Labor and Conservative party voters.

The data presented so far demonstrate that two domestic issues, taxation and abortion, are considered of foremost importance by the respondents and, equally important, that both issues divide different parties in different ways. To assess their effect on the voter's choice of party, we must ask how stable voter attitudes have been on these issues, and to what extent stand on issues affects voter preference.

We have adequate data on the stability of opinion over time only for the abortion issue. Unfortunately, questions dealing with taxation were not phrased identically in previous panel interviews. We do, however, have panel data for a related issue, namely the question of whether allocations for social security should be reduced, maintained, or expanded. This issue certainly has consequences for taxation policies, and like the taxation issue it may be considered a reasonable indicator of attitudes toward welfare policies. With respect to the social security issue, extensive shifts in opinion took place from 1965, when the question was first asked, to 1973. Only 35 percent of the respondents in 1973 still held the opinions they had expressed in 1965. The percentage of voters wanting social security measures to be cut back grew from 8 percent in 1965 to 21 percent in 1973, the percentage who wanted social security to be maintained grew from 36 percent to 50 percent, and the percentage of respondents holding that such measures should be extended declined from 43 to 18 percent. Support for welfare policies did indeed diminish.

With respect to the issue of abortion the opinions of 54 percent of the respondents remained stable over the four-year period, 1969–73. Several remarks can be made about the changes that occurred: (1) opinions became more liberal on this issue more often than they became more restrictive; (2) few voters changed their standpoint radically; and (3) the largest number of changes took place from abortion for medical reasons to abortion for nonmedical reasons, and from this last to self-determined abortion. Thus the proportions choosing the two most liberal alternatives (self-determined abortion and abortion for nonmedical reasons) increased from 53 percent in 1969 to 60 percent in 1973. The proportion who advocated self-determination in the matter of abortion increased from 15 to 26 percent.

To analyze the relationship between opinion on issues and change in vote preference we will first explore the gains and losses of the parties for the various opinion categories on the two salient domestic issues, abortion and taxation. We will then briefly examine movements of voters between parties, by opinion on the same issues.

With respect to changes in the distribution of party strength for various opinion categories, Table 2–8 indicates that the Christian People's party registered its largest gains among voters with a restrictive view on abortion. Support for the Socialist Election Alliance, conversely, went with increasing liberality on abortion. The Labor party lost votes in all opinion groups on this issue, and the Conservative party suffered its greatest losses among defenders of free abortion. Anders Lange's party attracted most votes in the latter opinion category.

Anders Lange's party also drew most of its votes among people who believed that taxes were too high and ought to be reduced. The Socialist Election Alliance gained even more in these groups, while the Labor party lost more votes, the stronger the opposition to the present tax level became. Differences in losses and gains among the parties are not so clear when it comes to the distribution of possible tax reductions. The Labor party lost most among people who wanted tax reductions to go to the lower-income brackets, while the Socialist Election Alliance and the Christian People's party gained most in this opinion category, but this tendency is slight.

Turning to shifts in voting between parties or groups of parties, we notice that the swings follow roughly the pattern we would expect on the basis of our earlier findings regarding voter preference and opinion on salient domestic issues. Thus the Christian People's party strengthened its position among groups with restrictive views on abortion and gained votes from both socialist and bourgeois parties. Of special interest is the fact that one-third of the nonvoters in 1969 who strongly opposed abortion turned out to vote for the Christian People's party in 1973. We also note that 21 percent of those who voted Conservative in 1969 and strongly opposed abortion defected to parties at the center other than the Christian People's party in 1973, while another 7 percent moved to the Christian People's party. This may be explained by the fact that opposition to abortion and a "No" to membership in the EEC often occur together, especially among the rural population. Consequently, many Conservative voters moved to the anti-EEC Agrarian Center party.

Among voters with more liberal views on abortion, the Labor party lost votes to the Socialist Election Alliance, while defectors from the Conservative party spread more evenly over all the other parties. In the group advocating free abortion, however, both Con-

Table 2-8

CHANGES IN PARTY SUPPORT, 1969–73, BY 1973 STANDPOINT ON SALIENT ISSUES

(in percentage-point gains and losses)

Issue Stand[c]	Socialist Election Alliance[a]	Labor Party	Liberal Party[b]	Christian Party	Center Party	Conservative Party	Anders Lange's Party[a]	Non-voters	N
Abortion[c]									
Restrictive view	+3	−10	−3	+8	−2	0	+2	+2	(426)
Liberal view	+5	−8	−4	+1	+2	−1	+2	+3	(388)
Free abortion	+10	−12	−1	+1	−1	−5	+5	+3	(295)
Tax level									
Taxes too high	+8	−15	+6	−3	−1	−3	+5	+3	(276)
Tax reductions possible	+6	−10	−2	+2	+1	−4	+3	+4	(522)
High taxes necessary	+4	−8	−1	+5	−1	−2	+1	+2	(272)
Distribution of tax reductions									
Favor lower-income group	+7	−12	−3	+4	+1	−3	+2	+4	(573)
Favor all groups	+5	−8	+9	−3	−3	0	+3	+3	(444)

a New party in 1973; thus, it can only have gained support.

b In 1973, the Liberals and the New People's party.

c Restrictive view: abortion should be either illegal or allowed only when a woman's health is in danger; liberal view: abortion for nonmedical reasons should be legal; free abortion: self-determined abortion should be legal.

Source: See footnote 4.

servative voters and nonvoters in 1969 moved to Anders Lange's party in greater proportion than average.

With respect to the issue of taxation, we find that 17 percent of the Labor voters who believed that taxes were too high swung to the Socialist Election Alliance; fewer of those who thought tax reductions were possible or accepted the current tax level did so. Only a small proportion of Labor voters moved to Anders Lange's party. This party gained relatively more from 1969 Conservatives and nonvoters holding that taxes could be reduced than from other groups. The center parties also gained more votes than others from the non-voters and 1969 Conservatives, regardless of opinion on the issue of taxation.

Our analysis suggests that, out of a long list of domestic issues, the two that came to dominate the election campaign also determined many of the swings in party preference. The issues of abortion and taxation explain a great many of the gains of the Socialist Election Alliance, the Christian People's party, and Anders Lange's party. But as we have seen, the voters were not only concerned with do-mestic issues. They also considered Norway's membership in the EEC to be a salient issue. We now turn to the question of how people re-acted to the EEC and to other foreign issues.

Foreign Issues and Vote Preference. Membership in the Western defense alliance (NATO) has been a cornerstone of Norway's foreign policy since 1949. During the cold war there was strong support for this policy and what opposition existed was not well articulated, but about 1960 opposition to NATO became more pronounced. To a large extent this opposition has come from the left, from the left wing of the Labor party and from parties to the left of Labor. In general, Norway's foreign relations have become a far more dominant theme in national political debate since 1960. In recent years the question of Norway's entry into the European Community has taken over from the NATO issue as the prime channel of concern about Norway's relation to the Western world.

The EEC dispute, which is related to practically all areas of na-tional politics, stirred tremendous antagonisms. It broke up old al-liances and friendships between and within parties and created political constellations unparalleled in modern Norwegian politics. One of the elements that the NATO and EEC debates have had in common is that urban radicals have constituted a major force in the opposition. Farm and fishery organizations have been another corner-stone of opposition to the EEC. Furthermore, the traditional Norwegian "countercultures"—the language movement, the temperance movement, and the lay religious movement—mobilized against Norwegian membership in the European Community.[14] The alliance in favor of EEC membership was equally strange: the core groups were the Conservative party, the moderate wing of the Labor party, and the corresponding economic organizations, respectively the organizations of business and the trade union movement.[15]

We shall first investigate the relationship between party preference and opinion on the EEC and NATO. Second, we shall study how these issues relate to each other in the minds of the electorate. Finally, we shall study changes in vote preferences between 1969 and 1973 according to opinion on the EEC.

At all elections from 1965 to 1973 our respondents were asked whether they thought Norway should remain a member of NATO or leave the alliance. As might be expected, the strongest opposition occurred on the left wing, among the Left Socialists. Among the bourgeois parties opposition to NATO was negligible and even in the Labor party it was weak. It is interesting that in all parties, even in parties to the left of Labor, support for NATO increased from 1965 to 1973. Excluding respondents with no opinion, some 85 percent of our sample indicated a pro-NATO position in 1973. The number who indicated no opinion, meanwhile, declined in all parties, almost without exception. This tendency may be partly due to a "panel effect": that is, repeated interviewing may conceivably have stimulated political interest in this issue. Nonetheless, we may assume that the tendency was partly due to an increasing awareness of and concern with foreign politics. The EEC debate between 1970 and 1972 presumably helped to stimulate this interest.

While differences between the parties' stands on NATO are rather limited, they are remarkably clear with regard to the EEC issue. It will be recalled that this issue had been settled by a referendum one year before our 1973 survey was conducted. Our sample slightly underrepresents the "Yes" group, which was 46.5 percent at the referendum. But our data seem to reflect the main tendencies in the development of opinion between 1969 and 1973 reasonably well: a sharp decline in the proportion who indicated "No opinion" and a substantial increase in the "Yes" percentage, which, however, never reached the majority level. The Socialist Election Alliance and the Agrarian Center party were almost unanimous in opposing EEC

---

[14] On the Norwegian countercultu.es, see Valen and Rokkan, "Norway: Conflict Structure."

[15] See Valen, "Norway: 'No'."

Table 2–9

SHIFTS IN OPINION ON NATO, 1969–73,
BY POSITION ON EEC AT THE REFERENDUM
(in percentages of respondents)

1969	1973			
	For NATO	Don't know	Against NATO	Total
1972 EEC Supporters				
For NATO	63	6	2	71
Don't know	13	8	0	21
Against NATO	5	1	2	8
Total	81	15	4	100
				(N = 469)
1972 EEC Opponents				
For NATO	42	6	1	49
Don't know	15	15	3	33
Against NATO	4	4	10	18
Total	61	25	14	100
				(N = 563)

Source: See footnote 4.

membership, while the Conservatives and the New People's party (the "Yes" wing that broke away from the old Liberal party) were heavily in favor of the EEC. Between 1969 and 1973 the Liberals and the Christians moved in the "No" direction, while Laborites became more favorable toward the EEC. Throughout the debate the three latter parties were severely split over this issue.

We have seen that between 1969 and 1973 opinion tended to become more favorable toward both NATO and the EEC. What was the relationship between these two issues? Table 2–9 presents changes in opinion on NATO separately for supporters and opponents (in 1972) of EEC membership. As might be expected, opponents of the EEC were less favorable toward NATO than EEC supporters, but even among the former a majority were in favor of NATO membership in 1973. Opinions on NATO were rather stable on the individual level—73 percent of EEC supporters and 67 percent of opponents indicated the same positions both in 1969 and in 1973—but in both groups there was a net swing of around ten percentage points in favor of NATO.

Table 2–9 indicates only a slight correlation between opinions on NATO and the EEC. If our table had been limited to the urban population, the correlation would have been considerably higher. The rural population tends to be split on these issues: in the referendum 84 percent of farmers and fishermen voted "No" to EEC membership, but according to our survey an even higher proportion of this group was in favor of NATO.[16] Thus the anti-EEC alliance of "red" workers and "green" farmers is severely split on defense policy.

When the EEC issue appeared on the agenda in the summer of 1970, the opinion polls indicated increasing volatility in the electorate. Opponents of the EEC particularly were inclined to change their party preference.[17] This pattern was very clear in 1973: around 40 percent of the EEC opponents in our panel (including both voting and nonvoting respondents) changed their party preference between 1969 and 1973, while the corresponding figure for EEC supporters was 28 percent. The importance of this issue is clearly reflected in differences in the marginal changes of support for various parties among supporters and opponents of the EEC.

If it were assumed that the EEC issue had a major impact upon the 1973 election, it could be predicted that parties in favor of the EEC would strengthen their position among EEC supporters but lose support among EEC opponents. For parties opposing the EEC, the opposite tendency would be expected: decline among EEC supporters and gains among EEC opponents. As far as the opponents are concerned, the data indeed support the hypothesis. Table 2–10 shows that the proportions of votes for the Labor and Conservative parties fell substantially within this group. At the same time the anti-EEC parties, the Christians, the Agrarians, and the Socialist Election Alliance, gained correspondingly. Among EEC supporters, the changes in party distribution were far less spectacular, and the trends are slightly inconsistent with the hypothesis. The Conservatives enjoyed some gains and the Agrarians suffered a moderate decline, but the trend seems to have been reversed for socialist parties: Labor declined by almost two percentage points, while the Socialist Election Alliance increased its share of the votes by approximately one percentage point. These findings indicate that the EEC issue had a much stronger impact upon the electoral choices of EEC opponents than upon those of EEC supporters.

[16] Ibid.

[17] H. Valen, "Local Elections in the Shadow of the Common Market," *Scandinavian Political Studies*, vol. 7 (1972), pp. 212-82, and Valen and Martinussen, *Velgere og politiske*, pp. 329-60.

Table 2–10

CHANGES IN PARTY SUPPORT, 1969–73, BY
STAND ON EEC AT THE REFERENDUM OF 1972
(in percentage-point gains and losses)

Party	Stand on EEC, 1972	
	For	Against
Socialist Election Alliance (Communist party plus Socialist People's party)	+1	+11
Labor party	−2	−15
Liberal party (Liberal party plus New People's party)	−4	−3
Christian party	0	+6
Center party	−1	+3
Conservative party	+1	−4
Anders Lange's party	+5	+1

Source: See footnote 4.

The contrast is even more striking when we consider the direction changes within the two groups, as presented in Table 2–11. The importance of the issue is clearly demonstrated in the split of the *Venstre*, the old Liberal party: Liberal supporters of the EEC who still supported one of the spin-off parties switched almost without exception to the New People's party, while EEC opponents largely remained within the majority Liberal party. For former Liberal voters who switched to other parties, the pattern differs between the two groups: EEC supporters largely moved to Labor and to the Conservatives, opponents tended to prefer the Christian and Agrarian parties.

A similar pattern is evident for other parties. The two pro-EEC parties, Labor and Conservative, maintained their positions among EEC supporters, although some exchanges of votes occurred between them, and both lost some votes to Anders Lange's party. Among EEC opponents both parties suffered heavy losses to anti-EEC parties: Labor defectors went in large numbers to the Socialist Election Alliance, to the Agrarian party, and to the Christians. The fact that the latter party took three times as many votes as the Agrarian party suggests an interaction effect with the abortion issue. It is worth noting that Conservative opponents of the EEC were most in-

Table 2–11

SHIFTS IN PARTY SUPPORT, 1969–73, BY STAND ON EEC AT THE REFERENDUM

(in percentages of respondents)

1969	1973									
	Left-socialists	Labor party	Liberal party	New People's party	Christian party	Center party	Conservative party	Anders Lange's party	Total	N
1972 EEC Supporters										
Left-socialists										(9)a
Labor	3	92	b	1	b	0	2	2	100	(238)
Liberal	4	17	4	48	2	2	21	2	100	(48)
Christian	0	6	6	0	69	0	19	0	100	(16)
Center										(13)a
Conservative	2	4	0	2	2	1	82	7	100	(114)
1972 EEC Opponents										
Left-socialists	96	0	0	0	0	4	0	0	100	(26)
Labor	25	59	1	0	9	3	1	2	100	(193)
Liberal	3	5	40	5	15	22	8	2	100	(40)
Christian	0	0	0	3	90	7	0	0	100	(60)
Center	0	1	1	0	8	88	1	1	100	(128)
Conservative	7	4	4	2	4	32	39	7	100	(44)

a Too few cases for computation of percentages.
b Less than .05 percent.
Source: See footnote 4.

clined to defect to the Agrarian party. These findings suggest that conservative elements opposed to the EEC were attracted to the Agrarians, radicals tended to go to the Socialist Election Alliance, while voters in the traditional countercultures (the language movement, the temperance movement, and the lay religious movement) were more inclined to prefer the Christians.

Only Anders Lange's party seems to have been unaffected by the EEC issue. According to Table 2–11, the likelihood that former Conservatives, Laborites, and Liberals would vote for Anders Lange's party in 1973 was identical for supporters and opponents of the EEC. We have seen that Anders Lange's party drew a large part of its votes from the pro-EEC side (Table 2–10). The explanation apparently is that the party was particularly attractive to conservative voters, and right-wing elements were far more inclined than radicals to support EEC membership.[18]

Interaction between Domestic and Foreign Issues. Our respondents selected three issues as particularly salient in the 1973 campaign: taxation, abortion, and the EEC. By comparing the results of the elections of 1969 and 1973 for groups of respondents classified according to position on these three issues, we have seen that the patterns of electoral change are indeed correlated with issue position. The relationship is particularly clear with regard to the EEC issue. We may ask, finally, how these issues are related to one another and what joint impact they have upon electoral change. Space does not permit a detailed analysis, but in Table 2–12 marginal changes in vote distribution between 1969 and 1973 are related to each of the domestic issues, separately for supporters and opponents of the EEC. Although the figures are rather small, they reflect interesting tendencies, which can be summarized briefly.

(1) When stand on abortion is related to voting, separately for EEC supporters and opponents, the abortion issue seems to have had almost no impact on the former group. But a clear pattern emerges among EEC opponents: people with a restrictive view on abortion were strongly inclined to move from the Labor party to the Christian People's party and to a lesser extent to the Center (Agrarian) party. People with more liberal views on abortion tended to prefer the Socialist Election Alliance or the Agrarians. To some extent position on abortion reflects the various components of the anti-EEC alliance: the rural population tends to hold a restrictive view on abortion, while urban radicals tend to be liberal. Interaction between the EEC

[18] Valen, "Norway: 'No'."

66

and abortion issues may thus explain why farmers and fishermen who defected from Labor did not go to the Socialist Election Alliance, but to the center parties. Because of its role in the EEC dispute, one would have expected the Agrarian party to gain heavily in rural areas. But its gains were moderate, and in fact the party lost a number of previous supporters to the Christian party. We may conjecture that the abortion issue strongly affected the interchange of votes between these two center parties. Even for the Conservative party, position on abortion seems to have had an effect on gains and losses. Among EEC opponents, the party lost relatively more from people in favor of free abortion than in other groups, and even among EEC supporters a slight tendency in the same direction is evident: the Conservative party's share of the votes declined by some three percentage points in the "free abortion" category, but increased by five percentage points among people holding a restrictive view.

(2) The impact on electoral change is less clear for the tax issue than for the abortion issue, but the former seems to have had a slight effect among both supporters and opponents of the EEC. As might be expected, Anders Lange's party was particularly attractive to people who opposed taxes. In fact, the party gained almost no support from people who accepted the present tax level. And this tendency is consistent, regardless of position on the EEC. The Conservatives lost more support among people strongly opposed to the existing level of taxation than among any other group.

For most other parties, Table 2–12 shows no regular tendency with regard to the tax issue, with the notable exception of Labor. On the pro-EEC side, the tax issue does not seem to have affected the Labor party's fortunes, but in the anti-EEC camp, where so many former loyalties were broken, dissatisfaction with taxes seems to have contributed to the defeat of the party. In this group the proportion voting Labor who accepted the present tax level was only half as great as the proportion who were most opposed to it. Interestingly enough, a great number of the Labor defectors in the latter category went to the leftist Socialist Election Alliance. This shift between socialist parties may simply be a consequence of a high income level. We have seen that a large number of middle-class people moved from Labor to the Socialist Election Alliance (Table 2–3). Presumably they were people with relatively high income taxes. We may assume that dissatisfaction with taxes is positively correlated with level of income. But since the Socialist Election Alliance did not advocate lower taxes, people hardly shifted from Labor to the Socialist Election Alliance for the purpose of reforming tax policies.

Table 2-12

CHANGES IN PARTY SUPPORT, 1969–73, BY STAND ON SALIENT ISSUES IN 1973

(in percentage-point gains and losses)

Stand on Issues, 1973		Left-socialists	Labor Party	Liberal Party[a]	Christian Party	Center Party	Conservative Party	Anders Lange's Party[b]	Non-voters	N
For EEC	Stand on abortion									
	Restrictive	0	−1	−9	+1	−4	+5	+4	0	(128)
	Liberal	+2	+1	−6	0	0	+3	+2	−2	(197)
	Free	+1	−2	+1	+1	−1	−3	+7	−5	(151)
Against EEC	Stand on abortion									
	Restrictive	+5	−12	−1	+12	+1	−3	0	−1	(257)
	Liberal	+9	−15	−1	+1	+8	−3	+2	+7	(180)
	Free	+21	−16	+3	+2	+5	−6	+3	−7	(119)
For EEC	Stand on tax level									
	Taxes too high	+1	+1	−2	−1	0	−4	+7	−2	(114)
	Lower taxes possible	+2	−2	−8	0	−2	+3	+5	0	(220)
	High taxes necessary	−1	0	−2	+2	−4	+3	+1	−3	(125)

Against EEC   Stand on tax level

Stand on tax level									
Taxes too high	+15	−21	0	+10	+3	−4	+3	−3	(142)
Lower taxes possible	+9	−13	+1	+5	+5	−5	+2	+1	(262)
High taxes necessary	+11	−10	+4	+8	+2	−3	0	−10	(132)

a In 1973, the Liberals and the New People's party.
b New party in 1973.
Source: See footnote 4.

However, Table 2–12 suggests that not only the Socialist Election Alliance but also the bourgeois parties profited from dissatisfaction with taxes among former Laborites, and these defections to the right are more likely to express a true protest against taxes and public expenditure in the welfare society.

Some Concluding Remarks

The problems dealt with in this paper certainly require more analysis than we have been able to offer so far. In particular, it would have been useful to link different parts of the analysis by relating issue data to social background variables. Nonetheless, several findings emerge from this limited analysis:

(1) The *Storting* election of 1973, which differed sharply from previous elections in postwar Norway, was dominated by three issues perceived as central by the electorate: taxation, abortion, and Norway's relation to the European Community. Most of the changes in voting between 1969 and 1973 seem to have been determined by the position of the various parties on these issues.

(2) The taxation issue, which coincides with declining support for social security, may be interpreted as an indication of general dissatisfaction with the policies of the welfare state. Anders Lange's party profited, while the Labor party and the Conservatives lost support because of this issue.

(3) The question of self-determined abortion, which brings into play the moral-religious conflict dimensions in Norwegian politics, was already an issue in 1969. In 1973 the opponents of self-determined abortion tended to move away from parties defending this policy, particularly the Labor party. The impact of the abortion issue was particularly visible among opponents of the European Economic Community. The reason is apparently that it was particularly the rural population that tended to be both anti-abortion and anti-EEC—which explains why the Christian People's party made greater inroads than the Agrarian Center party into Labor's support among farmers and fishermen.

(4) Yet most important was the European Economic Community issue, which had dominated Norwegian politics since 1970. While only minor changes occurred in party distributions on the pro-EEC side, opponents of the EEC were inclined to shift party. This tendency accounts for the fact that the anti-EEC

parties—the Socialist Election Alliance, the Christian People's party, and the Center party—won the election. Furthermore, electoral changes related to social background variables correspond with those related to the EEC issue. Farmers and fishermen continued to move from Labor to the Christian and Center parties, and younger radicals with higher education continued to move from Labor to left-socialist parties. Since urban radicals and the farming and fishing populations were the cornerstones of the opposition to the EEC, it was natural enough that these long-term tendencies were reflected in the 1973 election. In fact, the EEC issue reinforced these general tendencies.

Concern over Norway's relationship with the European Economic Community had a decisive impact upon the 1973 *Storting* election. It was the major cause not only of the changes in the party system, but also of Labor's severe setback in the election. Without the EEC issue, whatever electoral changes had taken place would probably have been moderate and 1973 would have more or less resembled a long series of *Storting* elections that preceded it.

In the Scandinavian context, analysis of the Norwegian data indicates that the results of the 1973 elections must largely be accounted for by national circumstances. Thus the similar electoral trends that appeared in Denmark, Norway, and Sweden in 1973 cannot have originated from any common source. It is true that taxation problems were greatly debated in all three countries, and, as we have seen, Norwegian voters perceived taxation as a salient issue. But our analysis suggests that in Norway the total effect of this issue was rather limited.

From a comparative point of view the great impact of the EEC issue in Norwegian politics is interesting. It is a good example of how a foreign-policy issue can relate to most areas of national politics. Although the Scandinavian countries are rather similar in their economic, social, and political structure, they differ sharply in their foreign policies. Systematic comparative analysis of the impact of foreign issues might contribute greatly to our understanding of the national variations in political developments in this part of the world.

3
RECENT ELECTORAL TRENDS IN SWEDEN

Bo Särlvik

The Electoral Stalemate in 1973 [1]

In 1973 the Social Democratic party in Sweden, like the Social Democratic parties in Denmark and Norway, met with severe electoral losses. Its support declined to its lowest level in about three decades.

Editor's Note: The names of the Swedish political parties have been translated in this volume as follows: *Vänsterpartiet Kommunisterna*, Communist party; *Socialdemokratiska Arbetarepartiet*, Social Democratic party; *Centerpartiet*, Center party; *Folkpartiet*, People's party (the Liberals); *Moderata Samlingspartiet*, Moderate party (the Conservatives); *Kristen Demokratisk Samling*, Christian Democratic party.

[1] This study of recent electoral trends in Sweden is based partly on data drawn from a nationwide interview sample survey conducted in connection with the 1973 election. I have also drawn on the findings of a series of similar studies of previous elections from 1956 to 1970. I directed all of these studies while I was associated with the Institute of Political Science, University of Göteborg, and they were all conducted in collaboration with the Swedish Central Bureau of Statistics. Reports on these studies have been published in the official election statistics reports and in scholarly publications. For the 1970 election, see Bo Särlvik, "Valet 1970" [Election 1970], in *Allmänna valen 1970* [The general election, 1970], vol. 3, *Sveriges Officiella statistik* [The official statistics of Sweden] (Stockholm: Statistiska centralbyran, 1973), pp. 47-109. For the 1973 election, see Olof Petersson and Bo Särlvik, "Valet 1973," in *Allmänna valen 1973*, vol. 3, *Sveriges Officiella statistik*, pp. 47-101. A comprehensive overview of developmental trends is given in Bo Särlvik, "Sweden: The Social Bases of the Parties in a Developmental Perspective," in Rose, ed., *Electoral Behavior: A Comparative Handbook* (New York: Free Press, 1974), pp. 371-434. In preparing the present paper, I have drawn heavily on analyses undertaken by my co-investigator in the 1973 study, Olof Petersson; these are a continuation of the corresponding analyses undertaken by myself for the previous elections, especially those in 1968 and 1970. See also Olof Petersson, "The 1973 General Election in Sweden," *Scandinavian Political Studies*, vol. 9 (1974), pp. 219-28. This article is primarily based on aggregate data and contains an analysis of regional variations in recent electoral change.

Table 3-1

RESULTS OF SWEDISH ELECTIONS, 1952–73

	1952	1954ᵃ	1956	1958ᵇ	1958ᵃ	1960	1962ᵃ	1964	1966ᵃ	1968	1970ᶜ	1973ᶜ
Results by Party (in percentages of votes cast)												
Communist party	4.3	4.8	5.0	3.4	4.0	4.5	3.8	5.2	6.5	3.0	4.8	5.3
Social Democratic party	46.1	47.4	44.6	46.2	46.9	47.8	50.4	47.3	42.3	50.1	45.3	43.6
Center party	10.7	10.3	9.4	12.7	13.1	13.6	13.1	13.4	13.7	16.2	19.9	25.1
People's party (Liberals)	24.5	21.7	23.8	18.2	15.6	17.5	17.1	17.1	16.8	15.0	16.2	9.4
Moderate party (Conservatives)	14.4	15.7	17.1	19.5	20.4	16.5	15.5	13.7	14.7	13.9	11.5	14.3
Total ᵈ	100.0	100.0	100.0	100.0	100.0	100.0	100.0	100.0	100.0	100.0	100.0	100.0
Voter Turnout (in percentages of the electorate)	79.1	79.1	79.8	77.4	79.2	85.9	81.0	83.9	82.8	89.3	88.3	90.7

a Local government (communal) elections.

b Election called after the dissolution of the second chamber of the *Riksdag*.

c In these years parliamentary and local-government elections were held simultaneously, under the new order. The statistics given pertain to the parliamentary elections.

d The total includes minor parties, for which percentages are not given in the table. The Christian Democratic party received 1.5–1.8 percent of the vote in the elections from 1964 to 1973. In 1966, local electoral coalitions of nonsocialist parties obtained 4.3 percent of the vote. Split-off Communist factions obtained 0.4 percent and 0.6 percent of the vote in 1970 and 1973 respectively.

Source: *Allmänna valen 1973* [General election, 1973], vol. 1, *Sveriges Officiella statistik* [The official statistics of Sweden] (Stockholm: Statistiska centralbyrån, 1974), p. 10.

Table 3–2

DISTRIBUTION OF SEATS IN THE *RIKSDAG*, 1970 AND 1973

Election	Com-munist party	Social Demo-cratic party	Center party	People's party (Liberals)	Moderate party (Conser-vatives)	Total Number of Seats
1970	17	163	71	58	41	350
1973	19	156	90	34	51	350

Source: *Allmänna valen 1973*, Del 3, p. 13.

Although the Social Democrats have been the governing party in Sweden since 1932, their electoral fortunes have fluctuated considerably in the course of the postwar period. In 1952, 1956, and 1966 they suffered setbacks that seemed to threaten their position as the party in power. Each time, however, the Social Democratic party regained its strength in subsequent elections. After their defeats in the parliamentary elections of 1952 and 1956, the Social Democrats managed to save their hold on governmental power partly by joining in a coalition with the Center (formerly Agrarian) party from 1951 to 1957 and partly by relying on their strength in the upper house of the *Riksdag*. In 1973 the situation that the Social Democrats faced was entirely different. This was their second electoral defeat in a row, and their support had declined from 50.1 percent of the vote in 1968 to 43.6 percent in 1973 (see Table 3–1).

The outcome of the 1973 election meant that there was no longer a socialist majority, either in the electorate or in the *Riksdag* (see Table 3–2). In the *Riksdag* the election had produced a perfect stalemate, with 175 seats for the socialist parties and 175 seats for the nonsocialist parties. The Communists had gained 2 seats, the Social Democrats had lost 7. In the nonsocialist bloc, the Center party had won 19 new seats and the Conservatives (officially the Moderate party) 10. The People's party (the Liberals), which had never really recovered from its disastrous tactics in the long battle over pension reform in the late 1950s, faced a new devastating defeat: it lost 24 seats and its share of the vote fell to 9.4 percent. For more than a decade the People's party had striven hard to achieve a workable "collaboration of the center" with the Center party, and in the period leading up to the 1973 election the party leadership had ostentatiously given first priority to laying the groundwork for a coalition government by the three bourgeois parties. As it turned out, this strategy had allowed the Center party to appear as the main alternative to the Social Democrats and to gain the support of an increasing number of nonsocialist voters.

By 1973 the Social Democrats' old coalition partner, the Center party, had become the largest rather than the smallest among the nonsocialist parties. During its period in opposition, the Center party not only had enjoyed an unbroken series of electoral successes, but also had broadened its social base. Thus it was no longer acting as a narrowly based agrarian interest party, and after the 1973 election it had replaced the People's party as the predominant party in the center of the political spectrum. Well in advance of the 1973 election, the three nonsocialist parties (the Center, People's, and Moderate parties) had made it clear that they intended to form a three-party coalition government if they achieved a majority in parliament, and the Center party had made no secret of its intention to play a major role in such a coalition. An entirely new parliamentary situation had thus emerged as a consequence of the change in the balance of strength *within* the nonsocialist bloc. The possibility of splitting the bourgeois bloc through collaboration with the Center party—which in the past had been one of the Social Democrats' most successful strategies—appeared to be foreclosed.

The constitutional reforms enacted in 1971, together with the modification of the proportional representation election system, were among the factors that made the parliamentary situation in 1973 profoundly different from that which had obtained after Social Democratic election setbacks in the past. The old two-chamber *Riksdag* had been replaced by a unicameral parliament with three-year election periods. Both the 1970 and the 1973 elections were conducted under an electoral system that entails a more strictly proportional distribution of the total number of seats in the *Riksdag* than the previous system.

The constitutional reform meant, in the first place, that there was no longer any upper chamber that could help a Social Democratic government bridge over a difficult period after a temporary decline in a national election. The upper chamber of the old *Riksdag* had been elected by county councils and major city councils under a system of successive renewal, one-eighth of its membership being elected each year. In addition to the stabilizing effect of this successive renewal system, which tended to level out fluctuations in party strength, two features of the upper chamber had underpinned the Social Democrats' position. One of these was the system of election by city and county councils: the Social Democrats were more successful in county elections than in national elections through most of the postwar period, and this was indirectly reflected in their strength in the upper chamber. The second was the fact that the two-tier proportional system for the upper chamber had a built-in tendency to overrepresent comparatively big parties, which also benefited the Social Democrats.[2]

The new electoral system gives fully proportional representation in the *Riksdag* to every party that receives at least 4 percent of the vote. One of the consequences of the new electoral order has been the greater parliamentary representation of the Communists, who were substantially underrepresented in the old *Riksdag*, since the 1970 election. The threshold rule for parliamentary representation could actually have had a disastrous impact for the Communists, whose support has sometimes dropped below 4 percent, but they passed the threshold both in 1970 and in 1973, and the indications from recent trends are that they will continue to do so in the foreseeable future.

In a sense, the change in the electoral system means that it is more difficult for the Social Democrats to attain a majority in the new unicameral *Riksdag* than it was in the old *Riksdag*. On the other hand, the change appears to have had a slightly favorable effect on the combined representation of the Social Democratic and Communist parties. The explanation for this effect lies in the fact that the Social Democrats used to be overrepresented under the old electoral order at the expense of the Communists, but their overrepresentation regularly amounted to one or two seats less than the corresponding Communist "loss" because of the lack of perfect proportionality.[3] Given

---

[2] For an overview of the Swedish political system, see N. Andrén, *Modern Swedish Government* (Stockholm: Almqvist & Wiksell, 1961). See also Nils Stjernquist, "Sweden: Stability or Deadlock," in R. Dahl, ed., *Political Oppositions in Western Democracies* (New Haven: Yale University Press, 1966). The new constitution is treated authoritatively in E. Holmberg and N. Stjernquist, *Vår nya författning* [Our new constitution] (Stockholm: PAN, 1973). Many important aspects of Swedish politics are illuminated in another study based on the same series of election surveys as this article; see S. Holmberg, "*Riksdagen representerar svenska folket.*" *Empiriska studier i representativ demokrati* ["The Swedish parliament represents the Swedish people." Empirical studies in representative democracy] (Lund: Studentlitteratur, 1974).

[3] For an analysis of the previous election system, see C. G. Jansson, "Mandatfördelningen vid andrakammarval," [Distribution of seats in the lower house] in *Författningsutredningen, V.: Organisationer. Beslutsteknik. Valsystem* [The government commission on constitutional matters, 5: organizations, decision-making, electoral system] (Stockholm: S.O.U., 1961), p. 21.

the balanced strength of the socialist and nonsocialist blocs in the *Riksdag*, this slight shift may actually have significant consequences for the preconditions for majority formation in the future.

After the 1970 election, the Social Democrats were able to continue in office in spite of the fragility of their parliamentary base. An anti-Social Democratic majority could only have been formed by the Communists' and the bourgeois parties' combining their votes or, possibly, by the Communists' abstaining from voting in order to allow the bourgeois parties to defeat the government. Such combinations may well emerge occasionally in votes on minor policy issues, but it was highly unlikely that the Communists would align themselves with the bourgeois parties when the fate of the government was at stake and thus help to bring down a Social Democratic government. The Communist party in Sweden has consistently proved to be more "reliable" —or more strategy-conscious—in this regard than left-socialist parties in Denmark and Norway. In any case, it would have been meaningless for the bourgeois parties in the 1970–73 period to form a government that could have been defeated by the socialist parties at any time.

In the stalemate that resulted from the 1973 election, the Social Democrats were thus denied all the reserve resources they had been able to draw on in the past: collaboration with the Center (Agrarian) party, their strength in the upper chamber, and the help of the Communists. The Social Democrats could have chosen to resign in order to recuperate during a period in opposition. After all, the bourgeois parties had more seats than the Social Democrats in the *Riksdag*, and immediately after the election all the bourgeois party leaders actually urged the Social Democrats to resign. But the Social Democrats did not resign. There may have been several reasons for this decision, but without any doubt the most important was the Social Democrats' strong belief in the political value of retaining their hold over the governmental machinery, even when this involved them in a cumbersome tactical game. The Social Democrats have certainly never shown any receptivity to the idea that a spell out of power could somehow be a purifying experience for a political party. To this must have been added another consideration: as long as they stayed in power they could always have recourse to dissolving parliament and calling a new election, and they had a good chance of calling an election on a policy issue that would maximize their chances of returning from such a contest with renewed strength.

Party Strategies under Minority Government

When the Social Democratic government made clear that it intended to remain in power, the opposition parties still had the option of bringing the government down. Even if the Communists supported the government, the bourgeois parties could exploit the "lottery" rule for tied votes in the *Riksdag* to defeat the government on a major political issue and thus force it to resign. Under the Swedish parliamentary rules, the speaker does not have a casting vote. Instead, a tied vote is resolved by a lottery between the two proposals on which the vote has been taken. (Alternatively, the matter can be sent to committee for a second time.) Theoretically, the bourgeois parties would obviously always have a fifty-fifty chance of defeating the socialists. On the other hand, the opposition parties had to take into account the unavoidable consequence of such a challenge, namely, that it would be countered by the dissolution of parliament and a new election. It soon became clear that the People's party wished to avoid an early election. After their electoral disaster the People's party needed time to review their political strategy and to find policy stands that would give them a vote-attracting political image of their own again. Consequently they had to avoid any head-on confrontation with the Social Democratic government for the time being.

Precarious as it may have appeared immediately after the election, the parliamentary situation of the Social Democratic government, therefore, proved to be workable. On question after question it turned out to be possible to avoid the threatening stalemate, when it came to voting in the *Riksdag,* by forming temporary voting coalitions that transcended the boundaries between the two blocs. The government thus survived its first year with the new *Riksdag* that began its term at the beginning of 1974. Given that regular elections would have to be held in 1976 even if the *Riksdag* were dissolved before then, and that none of the parties appeared anxious to mount election campaigns in both 1975 and 1976, the prospects for the Social Democrats' continuing in office until 1976 gradually became more and more favorable.

The prime minister, Olof Palme, who used to be known (at least to his opponents) as a politician who preferred confrontation to conciliation, has proved himself to be a skillful tactician. His government has maneuvered with great caution on issue after issue so as to secure the support of at least one of the opposition parties for compromise solutions, always managing to make the necessary concessions without sacrificing the main objectives of the government's program. In some instances the Conservatives (the Moderate party) have become isolated in a minority position. Even more notable, however, are the occasions when a majority has been formed through agreements between the Social Democrats and the People's party on important economic and financial questions. Having recognized that it ran the risk of losing political significance in the shadow of the Center party, the People's party was apparently deliberately seeking to enhance its political role and its influence on substantive policy making by trying to work out compromises with the Social Democrats, even at the expense of its relations with other bourgeois parties. This change was so apparent that political commentators were seriously speculating that the People's party might take over the Center party's old role as the natural coalition partner of the Social Democrats.

The situation during the 1973–76 election period was much too uncertain to warrant the conclusion that the positions of the parties had undergone any definite or lasting change.[4] But clearly the options for parliamentary coalition formation appeared more open than they used to be. In parliamentary politics, not much of the bourgeois unity of 1973 appeared to have survived the failure to depose the Social Democrats from their governing position. At the left end of the political spectrum the real importance of the Communists had been reduced in spite of their moderate gain in the 1973 election. While their nineteen seats in the *Riksdag* were important for the overall balance of strength, the Communists were not in a position to secure a majority vote for any government proposal. To find a minimum winning coalition, the Social Democrats had to seek the collaboration of at least one nonsocialist party, and once they had achieved this, they did not really need the support of the Communists. The Communists thus found themselves in the embarrassing position of being bound to give general support from the left to a government which most of the time worked on the assumption that it wanted to reach an understanding with the political center.

It is obvious that this situation could have become extremely dangerous for a governing Social Democratic party in a harsh economic climate. In similar situations, governing socialist parties have often lost support to the Communists. However, the economic climate since the election was on the whole favorable: after two years of economic recession, the Swedish economy showed clear indications of renewed growth through the period 1974–76. If anything (accord-

---

[4] Apart from editorial revision this manuscript was completed in August 1975. The developments that led up to the 1976 election and the results of that election are treated in a postscript to this chapter.

ing to the somewhat uncertain evidence of the opinion polls), the Social Democrats' electoral prospects seemed in 1975 to be slightly better than they were at the time of the 1973 election.

Uncertainty and Stability in the Party System

We stressed at the outset that the Swedish election of 1973 bore a resemblance to the contemporaneous elections in Denmark and Norway in the sense that it resulted in a marked weakening of the Social Democratic party and in a remarkably uncertain parliamentary balance of strength. But the overall impression is that the differences are at least as important. Although voter turnout for the Swedish election was unusually high (90.7 percent; see Table 3–1), the contest lacked the political intensity of the 1973 elections in Denmark and Norway. The Swedish campaign was not very bitter or even very exciting. The significance of the shifts in party strength that occurred is unquestionable, but these were not due to any marked increase in the overall volatility in the voters' party preferences. With the aid of interview survey data covering a long series of parliamentary elections, we are actually in a position to gauge the flows of the vote that underlie the aggregate election results.[5] These survey data indicate that about 14 percent of those eligible to vote in 1973 had changed their party preference since 1970. About the same proportion shifted their allegiance between 1968 and 1970 (14 percent) and between 1964 and 1968 (15 percent). What sets the 1973 election apart from the postwar elections that preceded it is the continuation of the decline in Social Democratic strength that had begun in 1970. Between 1970 and 1973 the Social Democratic vote declined by only two percentage points—but this drop was a politically significant step in an ongoing erosion of the party's electoral support.

In quantitative terms, the shift of voters away from the People's party (6.8 percentage points) was much more impressive. It should, of course, be kept in mind that changes in the relative voting strengths of the bourgeois parties are a recurrent phenomenon in Swedish politics. In almost all of the postwar elections, the internal competition among the nonsocialist parties has entailed a loss of strength for at least one of them, even when together they have been able to make gains at the expense of the Social Democrats. In all of the elections since 1956, including 1973, covered by our national interview surveys, about half of all vote shifts from one election to the next

---

[5] See footnote 1.

have consisted of flows among the bourgeois parties. This is one of the circumstances that helps to explain why the bourgeois parties have found it so difficult to present a concerted policy alternative to the governing Social Democrats. Not only have they disagreed over the precise contents of such an alternative, but also at any given time at least one of the partners in the prospective bourgeois coalition has been preoccupied with the desire to recover its losses to another bourgeois party in the previous election—and all of them have had grounds for giving some thought to improving their relative weight in the bourgeois bloc.[6]

To return to our comparison between the Swedish election, on the one hand, and the developments in Denmark and Norway, on the other, the divergence in the Swedish case consists of the absence of any real upheaval in the party system. No new parties emerged and the two-bloc division of the party system has seemed to be temporarily inoperative rather than obliterated. Were the 1976 election to result in a bourgeois majority, there was little doubt that bourgeois unity would be revived in a majority government. On the other hand, were the 1976 election to result in the kind of balance of strength that existed in 1970, the emergence of a new pattern in parliamentary politics would be a real possibility. In that eventuality, the Social Democrats would have to consider whether they would prefer to reach some kind of long-term understanding with one of the centrist parties or to rely on a somewhat hazardous and possibly damaging alliance with the Communists. In the light of recent trends, one might well conjecture that under those circumstances the Social Democrats would choose to approach the People's party rather than the Center party in order to form a stable governmental base.

Rational as this kind of strategy consideration may appear, it is abstract and unrealistic as long as one does not take the voters' reactions into account. The nonsocialist sector of the electorate has been notoriously volatile. The relative stability of the balance of strength between the two blocs has been grounded in the bourgeois voters' consistent opposition to Social Democratic rule rather than in their exclusive attachment to specific bourgeois parties.

Strength of Party Attachment. As we can demonstrate with our interview survey gaugings, this relative lack of strong party attachment among the nonsocialist voters still prevails. This is brought out in Table 3–3, which is based on data drawn from the national election

[6] See B. Särlvik, "Political Stability and Change in the Swedish Electorate," *Scandinavian Political Studies*, vol. 1 (1966), pp. 188-222.

Table 3-3

STRENGTH OF PARTY AFFILIATION, SWEDISH NATIONAL ELECTIONS, 1968, 1970, AND 1973

(in percentages of respondents)

| | Voted for | | | | | | | | | | | | | | |
| | Communist party | | | Social Democratic party | | | Center party | | | People's party (Liberals) | | | Moderate party (Conservatives) | | |
Strength of Party Affiliation	1968	1970	1973	1968	1970	1973	1968	1970	1973	1968	1970	1973	1968	1970	1973
Strong attachment	23	28	26	51	44	44	29	31	21	19	25	27	37	33	27
Weak attachment	10	21	20	25	33	33	24	26	23	31	25	24	26	31	31
Only general preference	41	30	31	18	18	17	27	33	32	34	34	28	21	17	22
Neither attachment nor preference	5	6	7	4	3	4	9	6	13	9	11	12	7	9	7
Identifies with a party other than voted for	21	15	16	2	2	2	11	4	11	7	5	9	9	10	13
Total	100	100	100	100	100	100	100	100	100	100	100	100	100	100	100
N	(39)	(97)	(98)	(1,458)	(1,165)	(1,051)	(469)	(551)	(589)	(370)	(329)	(185)	(286)	(218)	(285)

Source: See footnote 1.

surveys in 1968, 1970, and 1973. In addition to interview questions about actual voting, respondents were asked a series of questions about "party identification." First they were asked whether they thought of themselves as adherents of any particular party. If so, they were also asked if they considered themselves strongly convinced supporters of that party. People who did not think of themselves as adherents of any party were asked whether they generally considered themselves "closer" to any party than to the others.

The classification of the voters in the three elections is based on these questions and provides an overview of the strength of party affiliation among each party's electors. The "strong attachment" category comprises electors who described themselves as very convinced adherents of the party they had voted for, while the "weak attachment" category includes those who thought of themselves as adherents of the party but would not describe themselves as "very convinced." The "only general preference" category comprises respondents who were content to say that they felt "closer" to the party they had voted for in the election, while those who failed to indicate any party preference in these general terms, but nevertheless had voted for the appropriate party, are included in the category "neither attachment nor preference." Finally, in all of the elections each of the parties received votes from voters who stated that they generally thought of themselves as adherents of or closer to a party other than that for which they had voted. Those appear in the category "identifies with a party other than voted for."

Table 3–3 shows that the proportion of voters with comparatively strong party attachments is much larger among Social Democratic voters than among those who supported one of the bourgeois parties or the Communists. The looseness of the bourgeois and Communist voters' attachment to the parties they had cast their votes for is also apparent in the relatively large proportion of voters who indicated that their sense of affiliation really related to another party.

In a multiparty system of the Swedish type, where parties are arrayed along a left-right axis and at the same time are grouped in two major blocs, any attempt by a party to break out of its traditional position or role entails the risk of losing voters who fail to recognize the party they used to support in its new position. Conspicuous changes in parliamentary strategy as well as participation in unfamiliar formal coalitions in office appear to involve this risk. The validity of this general assumption about the party system is substantiated, for example, by the case of the Center-Social Democratic coalition of 1951-57. The Center party actually experienced a sequence of heavy losses in elections during the coalition period in spite of the fact that, through its participation in the coalition, it must have secured quite substantial concessions to the agrarian sector, which at the time provided the bulk of its voting support. The continued decline of the People's party that has been recorded in opinion polls since the 1973 election now bears witness to the party's attempts to gain political significance through an at least partially independent policy of conciliation toward the Social Democrats. This has proved to be a liability in the eyes of large numbers of its one-time voters and potential supporters in the bourgeois sector of the electorate.

It is in this context that the fluidity of partisan attachments in the bourgeois sector of the electorate has a bearing also upon the prospects of new coalition patterns in parliamentary politics. If, for example, a People's party move toward collaboration with the Social Democrats were seen as unnatural by previous People's party voters, most of them would not be restrained by any strong party identification from switching their votes to a more reliable anti-Social Democratic alternative among the bourgeois parties.

The Voters' Second Choices and the Left-Right Axis. We shall make use of another kind of survey data to illuminate how prevailing views in the electorate on the positioning of the parties may affect the parties' strategy choices under the present conditions. These data were obtained by asking respondents, after the aforementioned party identification questions, which party they liked "second best." Their responses may be understood as measures of the distances the voters perceive between themselves and the parties they do not vote for but consider either opponents or natural allies of their preferred party. The results, set forth in Table 3–4, show how each party's identifiers (including those who merely felt "closest" to a party) distributed their second preferences.

The bulk of the Social Democratic voters considered the Center party their second preference. While this no doubt reflects a tradition of collaboration between the Social Democrats and the Center (Agrarian) party, it also helps to explain why the Social Democrats were so vulnerable when the Center party shifted to the role of the main opposition party, bent on winning votes from the Social Democrats as well as from the other nonsocialist parties. The Center (Agrarian) party had been an ideal coalition partner for the Social Democrats as long as the two parties were espousing compatible policy goals but catered to essentially different sectors of the electorate.

Table 3–4

CHOICE OF "SECOND-BEST PARTY,"
BY PARTY IDENTIFICATION

(in percentages of respondents)

Second-best Party	Party Identification				
	Com- munist party	Social Demo- cratic party	Center party	People's party (Liberals)	Moderate party (Conser- vatives)
Communist party	—	21	2	1	1
Social Democratic party	75	—	29	9	2
Center party	7	44	—	55	61
People's party (Liberals)	0	7	32	—	28
Moderate party (Conservatives)	0	2	21	22	—
No party, minor party, or no response	18	26	16	13	8
Total	100	100	100	100	100
N	(91)	(1,116)	(509)	(187)	(252)

Source: See footnote 1.

It is not surprising that, when the relationship between the two parties later became distinctly competitive, many previous Social Democratic voters were prepared to look upon the Center as a "not too different" party that offered attractive alternatives in policy domains like regional economic development and the environmental issues.

The internal duality of the Center party, on the other hand, becomes apparent in the quite even dispersal of its supporters' second preferences among Social Democrats, Liberals (People's party) and Conservatives (Moderate party). The two alternatives most favored by Center voters—the Social Democrats and the People's party—attract about equal shares of the "second best" ratings. Actually, the data can be read in two complementary ways. Either one can conclude that the majority of the Center party see another bourgeois party as their closest alternative, or one can stress that an even larger majority of the Center party voters actually prefer either the Social Democrats or the People's party over any of the parties at the two ends of the party spectrum. It is ironic that the joint effect of the prevailing two-bloc conception of the party system and the Center party's record of a close relationship with the Social Democrats is to place the Center party in a position where either staying in a concerted bourgeois bloc or attempting to break away from it involves electoral risks for the future. If it established too close a relationship with the Conservatives in a three-party bloc, the Center would allow the Social Democrats to recoup some of their losses; on the other hand, the Center party could hardly maintain its role as the leading opposition party if it did not stress the credibility of a bourgeois majority alternative to the Social Democrats. At least so far, the Center party has been successful in claiming that it is aiming at a bourgeois three-party government with a program based on the policies agreed on by the centrist parties. Naturally, this is a formula that can hardly win the wholehearted approval of the Conservatives.

The data also throw light on the People's party's difficulties in the present situation. Most People's party supporters apparently consider the Center their closest political alternative. This fact has certainly facilitated the policy of collaboration in the center embraced by the party leadership in recent years. But at a time when the Center party is gaining in importance in the political arena at the expense of the People's party, this also involves the risk that the outflow of votes to the Center party will continue, simply because the latter is now playing the leading role in the political center. At the same time, one can safely gather from the distribution of second preferences among People's party supporters that the leadership would run the risk of estranging a major part of its remaining electoral support should it attempt to move toward a policy of closer and lasting collaboration with the Social Democrats. Less than one-tenth of the People's party supporters rated the Social Democrats as their second preference, while more than twice that proportion felt closer to the Moderate party (Conservatives). Nor do most Social Democrats appear to be inclined to think of the People's party as a natural ally. When asked about their second choice, only 7 percent of the Social Democrats cited the People's party. The emergence of the Center party as a party with a broad electoral appeal has affected both the Social Democrats and the People's party, but the latter has clearly been most vulnerable because of its peculiar difficulty in defining any distinctive social or ideological boundary between itself and the Center party. In the absence of distinctive policy differences, the

Center party has then had the advantage that it was perceived as a fresh and untried alternative by any bourgeois voters in the political center who were beginning to despair of the People's party's chances of bringing Social Democratic rule to an end.

The overall pattern of second preferences coincides quite well with the left-right ordering of the parties. Generally, voters were most likely to rate as second best their own party's adjacent neighbors on the left-right axis. There is also a tendency—most conspicuous in the case of the Social Democrats—for the second-best ratings to tail off, the further away a party is positioned on the ideological axis. With the exception of the Communists and the Conservatives at the two extremes of this axis, each party is adjacent to two others, one on either side. An elector's choice between these two alternatives for second best is, of course, always compatible with a conception of the party system as an array of parties ordered from left to right along one ideological dimension.

It is an interesting feature of these data that the relative magnitudes of the second-best ratings given to each of the two adjacent alternatives afford complementary information about the relative distances among the parties. In other words, they tell us whether most of a given party's supporters look to the right or to the left for political allies. We have already noted that Center party supporters show a strikingly ambiguous distribution of their second preferences, which in itself can be taken as an indication of the uncertainty that characterizes the relations among the parties in the current situation. We have also pointed out that People's party supporters show a distinct preference for the other party in the political center. It is, furthermore, noteworthy that Social Democrats are likely to rate the Center party, rather than the Communist party, as their second choice. Again, this has something to do with the Social Democrats' reluctance to rely entirely on collaboration with the Communists for the building of a majority base.

We have gathered this kind of data for a series of elections and are thus in a position to evaluate the persistence of the preference pattern that appeared at the 1973 election.[7] Since the elections of the 1960s and 1970, for example, the number of voters who cited the People's party as their second choice has declined. This is perhaps

---

[7] For a discussion of the interpretation of this kind of data as measures of interparty distances, see B. Särlvik, "Voting Behavior in Shifting 'Election Winds'— an Overview of Swedish Elections 1964-1968," *Scandinavian Political Studies*, vol. 5 (1970), pp. 241-83. See also further analysis in Särlvik, "Sweden: Social Bases."

particularly interesting in the case of the Center supporters, many of whom are previous People's party voters. In the period 1964–70 they were noticeably more likely than in 1973 to rate the People's party as second best. In all previous studies, furthermore, the Conservatives were more likely to consider the People's party second best than they were to choose the Center party. Since the reversed ordering actually contradicts the pattern to be expected under perfect unidimensionality (in the technical sense of nonmetric dimensional analysis), one may wonder why this erratic deviation should appear in 1973. In the absence of hard evidence in the data to support any definite conclusion, we may only conjecture that the successful Center party managed to overshadow the People's party to such an extent that the Center naturally came to the minds of a good many Conservatives as the second most important (and therefore the second-best) opponent of the Social Democrats.

Voters' perceptions of the distances among the parties are bound to influence the way they respond to changes in party strategies, especially where their own party is concerned. Likewise, anticipation of such electoral responses must enter into the party leaderships' deliberations concerning their collaboration with other parties. Precisely for this reason it is noteworthy that our series of election surveys also includes one instance of a decisive change in party strategies being followed by an accommodating change in the voters' evaluations of the parties. This occurred at the termination of the Social Democratic-Center (Agrarian) coalition of 1951–57. At the time of the 1956 election, most of the Center party's voters (54 percent) embraced the coalition, selecting their party's ally as their second choice. At the same time, only a small proportion of the People's party's supporters (8 percent) would give a second-best rating to the Center party, and the large majority of them clearly thought of the Conservatives as closest to their own party position. The data from the 1964 election, when the two centrist parties had established a close collaboration in opposition, illuminate how sharply the change in party politics transformed the picture of the party system among centrist bourgeois voters. The predominant second-best choice of voters of both of these parties now became the other partner in the center bloc: 46 percent of Center party voters rated the People's party as second best and 49 percent of the People's party voters chose the Center party. Clearly the positions taken by party leadership and the evaluations of parties by the electorate are interdependent.

The Social Bases of the Parties

As we have seen, two trends revealed by the election outcomes of 1970 and 1973 combined to bring about a delicately balanced situation in parliament: one was the decline of the Social Democratic party's strength; the other was the surge towards the Center party.

Only the latter of these shifts was bound up with a redrawing of the social bases of the parties, and this was so only in that the Center party continued to emerge from its agrarian past and made further inroads into nonrural social groups, especially the urban middle class of the self-employed and salaried employees. As a result, the social profile of the Center party increasingly resembles that of the People's party. Yet the Center party still has a hard core of electoral support in the farming population (and its predominance in that sector is about as strong as it was before). It also has a more substantial working-class base of support than the People's party enjoyed during its peak period in the 1940s and 1950s. The drastic change that has occurred in the composition of the Center party's electoral support is shown in Table 3–5. The farm vote now makes up only just above one-fifth of the Center party vote, while about one-third is drawn from the working-class strata (groups 5, 6, and 7 in the table, thus including shop assistants and so on). About 45 percent of the party's votes are cast by employers and salaried employees in the urban middle classes.

In studies of trends in the electoral support of Western working-class parties, it has become almost customary to look for causes either in changes in the class structure or in the socialist party's ability to win sympathy in the middle class. None of these explanations is really pertinent to the variations in the Social Democratic vote in Sweden, however. As we have shown elsewhere, there is no indication that the affluent working class is especially prone to drift away from the Social Democrats toward the bourgeois parties. If anything the Social Democrats have their staunchest support among well-paid manual workers.[8] Since the party has not had any substantial support in the farming population since the 1930s, it has been virtually unaffected by the shrinkage of the agricultural sector during recent decades. In the period of fast economic growth that lasted through most of the 1960s, the Social Democrats managed to accommodate the growth of the urban middle-class strata by attaining an increasing share of their vote. But there is no evidence that the

---

[8] For further analysis, see Särlvik, "Sweden: Social Bases." See also data and analyses in the election survey chapters of the official election statistics reports.

Table 3–5

SOCIAL COMPOSITION OF THE
CENTER PARTY VOTE, 1956–73

(in percentages of respondents)

Socioeconomic Stratum	Election					
	1956	1960	1964	1968	1970	1973
(1) Managers and owners of large enterprises, higher-salaried employees, professionals	0	2	1	6	3	6
(2) Owners of small enterprises, self-employed	5	11	10	11	10	9
(3) Farmers	77	57	48	29	23	21
(4) Salaried employees in lower positions (excluding those in category 5)	4	8	9	18	23	27
(5) Shop assistants, certain employees in transport and service occupations	1	4	7	9	11	10
(6) Workers (excluding those in category 7)	2	10	17	19	22	21
(7) Workers in agriculture, lumbering and fishing	11	8	8	7	6	3
(8) Students	a	a	a	1	2	3
Total	100	100	100	100	100	100
N	(83)	(194)	(359)	(469)	(822)	(582)

a For the elections of 1956-64, students are classified according to their fathers' occupations.

Source: See footnote 1.

Social Democrats' gains and losses have been limited to variations in their vote within the middle-class strata. The data displayed in Table 3–6 show that the Social Democratic gains from 1964 to 1968 were derived from increasing support in most social strata, just as the decline from 1968 to 1973 was apparent in most strata.[9]

[9] It might be noted that the increase from 1968 to 1973 among farmers relates to a very small proportion of the vote, that is, an increase from 6 percent to 9 percent. There is also a Social Democratic gain between 1968 and 1973 among farm workers. Numerically this a very small category in the 1973 sample, however: the number of cases is 67.

Table 3–6

CHANGES IN SOCIAL DEMOCRATIC SUPPORT, BY SOCIOECONOMIC STRATUM, 1964–73

Socioeconomic Stratum	Social Democratic Vote			Socio-economic Distribution of the Electorate, 1973[a] (in percentages of respondents)
	1973 (in percentages of respondents voting)	Change 1964–68 (percentage point gain or loss)	Change 1968–73 (percentage point gain or loss)	
(1) Managers and owners of large enterprises, higher-salaried employees, professionals	16	+6	+2	8
(2) Owners of small enterprises, self-employed	21	+6	−11	7
(3) Farmers	9	−1	+3	8
(4) Lower-salaried employees (excluding those in category 5)	37	+1	−10	25
(5) Shop assistants, certain employees in transport and service occupations	61	+3	−6	13
(6) Workers (excluding those in category 7)	69	+1	−10	35
(7) Workers in agriculture, lumbering, and fishing	64	+4	+7	3
(8) Students	18	—	−16	1
				100

[a] The data base is the total 1973 survey sample, including nonvoters (N = 2,596). In addition to information about party choice obtained in interviews, information about respondents' participation in these elections was obtained from the electoral registers after each election.
Source: See footnote 1.

When these shifts are seen in the context of contemporary economic development, they appear to be linked to changes between "good times" and "bad times." The Social Democrats decline in periods of fast-rising prices and gain strength in periods of stable prices and economic growth. The state of the economy is not the only factor that influences Social Democratic support, however. Major controversies over policy issues (like the pension question in the 1950s) are also reflected in the election outcomes. The point we feel warranted to make is that variations in the Social Democrats' voting support are bound up with short-term political and economic developments rather than with changes in the structure or values of society. The Social Democrats' decline in the early 1970s may be seen as an expression of electoral dissatisfaction with the "stagflation" of the economy during these years. The fact that the Swedish economy escaped relatively unscathed from the international economic crisis of 1974–75 may account for the Social Democratic recovery reported in the opinion polls through the last year.

Table 3–7, which shows the social composition of the Social Democratic vote rather than the extent of Social Democratic support within each stratum, allows us to look at the social base of the Social Democrats in another perspective. As the table indicates, the composition of the Social Democratic party's support was largely stable, both during the economic upturn in the 1960s and during the downturn in the early 1970s. Its gains in the middle class during the 1960s did not much alter the predominance of the working class among its support groups. Thus, if we define the working class as strata numbers 5 through 7 in the table, we find that its share of the Social Democratic vote declined from 78 percent in 1956 and 1960 to 72 percent in 1973.[10]

To some extent the changes in the Social Democratic share of the vote reflect compensating gains and losses for the Communist party. As long as one is concerned only with the socialist-bourgeois two-bloc division of the vote, most of the shifts during the postwar period therefore appear to have been vacillations around an equilibrium level. The socialist parties together have fairly consistently won well

[10] The socioeconomic classification employed here is the same as the classification constructed for our analysis in the 1973 official election statistics report. This differs slightly from the classification used in previous election reports, but the new classification has been applied to the previous survey data in all instances where these are referred to here. For an interesting attempt to study changes in the social bases of parties with the aid of aggregate ecological data, see also L. Lewin, B. Jansson, and D. Sörbom, *The Swedish Electorate 1887-1968* (Uppsala: Almqvist & Wiksell, 1972).

Table 3–7

SOCIAL COMPOSITION OF THE
SOCIAL DEMOCRATIC VOTE, 1956–73

(in percentages of respondents)

Socioeconomic Stratum	Election					
	1956	1960	1964	1968	1970	1973
(1) Managers and owners of large enterprises, higher-salaried employees, professionals	1	1	1	2	2	3
(2) Owners of small enterprises, self-employed	3	3	4	4	4	3
(3) Farmers	4	2	1	1	1	1
(4) Lower-salaried employees (excluding those in category 5)	14	16	20	20	20	20
(5) Shop assistants, certain employees in transport and service occupations	14	17	15	16	17	16
(6) Workers (excluding those in category 7)	56	56	53	51	50	52
(7) Workers in agriculture, lumbering, and fishing	8	5	6	5	4	4
(8) Students	a	a	a	1	2	1
Total	100	100	100	100	100	100
N	(454)	(663)	(1,248)	(1,458)	(1,801)	(1,047)

a For the elections of 1956-64, students are classified according to their fathers' occupations.

Source: See footnote 1.

over 70 percent of the working-class vote, while the nonsocialist parties have received about the same share of the middle-class vote.

An overview of this social division of the vote is presented in Table 3–8. Three different methods have been used to gauge the class polarization of the vote at each of the elections from 1956 to 1973 (see notes to Table 3–8). Regardless of the type of measurement one chooses, the data suggest that there occurred a slight decline in the social polarization of the parties' voting support from the early 1960s. This was due to the growth of the socialist vote in the middle class as well as to a simultaneous increase in the nonsocialist vote

Table 3–8
SOCIAL POLARIZATION OF THE VOTE, 1956–73

	Election					
	1956	1960	1964	1968	1970	1973
(1) Percent voting for Social Democrats or Communists in:						
Working class	76	80	77	76	72	73
Middle class	23	25	30	34	32	29
(2) Index of class voting	53	55	47	42	39	44
(3) Squared eta coefficient for 7 socioeconomic strata	.33	.37	.30	.25	.21	.23
(4) Coefficient of contingency for 7 strata and 5 parties	.64	.64	.60	.52	.51	.50

Note: (1) This class dichotomy is based on the socioeconomic strata classification employed in Table 3-5—middle class comprises groups 1 through 4 in that table, working class comprises groups 5 through 7. (2) This is Alford's Index of Class Voting, that is, the Social Democratic and Communist percentage share of the vote in the working class *minus* the corresponding percentage for the middle class. (3) The entries in this row have been obtained from a one-way analysis of variance across all the socioeconomic groups appearing in Table 3-9 excluding students. The party bloc division is treated as a dichotomous dependent variable. The squared eta coefficient can be interpreted as the explained proportion of the variance in the dependent variable (analogous to the square product moment correlation coefficient). (4) The entries in this row are, for each election, the coefficient of contingency calculated for a table comprising seven columns for the socioeconomic groups in Table 3-5 and five rows for each of the parties (minor parties and missing-data cases are excluded).

Source: See footnote 1.

among the working class. None of these trends is remarkably strong, but their combined effect on the statistical relationship between social status and voting is, indeed, noteworthy.

We shall conclude this investigation of the social bases of the parties with a brief note on another aspect of the voters' social situation, namely, age. As Table 3–9 shows, the Social Democrats experienced heavy losses among students between 1970 and 1973. This is, of course, one of the most interesting components of the young vote, since students now make up a much larger proportion of this age group than they did fifteen years ago. The lowering of the voting age to twenty in 1973 and to eighteen in 1976 also means that the young vote has gained much more weight numerically than it had before in the electorate. Among students the Social Democratic losses

Table 3–9
PARTY CHOICE OF STUDENTS, 1968, 1970, AND 1973

Party Choice (in percentages of student respondents voting)	Election		
	1968	1970	1973
Communist party	5	12	18
Social Democratic party	34	38	18
Center party	12	17	27
People's party (Liberals)	29	18	7
Moderate party (Conservatives)	17	13	28
Christian Democratic party	0	1	2
Other	3	1	0
Total	100	100	100
N	(41)	(93)	(56)
Student nonvoters (in percentages of student respondents)	9	8	7
N	(47)	(102)	(69)

Source: See footnote 1.

were accompanied by gains for the Communists as well as the Center party. While the Communist upturn may perhaps be credited to the students' general radicalization and discontent with certain aspects of the government's educational policies, it is likely that the Center party's gain has more to do with the party's concern with environmental policies, as well as with its general attractiveness in 1973. The Social Democratic decline among young voters was not limited to students, although it was especially marked in that group. If one looks at the entire group of voters aged twenty to thirty years, it emerges that the Social Democrats lost fourteen percentage points in this age group as compared with eight percentage points in the voting electorate as a whole. (These comparisons are, of course, based on our survey data.)

Among voters who are aged between twenty and thirty, the Social Democrats are now weaker than they are in the electorate as a whole (42 percent as compared to 46 percent according to our survey data), while the opposite is true for the Communists and the Center party. It remains to be seen whether this merely means that young voters with less hardened party identifications responded especially strongly to the short-term factors that prevailed in 1973, or whether it is an indication of a more lasting erosion of the Social Democrats' standing in the electorate.

The Voters' Views

What are the voters' demands on the political system? In other words, what are the matters that concern voters at the time of an election and, in their view, ought also to concern parties and politicians? How is the government's record evaluated in the light of those demands? And what are the connections between voter demands and election outcome?

We shall attempt to answer these questions with the aid of interview data drawn from our national sample survey of the 1973 election. Most of the data to be employed here were obtained from open-ended questions asked in the introductory part of the interviews, hence, before we could have influenced the respondents by the topics raised in our more specific queries. The purpose of these questions was to chart the voters' grounds for satisfaction or dissatisfaction with the government's record, as well as the policy demands they rated as the most important for the next few years. Given the richness of the data, our chart is probably quite comprehensive, although we cannot claim that it is entirely exact in its details. The strength of this measurement technique lies in its capacity to reflect the relative importance of various policy areas and to register the balance of opinions on the government's record among those who are sufficiently concerned about a policy domain to comment on it spontaneously. But the percentages appearing in the following tables should not be assumed to indicate the proportions of voters who could have expressed an opinion about a policy area if they had been specifically asked to do so. These properties of the measurement technique must be taken into account when inferences are based upon the data.

Evaluation of the Social Democrats' Record in Office, 1973. The first of the questions in this sequence is related to the voters' evaluations of the policies pursued by the Social Democratic government. (The two interview questions, probes aside, were phrased as follows: "I would like to ask your views on the present government. First, I would like to ask if there is anything you particularly like about the Social Democratic government. . . . And is there anything about the Social Democratic government that you dislike?) In a subsequent question, respondents were asked what they personally considered most important for the parties, the government, and parliament to try to achieve or to change in the country in the next few years. Under the new constitutional order, representatives at both the national and the local levels are elected in contemporaneous parliamentary and local elections. In order to record demands directed to both levels of the political system, we therefore asked the same kind of question (somewhat later in the interview) about what ought to be achieved or changed in the voter's local government commune in the next few years. Answers to these open-ended questions were classified with a content-analysis coding scheme. Responses were classified according to the policy areas referred to in each answer. Obviously, this means that, when necessary, several codes were assigned to a single answer.

We have presented the data related to voter demands on both national and local politics in a compact form in Table 3–10 (see the explanatory legend to the table). Three policy domains dominate the voters' conception of *national* politics: taxation (mentioned by 22 percent), regional economic development (38 percent), and various aspects of social welfare reform policies. The latter domain comprises three categories in the table: social welfare, pensions and old-age care, and family welfare policies. To supplement the percentages given in the table, we have calculated the proportion of all voters who referred to at least one of these three areas. This proportion amounts to 36 percent. (A very large majority, but not all, of these responses expressed demands for new or expanded social services.) As the bottom row of the table shows, a large majority of the respondents expressed demands on both national and local politics (84 percent and 72 percent, respectively).

The demands directed to the two levels coincide in some regards, but there are also some interesting discrepancies. (Most percentages are lower for local politics, partly because more respondents referred to several policy areas in their answers about national politics.) Employment and social welfare rank high in both instances. In the case of social welfare, demands on the local level are especially concentrated in one area, namely, "family welfare policies." The high degree of concern over this area in local politics relates primarily to the need for the expansion of communal child-care institutions. This is an example of a demand that quite directly reflects societal change, in this instance the growing number of gainfully employed women. At the commune level, furthermore, references to "communications and planning" are quite frequent, most of them actually related to purely local matters. Finally, it is striking that local taxation attracts almost no attention. Although the local tax amounted to half or more of the total income tax for low- and middle-income earners, voters obviously did not see taxation as an important issue in the context of local politics. It should also be noted that a large number of the references to taxation in national politics had to do with indirect taxation (the value added tax, VAT) rather than income tax.

Our measurements of the voters' evaluations of the Social Democrats' record in office are brought together in Table 3–11 in an overview of favorable as well as unfavorable judgments on governmental policies in different areas (see legend to Table 3–11). On the whole, this table confirms the picture of the voters' concern about various policy areas presented in Table 3–10. Taxation, unemployment and regional development, and social welfare prove again to be the policy areas most often mentioned.

As can be seen in Table 3–11, the balance of opinions about the Social Democratic government was distinctly negative for two of the policy areas that were of most concern to the public at the time of the 1973 election, namely, taxation and employment and regional policies. Expressions of disapproval of the government were much more frequent than expressions of approval among the comments bearing on these areas. The image of the Social Democrats' achievements in social welfare, on the other hand, was decidedly favorable. We shall soon see, however, that neither this general appreciation nor the frequency of demands for specific measures in the social welfare area can be taken as evidence that the electorate was in the mood to expand the social welfare system.

The lack of appreciation of the Social Democrats' taxation policies can be seen as a more or less permanently negative feature of the public's image of the party. Precisely for this reason it cannot in itself be taken as an explanation of the downturn in the party's electoral fortunes. We obtained the same balance between positive and negative judgments on the subject of taxation at the 1968 election, when the Social Democrats won an absolute majority in the electorate.

If social welfare was an established electoral asset and taxation an equally fixed liability for the Social Democrats, the unfavorable balance of opinion over their employment policies was a new phenomenon in 1973. According to Table 3–12, positive and negative opinions on the Social Democrats' record in the area of employment were exactly balanced in 1968, while in 1973 only 21 percent of all comments were favorable and 79 percent were unfavorable to the Social Democrats. It is noteworthy that the shift occurred not only

Table 3-10

VOTERS' DEMANDS ON NATIONAL AND LOCAL GOVERNMENT, 1973 ELECTION

Policy Area	Type of Election	Respondent's Party					
		Communist party	Social Democratic party	Center party	People's party (Liberals)	Moderate party (Conservatives)	All Voters and Nonvoters
Taxation	NAT	18	17	24	25	37	22
	LOC	1	2	2	3	7	2
Social welfare (excluding pensions, family welfare)	NAT	16	17	14	20	16	16
	LOC	19	10	9	11	10	10
Pensions, old-age care	NAT	16	15	13	12	7	13
	LOC	5	7	6	9	7	7
Family welfare	NAT	14	11	15	18	19	14
	LOC	29	33	28	30	27	29
Employment, regional policies	NAT	43	37	43	39	34	38
	LOC	20	19	23	17	15	18
Housing	NAT	10	7	7	7	5	7
	LOC	12	10	13	14	14	11
Other economic, including agriculture	NAT	5	3	9	7	8	5
	LOC	0	0	1	2	1	1
Environment	NAT	14	7	13	12	8	9
	LOC	9	3	4	6	5	4

Communications, planning	NAT	5	2	3	3	1	2
	LOC	31	18	21	20	25	20
Law and order, morals, religion	NAT	3	7	8	15	16	10
	LOC	0	2	3	5	5	3
Socialism/liberalism (general ideological principles)	NAT	24	9	9	4	14	10
	LOC	1	0	0	1	0	0
Percentages of respondents who mentioned at least one policy area	NAT	90	81	87	89	91	84
	LOC	88	72	76	72	77	72

Note: Responses to two open-ended questions concerning national and local politics, respectively, have been classified according to "policy area." The entries in the table are percentages of the respondents from each party who mentioned each policy area in national politics and in local politics. Since the data are based on two interview questions, the percentages for national and local demands should be added separately. The column sums for each of the questions do not add up to 100 percent because some respondents mentioned more than one issue area, while others mentioned none. A few policy categories that were mentioned by only very small numbers of respondents have been omitted from the table. NAT = national politics; LOC = local politics.

Source: See footnote 1.

Table 3-11

VOTERS' EVALUATIONS OF THE GOVERNMENT'S PERFORMANCE, BY PARTY, 1973

Policy Area	Evaluation	Respondent's Party					
		Communist party	Social Democratic party	Center party	People's party (Liberals)	Moderate party (Conservatives)	All Voters and Nonvoters
Taxation	+	2	2	1	0	0	1
	−	22	20	31	33	33	25
Social welfare (excluding pensions, family welfare)	+	42	39	31	24	23	32
	−	14	16	24	18	25	19
Pensions, old-age care	+	20	34	26	23	19	27
	−	4	3	3	3	5	3
Family welfare	+	11	18	12	8	8	13
	−	7	5	11	10	14	9
Employment, regional policies	+	4	7	3	4	2	5
	−	22	13	24	21	18	17
Housing	+	1	2	1	0	0	1
	−	7	4	5	5	3	4
Other economic, including agriculture	+	1	1	0	0	0	1
	−	5	3	11	4	9	6
Environment	+	1	1	1	0	1	1
	−	4	1	2	2	1	1

Policy area		+ / −						
Communications, planning	+	3	1	1	0	1	1
	−	1	1	2	1	1	1
Law and order, morals, religion	+	0	1	1	1	1	1
	−	5	5	6	14	11	8
Foreign affairs, defense	+	17	5	5	2	1	4
	−	4	3	5	7	8	4
Socialism/liberalism (general ideological principles)	+	7	7	5	5	4	6
	−	13	5	12	14	19	10
Socioeconomic group interests	+	3	8	4	4	2	5
	−	2	2	4	7	4	3
Percentage of respondents who mentioned at least one policy area	+	77	86	63	56	50	70
	−	81	60	86	88	88	73

Note: The table is based on responses to two open-ended questions concerning the "good points" and "bad points" of the Social Democratic government. Responses are classified according to policy areas. Entries are percentages of responses which mentioned each policy area as a "good point" (+ row) or a "bad point" (− row). Each percentage is based on the number of respondents who voted for the party indicated. Since the data are based on two interview questions, the percentages for "good" and "bad" evaluations should be added separately. The column sums for each of these questions do not add up to 100 percent because some respondents mentioned more than one policy area, while others mentioned none. Policy categories mentioned by only very small numbers of respondents have been omitted from the table.

Source: See footnote 1.

Table 3–12

VOTERS' EVALUATIONS OF THE GOVERNMENT'S RECORD
ON EMPLOYMENT AND REGIONAL POLICIES,
BY PARTY, 1968 AND 1973

	Respondent's Party				
Evaluations	Social Demo-cratic party	Center party	People's party (Liberals)	Moderate party (Conser-vatives)	**All Voters and Nonvoters**
1968					
Favorable mentions, in percentages of total	68	29	39	33	50
Total number of mentions of issue	(230)	(102)	(51)	(40)	(464)
1973					
Favorable mentions, in percentages of total	34	13	15	10	21
Total number of mentions of issue	(207)	(160)	(46)	(58)	(563)

Note: This table is based on open-ended interview questions concerning the "good points" and "bad points" of the Social Democrats in 1968 and 1973. The entries are, for each year, the total number of references to employment and regional policies made by respondents from each important party and by all respondents, and the percentages of all such references that were favorable— that is, expressed approval of the policies pursued by the Social Democrats.
Source: See footnote 1.

among opposition voters, but also among the party's own voters in 1973. It must, of course, be kept in mind that Table 3–12 only takes into account the electors who actually referred to employment and regional economic development as a "good" or "bad point" about the Social Democrats; this means that the data probably reflect the balance of opinion among those voters who were most concerned with these problems. The Social Democrats have for a long time built much of their prestige on their claim to being the party that maintains full employment. This claim is probably still essential to the party's appeal, but our data suggest that in the 1973 election campaign the Social Democrats encountered a damaging reassessment of their ability to handle the current employment problems.

Although the mass media's reporting of the public debate in the late 1960s and the early 1970s sometimes conveyed the impression that radical views were gaining strength, the evidence of the election results points in the opposite direction. The socialist—Social Democrat and Communist—share of the vote fell between 1968 and 1973. The survey data provide further indications that the shift of the vote was accompanied by a shift in the public's mood. We have monitored the views of the electorate on several aspects of welfare state policies and economic issues in a series of election studies, and our data indicate a shift "to the right" from 1968 to 1973.

The most striking shift occurred in the balance of opinion on the need for further social welfare reforms. This trend is shown in Table 3–13: the proportion of "positive" views on social welfare reforms fell from 52 percent in 1968 to 32 percent in 1973, while the proportion of "negative" opinions climbed up from 41 percent to 60 percent. The shift appears among supporters of all parties, notably among Social Democratic voters. As we saw in Tables 3–10 and 3–11, the achievements of the welfare state were generally approved of by voters who were concerned enough to single out this area as one in which to evaluate the government's performance, and a variety of new reforms enjoyed support in many sectors of the electorate. At the same time, however, the data in Table 3–13 indicate that support for any further general expansion of the social welfare system was diminishing.

We have brought together several measures of opinion on issues that are related to the left-right cleavage in Swedish politics in Table 3–14, employing a balance-of-opinions index, which helps to bring out trends in electoral opinions. The table shows that opinion on state economic control has shifted to the right less markedly than opinion on social welfare, but in both areas the trend is consistent.

Foreign Policy and the International Context. Foreign policy and events in the international arena were far from the focus of attention during the 1973 campaign. Sweden's relationship with the EEC, which had been a source of dissension in the past, was treated more or less as a settled question. The American involvement in Vietnam was clearly very much present in people's minds as well as in the mass media, but neither the war as such nor the frozen diplomatic

Table 3–13

VOTERS' VIEWS ON WELFARE STATE POLICIES, 1968–73

(in percentages)

Survey Result	Communist party	Social Democratic party	Center party	People's party (Liberals)	Moderate party (Conservatives)	All Voters and Nonvoters
1968						
Agree	13	28	56	54	71	41
Ambiguous/undecided	10	7	6	7	6	7
Disagree	77	65	38	39	23	52
Total	100	100	100	100	100	100
N	(39)	(1,421)	(461)	(360)	(280)	(2,866)
1973						
Agree	22	47	76	68	78	60
Ambiguous/undecided	8	7	6	7	7	8
Disagree	70	46	18	25	25	32
Total	100	100	100	100	100	100
N	(93)	(988)	(567)	(178)	(266)	(2,421)
Change, 1968–73 [a]	−9	−19	−20	−14	−7	−19

[a] Percentage who agreed in 1968 *minus* percentage who agreed in 1973. Thus, a negative entry indicates a shift to the right.

Note: Respondents were invited to agree or disagree with the statement: "Social reforms have gone so far in this country that in the future the state should reduce rather than increase social benefits and support for its citizens."

Source: See footnote 1.

relationship between Sweden and the United States was turned into a campaign issue.

The survey data suggest that foreign policy had hardly any appreciable direct impact on voting behavior or the election outcome. The proportion of respondents who expressed any concern with foreign policy in our survey of voter demands was so slight that foreign policy has been omitted from Table 3–10. Admittedly, the phrasing of the survey question may have induced people to think primarily about domestic policies. But foreign policy was mentioned only slightly more often in the evaluations of the government's performance set forth in Table 3–11. Among the few comments on foreign policy that were made, negative and positive evaluations were quite evenly balanced (see Table 3–11).[11] More detailed survey data on Sweden's policies toward the EEC and the United States support the thesis that the division of opinion on foreign policy cannot account for the Social Democrats' electoral setback. If anything, the impact of foreign affairs should have been slight but in the opposite direction.

By 1973 the relationship between Sweden and the United States had been strained for some years. Both the Johnson and the Nixon administrations had shown clear signs of dissatisfaction with the reception afforded to American political refugees by Sweden as well as with the Swedish government's generally critical attitude toward the Vietnam War. The enmity between the two countries reached a climax after Prime Minister Palme's harsh condemnation of U.S. bombing in Vietnam on Christmas 1972. The ensuing withdrawal of the American ambassador from Sweden and the severing of relations in general naturally aroused some opposition in Sweden.

The responses to an interview question in our election survey about the government's criticism of the American role in Vietnam followed a distinctly partisan pattern. The government's standpoint was generally endorsed by Communists and Social Democrats but more than half of the Center and People's party voters who expressed views disapproved of the Swedish government's policy, as did an even larger proportion of Conservative voters. Nevertheless, the government had substantial minority support among opposition party voters. This meant that the division of opinions in the electorate was weighted in favor of the government, though not overwhelmingly so.

In general, worry about U.S. Indochina policy was frequently mentioned in response to open-ended questions about the international situation. Other interview questions show that quite large proportions of the electorate believed that the United States had become increasingly belligerent as well as increasingly unfriendly toward Sweden.[12] A very large portion of the electorate found it difficult to apportion the blame between the two sides in the Vietnam War, but those who did choose sides were mostly critical of the United States.

[11] The data in the election survey provide the basis for the statement that there was widespread concern among the public about international affairs. Thus, for example, an open-ended question about what worried people in international politics indicated a surprisingly high level of awareness and concern. It goes beyond the scope of this article to treat these data.

[12] A selection of additional data from the election survey which pertain to international opinions are published in O. Petersson, "Stormaktspolitik i svensk opinion" [Great power politics in Swedish opinion] Internationella studier [International studies], vol. 4 (1975). These data are drawn from a comprehensive study of this topic to be published by Petersson.

Table 3-14
LEFT-RIGHT BALANCE OF OPINIONS, 1968 AND 1973

Interview Statement	Year	Respondent's Party					
		Communist party	Social Democratic party	Center party	People's party (Liberals)	Moderate party (Conservatives)	All Voters and Nonvoters
The risk of unemployment is reduced if the state gets more influence over banks and business enterprises.	1968	+79	+43	−22	−31	−63	+8
	1973	+66	+46	−46	−62	−73	−4
Private enterprise fulfills its tasks if it is left free of interference by the state.	1968	+72	+28	−56	−51	−74	−10
	1973	+44	+14	−64	−67	−80	−25
Those who are in leading positions in banks and industry get much too much influence if the state is not able to control private enterprise.	1968	+72	+70	+19	+8	−34	+40
	1973	+84	+67	+12	−12	−30	+32
Social reforms have gone so far in this country that in the future the state should reduce rather than increase social benefits and support for citizens.	1968	+64	+37	−18	−15	−48	+11
	1973	+48	−1	−58	−43	−53	−28

Note: This table presents an overview of data drawn from a series of interviews. Respondents were asked whether they agreed or disagreed with the statements expressing generally "rightist" or "leftist" views on economic policies and social welfare listed in the left-hand column. The entries in the table are balance-of-opinions index values; a *plus* sign indicates predominance of "leftist" responses, while a *minus* sign indicates predominance of "rightist" views. The index is based on the percentage distribution of "leftist," "ambivalent," and "rightist" responses; the index value is obtained by subtracting the "rightist" percentage from the "leftist" percentage.

Source: See footnote 1.

Again the data indicate that partisanship and views on foreign policy were linked, but not in the sense that many votes were swayed by foreign policy issues. Rather, foreign policy issues were perceived, at least partly, in the light of a broader ideological outlook.

Sweden's relationship to the EEC has been the only other foreign policy question of sufficient importance to cause dissension in party politics in recent years.[13] When the European Free Trade Association (EFTA) began to crumble as a consequence of Britain's renewed attempts to win entry into the EEC, it was obviously necessary for Sweden to reconsider its relations with the European Community. At the time of the 1970 election, it was still considered a possibility that Sweden would achieve membership status with certain qualifications intended to preserve its neutrality; the government had actually requested negotiations with the EEC to this effect. In the end, however, Sweden decided to stay out of the EEC and instead a trade agreement was concluded. The ground for this decision was primarily that only by this means could the country maintain the credibility of its neutrality. This was the standpoint taken by the Social Democrats as well as the Center party, while the People's party and the Conservatives wished to explore further the feasibility of acquiring full membership in the EEC. It was not the first time that somewhat different conceptions of the country's neutrality had aligned the parties this way. Nevertheless, the EEC issue did not develop into a major divisive issue in Sweden, as it did in Denmark and Norway. And since the bourgeois parties were themselves divided on this question, they did not bring it into the foreground in the 1973 election campaign.

At the time of the 1970 election, the EEC issue aroused little interest; 44 percent of a survey sample said they had no definite view of the matter. Among those who had a view, on the other hand, most were in favor of Sweden's joining the Common Market, with the exception, of course, of the Communists. The latent controversy was visible in 1970 only in that the pro-EEC majority was much smaller among Social Democrats and Center party voters than among Conservative and People's party voters.

To the extent that voters had views at all on Sweden's relationship with the EEC in 1973, our survey data suggest that acquiescence, if not satisfaction, with the country's staying out of the community prevailed. Of the small minority who wanted any change, the Communists, of course, were most hostile to and the Conservatives most

---

[13] See M. Bergquist, *Sverige och EEC* [Sweden and the EEC] (Stockholm: Norstedt, 1970). Although this study concentrates on the period 1961-62, the author's analysis of the arguments is largely valid also for the later phases of the EEC debate.

in favor of closer ties with the EEC. As in 1970, a very large proportion of the voters confessed to having no opinion on the matter.

Swedish voters—unlike the Norwegians and Danes—saw the relationship with the EEC as primarily a foreign policy issue whose economic implications were secondary. Public opinion never became strongly mobilized along sectional or interest-group lines. Instead, party standpoints largely determined the voters' attitudes on Sweden's membership. The reason may have been that no conflict between party standpoints and interest-group views really emerged. Thus, farming interests were skeptical about membership, but their views were readily channeled through the Center party, and the fact that the Social Democratic party came out against membership prevented the kind of internal split in the labor movement that occurred in Norway and in Denmark. Although the electoral upheavals in Norway and Denmark were contemporaneous with the Social Democratic decline in Sweden, the setting was different in the Swedish case.

A Scandinavian Trend?

The coincidence of the weakening of the Social Democratic parties in Denmark, Norway, and Sweden in 1973 is so striking that one is almost bound to consider whether it reflects a common political trend, perhaps even the beginning of the end of the party system that has been characteristic of Scandinavian politics for some decades. The broad features of this system are well known: a strong Social Democratic party and a set of nonsocialist parties, which, in addition to the main socioeconomic cleavage, also reflect an urban-rural cleavage and differences in cultural values. In all three of these countries, society has shown a remarkable capacity for assimilating fast technological and industrial development, while striving for consensus politics, maintaining a stable party system, and implementing tension-reducing welfare state policies. The Social Democratic predominance during the postwar era has been most consistent in Sweden and least so in Denmark, but even in Denmark the Social Democrats have been seen more or less as the "natural" government party.

There is evidence of other parallel trends in two or more of these countries. In Denmark as well as in Norway, parties to the left of the Social Democrats have had significant successes. In Norway, the left-socialist alliance gained more than 10 percent of the vote in 1973, and in Denmark the combined strength of the left-socialist and the Communist parties has hovered around 10 percent since 1966. In Sweden the Communists and the "Marxist-Leninist" splinter parties have been stepping up their propaganda and their organizational activities since the late 1960s. Their views received more attention in the mass media than ever before, and they have, no doubt, a highly visible and articulate support base within the increasing student population. In elections in Sweden, the success of the "left of the Social Democrats" parties has been much less spectacular, however. The lively debate over the causes and significance of the growth and intellectual activity of the left fringe may have created the impression of a shift to the left, a radicalization, of the electorate as a whole. Precisely for this reason it needs to be stressed that the net effect of the flows of the vote in all of these countries in the 1970s has been a *shift to the right,* as evidenced in the overall decline in the socialist share of the vote.

In Denmark and Norway, this shift has been accompanied by quite dramatic dislocations of the party system and a marked tendency toward fractionalization. To some extent dissatisfaction with welfare state policies has been channeled through populistic and antisocialistic new parties. The strains on the party system have been much less intensive in Sweden. One reason for this may be that, while the new populistic parties in Denmark and Norway provided an outlet for middle-class frustration over nonsocialist coalition government, in Sweden the bourgeois voters had not yet had the experience of disillusionment with bourgeois government for the simple reason that the parties they supported had remained in opposition. Perhaps an even more important source of dissension in Denmark and Norway, which affected Sweden much less, was the relationship with the EEC. In Norway, where the EEC controversy was to some degree linked to the long-term split within the Labor party over the country's NATO membership, the EEC referendum split not only the Social Democratic party but also the Liberal party. In Denmark, the crisis appears to have culminated when the impact of EEC membership, on food prices, for example, made itself felt.

The economies of all three countries were obviously affected by trends in the world economy. In Sweden rising prices and unemployment caused by structural economic change certainly had a decisive impact on the outcome of the 1970 election. Then at the time of the 1973 election, recessionary trends in the economy caused an increase in the level of unemployment that was quite alarming by Swedish standards. (By the standards of most European countries, the unemployment rate was still fairly low.) External economic factors weakened confidence in the welfare state's capacity to maintain

112

economic growth and full employment and at the same time fueled dissatisfaction with progressive taxes when nominal wages and salaries went up owing to inflation. These developments appear to have been among the causes of the Social Democratic party's decline in all three Scandinavian countries.

We have seen in the foregoing section that the Social Democrats' setback in Sweden was accompanied by a shift toward the right in the electorate's views on social welfare policies and state economic control. There is some evidence in the survey data that at the same time the voters' attitude toward the parties and politicians became slightly more distrustful. The data are presented in Table 3–15 in the form of balance-of-opinions index values based on interview questions asked in 1968 and 1973. The questions were designed to tap feelings of cynicism about the party system and were presented in the form of statements expressing such feelings. The relatively high frequency of "cynical" views to some extent may be due to this question format, which perhaps called forth the well-known "response acquiescence" effect. The point is, however, that the *balance* shifted, weakly but consistently, toward increasing distrust in 1973. (See the explanatory note to Table 3–15.) It is also noteworthy that feelings of distrust were consistently more widespread among bourgeois voters than among Social Democrats on both occasions. Given the long Social Democratic rule, one may surmise that attitudes toward the ruling party have gradually come to encompass politics in general. It also seems likely that the increase in distrust, like the outcome of the election, was caused by dissatisfaction with the government's ability to handle the country's economic problems. The Swedish party system did not, however, come under the kind of attack that the established parties in Denmark and Norway experienced during the referendum campaigns and the 1973 election campaigns.

The signs of uncertainty in the party system which have recently affected all three countries to varying degrees might be taken as evidence that their tradition of political stability has depended upon the presence of a strong Social Democratic party which did not have to fear any serious competition from the left. When the strength of the Social Democrats is undermined, governmental stability depends on the nonsocialist parties' ability to offer an alternative of comparable strength and cohesiveness. If the nonsocialist parties fail to achieve this, the two-bloc party system is bound to disintegrate and make way for a more flexible and less stable multiparty type of parliamentary politics.

Table 3-15

LEVEL OF TRUST IN PARTIES AND POLITICIANS, 1968 AND 1973

Interview Statement	Year	Balance of Opinions Index					
		Communist party	Social Democratic party	Center party	People's party (Liberals)	Moderate party (Conservatives)	All Voters and Nonvoters
Parties are interested in people's votes but not in their views.	1968	+18	+29	+7	+17	+15	+19
	1973	−5	+10	−1	−1	−3	−2
One can never be sure that any of the parties intend to keep their promises.	1968	−16	−18	−30	−26	−29	−26
	1973	−32	−22	−42	−29	−30	−31
Those who sit in the *Riksdag* and make decisions do not pay much attention to ordinary people's views.	1968	−27	+12	−10	−3	−5	+3
	1973	−37	−6	−28	−16	−15	−12

Note: These data were obtained from a series of interview questions. Respondents were asked whether they agreed or disagreed with the statements about parties and politicians listed in the left-hand column. For each of these statements, agreement has been taken as an expression of "distrust," disagreement an indication of "trust." For each category of voters and for each of the statements, we have calculated the distribution in percentages of trust, distrust, and "ambiguous response." The balance-of-opinions index has been obtained by subtracting the distrust percentage from the trust percentage. A plus sign indicates predominance of trust, while a minus sign indicates predominance of distrust. (This is, of course, equivalent to the mean value that would be obtained if all trust answers were scored +1, all distrust answers −1, and all ambiguous responses zero.)

Source: See footnote 1.

From this perspective, it is the differences rather than the similarities in the recent political trends in the three Scandinavian countries that merit attention. The drift toward the fragmentation of the party system is far more pronounced in Denmark than in Norway, while in Sweden the party configuration has remained largely unaffected. The growth of the "left of the Social Democrats" parties has been much more marked in Denmark and Norway than in Sweden in terms of electoral support, while the increased strength of the Communists in the Swedish *Riksdag* is primarily the result of a change in the electoral system. In the case of Sweden, the electoral upheaval in 1973 essentially amounted to an impressive transference of votes to one of the parties in the center of the party system. The outcome has been considerable uncertainty in parliamentary politics, but it would take nothing more than a decisive outcome in the 1976 election—in favor of either the socialists or the nonsocialists—to restore the two-bloc political division.

Postscript: The 1976 Election *

When the Swedish *Riksdag* met on October 4, 1976, after the election of September 19, the Social Democratic government under Olof Palme had already resigned as a consequence of the election outcome. It was staying in office as a caretaker cabinet, awaiting only the formal investiture of Torbjörn Fälldin as prime minister in a coalition government formed by his own Center party, the People's party (Liberals), and the Conservatives. The election had resulted in a majority for this coalition comprising 180 of the 349 seats in the *Riksdag* (see Table 3–16). At the time of their defeat in 1976 the Social Democrats had been in office, either in one-party cabinets or as the dominant party in coalitions, since 1932.

The significance of the 1976 election as a turning point in the history of the Swedish parliamentary system lies not only in the fact that the Social Democrats lost power after forty-four years in office. The formation of a nonsocialist government based on parties with a majority in the *Riksdag* is in itself remarkable, since it is the first of its kind since the establishment of a democratic parliamentary system in Sweden in the final years of World War I. After the Liberal-Social Democratic coalition broke up in 1920, a succession of short-lived minority governments held power until the beginning of the

* Editor's Note: The body of this chapter was written and revised in 1975. The postscript, written in October 1976, tests the author's earlier findings against the results of the September 1976 Swedish election.

Table 3–16

1976 ELECTION RESULTS: SEATS, VOTE, AND CHANGE IN VOTE

Result	Party					
	Communist party	Social Democratic party	Center party	People's party (Liberals)	Moderate party (Conservatives)	Christian Democratic party
Seats in *Riksdag*, 1976	17	152	86	39	55	
Percent distribution of vote, 1976 a	4.8	42.7	24.1	11.1	15.6	1.4
Change, in percentage-point gains and losses:						
1973 to 1976	− 0.5	− 0.9	− 1.0	+ 1.7	+ 1.3	− 0.4
1970 to 1976	0	− 2.6	+ 4.2	− 5.1	+ 4.1	− 0.4
1968 to 1976 b	+ 1.8	− 7.4	+ 7.9	− 3.9	+ 1.7	− 0.1

a The total does not add up to 100 percent because of the exclusion of a split-off Communist party (0.3 percent) and a small proportion of "others."

b The small proportion of votes received by electoral coalitions of nonsocialist parties in 1968 has been divided up among the nonsocialist parties according to the number of votes cast for each party's list of candidates under such coalition labels.

Source: For the 1976 election, see *Fran Riksdag & Departement* [From the *Riksdag* and departments], official weekly journal published by the government information board, no. 29 (1976). For previous elections, see *Allmänna valen 1973*, vol. 1, p. 10.

Social Democratic era in the 1930s. Although individual bourgeois parties staffed several of these governments, Prime Minister Fälldin's cabinet is unprecedented in that it is the first coalition government formed exclusively by nonsocialist parties. (The only partial exception is a minority government in the 1920s that was formed by the Liberals during the period when they were split into two small parties.)

In the body of this chapter we stressed that the conception of the Swedish party system as essentially consisting of a socialist and bourgeois bloc has come to be generally accepted, in spite of the fact that the boundary between the blocs is sometimes transgressed in parliamentary politics. But as far as the working of the parliamentary system is concerned, the two-bloc division until now has had its ground in the declared intention of the bourgeois parties to form a coalition government if and when they attained a parliamentary majority. The underlying expectation was that the Swedish party system would reflect changing electoral results according to the classic two-party parliamentary model, rather than the more unstable pattern of center-left or center-right coalitions that often has emerged in multiparty systems. But this expectation was theoretical, based on an understanding of the dynamics of the system. Only now has an alternative to Social Democratic predominance materialized in the form of a bourgeois bloc government.

Analysis of the Election Results. What are the likely consequences of the 1976 election outcome for the functioning of the parliamentary system and the party system? There appear to be four main alternative scenarios, and although we are not in a position to predict which of them will come true, we can usefully consider their implications. In the first place, it is entirely possible that the Social Democrats will return to power after the next election in 1979; the 1976 bourgeois government would then stand out as an interlude in a continuing era of Social Democratic predominance. It is equally possible, however, that the 1976 election has inaugurated a new electoral era that will last for a decade or more, with a continuous bourgeois majority in the electorate and the nonsocialist bloc normally in power. It is at least a plausible conjecture that this would ultimately lead to the creation of a large, united liberal-conservative party. As a correlate, it may be conjectured that the failure of the three coalition parties to merge might prevent them from attaining a level of stability in power at all comparable to that of the previous Social Democratic governments. The third possibility would consist in a modified version of the classic two-party parliamentary system, where the two blocs would alternate in power with a normal frequency of, say, one or two election periods.

Finally, it is quite conceivable that the two-bloc system might break up after only a few years of nonsocialist coalition government either before or, more likely, after the next election. This could take the form of a split between the two centrist parties—the Center party and the People's party (Liberals)—and the Conservatives. To complicate matters further, it is not entirely unthinkable that the Social Democrats might entice one of the two centrist parties to join them in a coalition. The Social Democrats might come to show considerable interest in that possibility if they deemed their prospects of winning a majority of their own to be slim and if, at the same time, they were reluctant to return to office as long as they needed the parliamentary support (without participation in government) of the Communist party. If, as one can expect, the three parties in the bourgeois bloc prove unwilling to merge into one party, there still remains the possibility that two of them, the Center party and the People's party, might realize their long-nurtured idea of merging into a united centrist party. Since this would be a comparatively big party, its formation would effectively preclude a coalition of the type that the Social Democrats might be most interested in, that is, a two-party coalition wherein the Social Democrats could play the leading role.

There are two further possibilities (both of which have precedents in Swedish parliamentary history) for cabinet formation in situations where the nonsocialist parties have a majority but are unable to form a cohesive bloc. One would consist in center-based minority governments. The other would be a minority Social Democratic government, "tolerated" by the center. For the time being at least, a minority cabinet formed by the Conservatives alone appears highly unlikely. It is notable that the provisions for cabinet formation in the new Swedish constitution actually are framed with a view to the situation that arises when no government with a majority base in the parliament can be formed. Thus, when a cabinet has resigned, it is the duty of the speaker of the *Riksdag*, after consultations with party leaders and vice speakers, to propose a new prime minister to the parliament. The proposal is considered approved unless a majority of the members vote against it. This procedure makes it feasible for one or more parties in the parliament to allow a minority government to be formed, even if they do not wish to give it open support. By abstaining at the vote such parties could indicate that they were prepared to "tolerate," rather than support, the new cabinet. Likewise, the procedure for a vote of censure affords protection for a minority government. A no-confidence motion is carried only if a majority of the total number of members votes for it; an opposition party can thus save a cabinet without actually supporting it by abstaining at the vote.

None of the eventualities discussed in the last paragraph is likely to come true in the course of the election period that has just begun. Given the high degree of party cohesion on important votes in the Swedish parliament, a majority of eleven is an entirely sufficient base for a stable government. There is little doubt that the three coalition parties are firmly determined to demonstrate that they are a credible alternative to Social Democratic predominance. Indeed, their failure to do so could easily unleash a dangerous confidence crisis within the half of the electorate that has waited so long for a change. But the three parties' experience of shared responsibility in government during this election period will certainly be of crucial importance for their willingness to present themselves again as a prospective governmental bloc at the time of the next election. This will determine which of the scenarios described above would follow, unless the Social Democrats prove able to return to office with a majority of their own.

The Electoral Trend. The shift to the right in the electorate, which began in the 1970 election and was confirmed in 1973, continued in 1976 with the small decisive move needed to ensure a nonsocialist majority in the *Riksdag* as well as in the electorate. The three nonsocialist parties in the new government received 50.8 percent of the vote, to which should perhaps be added the 1.4 percent of the vote cast for the Christian Democratic party. It would be wrong to state that this outcome could have been safely predicted from the trend in the 1970 and 1973 elections, however. In the 1960s the Social Democrats proved themselves capable of recovering from the decline they had suffered in the 1950s as well as from temporary setbacks. Thus, as late as 1968 the Social Democrats attained their best parliamentary election result of the postwar period only two years after a shattering loss of electoral support in the 1966 local government elections. Moreover, as late as the spring of 1975, opinion polls appeared to give the Social Democratic party a very good chance of surviving the next election, albeit with only a slim majority in the *Riksdag* dependent on Communist support.

The electoral change that finally shifted the balance was small, indeed. As Table 3–16 shows, the Social Democrats lost 0.9 percentage points from their share of the total vote at the 1973 election. Including the Communist loss, there was an electoral swing of 1.4 percentage points away from the socialist parties. As Table 3–16 also shows, it was a cumulative, sustained voting trend through the elections in 1970, 1973, and 1976 that eroded the ground for the Social Democratic government. From its level in 1968—when the Communist vote fell to rock bottom because of the events in Czechoslovakia—the Social Democrats' support has receded fom 50.1 percent to 42.7 percent of the vote, a decline of 7.4 percentage points. Had the swing occurred at a single election it would certainly have been considered a major political reversal.

This calls for answers to two different questions, or explanations on two different levels. First, what were the forces that brought about the declining trend in the Social Democrats' support in the 1970s? And second, given the narrowness of the resulting defeat, what short-term factors checked the Social Democrats' attempts to stop the downward drift and recover enough ground to defend their position as the governing party?

In the body of this chapter, we attributed the weakening support for the Social Democratic government in the early 1970s, more than anything else, to dissatisfaction caused by "stagflation" in the economy, that is, the combined effect of rising prices and slackening economic growth. As witnessed by the OECD economic survey on Sweden in 1976, the government's management of the economy during the years following the 1973 election was remarkably successful in some important respects.[14] Unemployment was brought down again to a very low level (from 2.6 percent of the labor force in 1973 to 1.6 percent in 1975), and industrial investment showed an upward turn that was in marked contrast to its development in many other countries. There was a significant rise in real personal income and, interestingly, a strong upturn in the personal savings ratio. Furthermore, the tax structure was changed so as to alleviate the steepness of the progressivity in the income tax for wage earners whose nominal income increases were partly a reflection of the inflationary trend. Consumer prices, however, continued to rise at about the average rate for OECD countries, which was, of course, quite high.

While the economy recovered from the 1970 recession, the Social Democrats did not. Why was this? To explore with any certainty how the state of the economy was evaluated by voters at the time of the 1976 election, we need survey data that are not yet available. But in light of the previous election study data we would venture the hypothesis that inflation was the feature of the economic situation that remained the decisive electoral liability for the Social Democratic government. In 1976, prices were still rising at a rate of around 10 percent per year. The government's success in bringing down unemployment may have been sufficient to fend off electoral disaster in 1976. But as long as prices continued to rise, the Social Democratic government was not able to restore confidence in its economic policy to anything like its level in 1968.

The development of voting intentions in the electorate in the period between the elections of 1973 and 1976 is outlined by the data in Table 3–17. The table is based on the large-scale national surveys which are conducted twice a year by the National Central Bureau of Statistics as a public service. Rather smaller but also reliable surveys

---

[14] OECD Economic Surveys: Sweden, April 1976.

Table 3–17

VOTING INTENTIONS IN THE SWEDISH ELECTORATE, 1973–76

(in percentages)

	Intended Vote						
Survey Date	Com- munist party	Social Demo- cratic party	Center party	People's party (Liberals)	Moderate party (Conser- vatives)	Others	Total
November 1973	4.8	43.9	26.6	8.7	14.0	2.0	100
May 1974	5.0	44.7	25.9	8.2	14.1	2.2	100
November 1974	5.1	44.6	25.1	8.5	14.3	2.4	100
May 1975	5.2	45.1	24.7	7.6	15.1	2.4	100
November 1975	5.0	44.3	23.9	8.9	15.3	2.6	100
February 1976	4.8	44.0	23.5	10.1	15.3	2.3	100
May 1976	4.8	42.3	22.8	10.8	16.9	2.3	100

Note: Respondents were asked how they would vote "if there were an election today." The total sample for each of these surveys comprises about 9,000 individuals. The sample is an unclustered probability sample representative of the electorate; it is rotated so that one-third of the sample is exchanged on each occasion. The percent distributions given in the table above have been adjusted so as to correct for systematic errors arising from the difference between the sample and the electorate in respect of party distribution in the last previous election, differential probability of participating in different population groups, and nonresponse. Confidence intervals are ±0.6 percent or less for each estimate.

Source: "Party Sympathy Surveys" conducted by the Swedish National Central Bureau of Statistics at the times indicated, published in the series *Statistiska meddelanden* [Statistical reports]; see also *Political Opinion Survey*, published by National Central Bureau of Statistics, June 1975.

are conducted monthly by a commercial polling agency (SIFO); minor fluctuations aside, this series of data presents the same picture of the development of opinion as the larger studies. As the situation in the national economy improved, the Social Democrats appear to have regained some support through 1974 and at least up to the spring of 1975. Then followed a relapse which became very marked in the spring of 1976. Thus, the Central Bureau of Statistics reported the Social Democrats to be down to 42.3 percent in May, while the SIFO surveys rated them slightly below 40 percent in both April and May. There was no indication of any compensating increase in Communist support. Instead, the opinion polls indicated that the Communists had fallen below 5 percent.

There is some survey evidence to support our conjecture that the Social Democrats' standing on the employment issue had improved by

1976 over its level during the most troublesome phase of the preceding recession. The evidence is provided by a series of SIFO data
based on an interview question whether electors thought a Social
Democratic or a bourgeois government would be more capable of
securing full employment (see Table 3–18). As is seen from the
response distributions at different times for this question, the balance
of opinions shifted clearly in favor of the Social Democrats from 1973
to 1976. But it is also clear that public confidence had not been
restored to its 1968 strength.

The main conclusion that could be drawn from the opinion polls
in the late spring of 1976 was that the balance of strength in the
electorate was as even as it had been at the 1973 election. The Social
Democrats' organizational machinery has a reputation for being able
to mobilize additional support once an election campaign gets under
way, and it was felt that it might do this again. On the other hand,
it might not.

Judging from the opinion polls, the Social Democrats did, indeed,
pick up some strength between May and the election, but probably
not very much and certainly not enough. Although most political
commentators would agree that the government defended its economic
policy record fairly successfully during the campaign, the main themes
did not come out quite in the way the Social Democrats would have
desired. The election campaign did not gain momentum until late
August. In the first weeks of the campaign, the bourgeois parties
concentrated their attacks on a scheme for the transferring of capital

Table 3–18
RESULTS OF SURVEYS ON THE EMPLOYMENT ISSUE, 1968–76
(in percentages)

Government Considered More Capable of Securing Full Employment	Response Distribution			
	1968	1970	1973	1976
Social Democrats	48	29	30	38
Bourgeois parties	28	35	40	27
No difference	14	20	16	17
Don't know	9	16	14	18

Note: Voters were asked whether they thought a Social Democratic or a bourgeois
government would be more capable of securing full employment.
Source: SIFO opinion polls, reported in *Svenska Dagbladet* [Swedish daily post],
July 3, 1976.

as well as economic power in private industries from the shareholders to wage-earner funds to be controlled by the employees through their trade unions. The scheme had been proposed by the manual workers' trade unions (the Swedish Federation of Labor, LO) and had received a positive though less committed response from the central organization of the white-collar workers (the Salaried Employees' Federation, TCO). The Social Democratic government endorsed the general aims of the scheme and appointed an investigative committee with the task of considering further the ways in which these aims could be achieved. If implemented, anything like this scheme could result in a profound change in the power structure in private industry without actual nationalization.[15]

Since the scheme could appeal to white-collar workers as well as manual workers, it clearly had the potential to become the next major policy initiative for the Social Democrats. On the other hand, there were unmistakable indications that the party leadership had reservations about the practicability of the scheme in the form that had originally been proposed. Here, for once, was a policy issue on which the public standpoints chosen by the unions and the party leadership were not entirely attuned. When the bourgeois parties turned the matter into a campaign issue, it became clear that, while the Social Democratic leadership proposed to realize the aims of the scheme sometime in the future ("not until after the 1979 election"), they were unwilling to commit themselves beyond that general statement. As a result the government's spokesmen ended up on the defensive, yet remaining evasive about their actual commitment, while the bourgeois opposition vehemently proclaimed that the scheme would mean the end of both a mixed economy and a free society.

The Nuclear Power Issue. In the second part of the campaign, all other political controversies were upstaged by the nuclear power issue. It had been clear for at least the last year that the Center party was opposed to the nuclear energy program which had been adopted by the government and was supported by the two other bourgeois opposition parties. The Center party leader, Fälldin, took the issue into the election campaign in a series of forceful speeches, warning, in particular, that the storage of waste from such nuclear installations would pose insoluble problems and involve enormous risks. As an alternative, Fälldin not only proposed a long-term energy program intended to make the country independent of nuclear power but also

---

[15] See the discussion of "economic democracy" in Galenson, in this volume, pp. 293-95.

demanded an immediate decision that no further nuclear installations be put into operation or constructed. Moreover, he said, the country's energy policy should be restructured so as to make it possible to close down existing nuclear power plants within the next few years. The Center party leader attached so much weight to the nuclear power question that he at least appeared to pledge that his party's participating in a new government would be made dependent on the coalition partners' acceptance of the Center party's energy program. Fälldin's move made it necessary for Palme to devote considerable attention to defending the government's energy program, but Palme also attempted to exploit this issue as one of the many on which the three bourgeois parties had proved unable to present an agreed policy for their prospective coalition.

Most observers of the campaign would agree that the nuclear energy debate made some impact on public opinion and that, on balance, public opinion probably shifted in support of Fälldin's standpoint. To what extent public concern about nuclear energy can have affected the election outcome is nevertheless a matter of uncertainty. By the standards of the 1973 election, the Center party actually lost electoral support in 1976. So did the Communists, who had tried to jump on the supposed bandwagon of opposition to nuclear power. In the Communists' case, however, the election setback was probably mainly the result of a drawn-out fight between party factions over entirely different ideological matters. Many observers, including leading Social Democrats, have pointed to the nuclear energy controversy as the issue that cost the Social Democrats the last 1 or 2 percent of the vote that could have saved the government. They may have two reasons for this. One is that the predominance of the nuclear energy question drew attention from the areas where the Social Democrats had hoped to meet with a much more positive public response to their own policy proposals, such as more leisure time for families with small children, further strengthening of the employees' bargaining power in industrial relations, and an extension of the minimum paid vacation from four to five weeks. The second reason why the nuclear energy issue may have been decisive for the election outcome is that the opinion polls during more than a year had forecasted that the Center party would lose a considerable part of the votes it had gained at the expense of the Conservatives and the People's party in the previous elections.

Political commentators generally attributed the downturn to disappointment among bourgeois voters over the passivity of the Center party in its role as the leading opposition party. The move to make nuclear energy a major issue in the campaign could thus have saved the Center party from an even bigger loss of electoral support. It may even have held back a small percentage of voters who had previously switched to the bourgeois parties but could have drifted back to the Social Democrats in 1976. To many who followed the last weeks of the campaign closely, this latter hypothesis is certainly plausible. There is, however, no evidence to support it in the measurements of movements in public opinion conducted by SIFO during the months preceding the election. The SIFO polls published during the campaign indicate only that the Center party, in the last weeks before the election, may have gained back a part of the support it was in danger of losing to other bourgeois parties, while the Social Democrats apparently were also gaining slightly. The last of these surveys was conducted in the last week before the election. On the other hand, results supporting the hypothesis are afforded by an interview survey conducted by the Central Bureau of Statistics during the last two weeks before the election. According to analysis based on successive two-day periods in the course of the fieldwork, the Center party did, indeed, gain at the expense of the Social Democrats in the final weeks. Thus, although the measurement uncertainty associated with this mode of analysis must be relatively big, one cannot exclude the possibility that the nuclear power issue helped to tilt the balance against the Social Democrats. If so, it would seem to have counteracted the effect of the earlier Social Democratic upturn that lasted from the late spring to the early phase of the campaign.

Sidelights on the Election. Voter turnout remained at the record high it attained in 1973, that is, about 91 percent. It is notable that this extremely high participation rate was maintained in spite of the fact that the voting age had been lowered since the previous election from twenty to eighteen years. Voters who because of this change were entitled to vote for the first time in 1976 made up around 8 percent of the total electorate. According to opinion poll data published during the summer, the party division among this age group appears not to differ very much from that of the electorate at large, although the Communist vote at the election may have been slightly stronger.

County council elections and communal elections are held on the same day as the *Riksdag* elections. By and large these elections are mirror images of the parliamentary elections in respect to turnout as well as the party division of the vote. Further analysis, for which neither data nor time has been available in the writing of this preliminary account, will probably reveal variations bound up with local politics. Already an inspection of the constituency data for the parliamentary election suggests that there were some regional variations in the election outcome. Thus, the Social Democrats appear to have done comparatively well in the north and in other regions where state efforts to maintain employment have been seen to have an impact.

A quantitatively small component of the electorate whose voting behavior is likely to attract much interest consists of the 220,000 foreign nationals who, for the first time in 1976, were entitled to vote in local elections. Their enfranchisement is due to a new law which grants voting rights to resident aliens who have lived in Sweden for at least three years. It also entitles them to hold elected office in local government, and in several towns with sizable immigrant populations one or two non-Swedish citizens were elected to the town councils. As most of the immigrants are industrial workers (Finns are the largest single national group), it is likely that their votes afforded a marginal advantage to the Social Democrats in industrial cities and towns.

Aside from the trends in the party division of the vote, it may also be noted that the trend towards equal representation of women in the parliament continued, although at a slow pace. After the 1970 election there were fifty-one female members in the parliament; the 1973 election brought their number up to seventy-four. In the 1976 *Riksdag* there will be seventy-six women members, with an additional five who will serve as substitute members, replacing cabinet ministers. (Cabinet members and the speaker are relieved of their duties as members during their terms of office, and their places are taken by substitute members with the same functions as ordinary members. Nonelected candidates on the party list ballots in the election are called to serve as substitute members, when needed, in the order in which they appear on the ballot.) The female representation (including substitute members) in the *Riksdag* is now 23 percent of the total membership. Of the twenty members of the cabinet, five are women.

Three-Party Coalition Government. Prime Minister Olof Palme tendered his and his cabinet's resignation to the speaker of the *Riksdag* on the day after the election. For the first time, the rules for cabinet formation under the new constitution (which came into force on January 1, 1975) were to be put into effect.[16] Under the new constitution it is incumbent on the speaker—rather than the king, as

[16] For an English translation of the new constitution, see *Constitutional Documents of Sweden*, published by the Swedish *Riksdag* (Stockholm: 1975).

head of state—to lead the proceedings at a change of government. When the change of government follows an election this responsibility rests with the speaker, chosen by the newly elected parliament on its first day in session, that is, the fifteenth day after the election. In the intervening two weeks the speaker of the previous election period is still in office. He is empowered to accept the resignation of a cabinet, and he is also entitled to convene informal consultations concerning the next government, but he is unable to initiate, formally, the formation of a new government. It follows that the resigning cabinet will always be requested to stay in office as a caretaker government. The *Riksdag* met on October 4. The speaker (a Social Democrat) was reelected, and after final consultations he proposed Fälldin as the new prime minister. Having received the required vote of approval in the parliament, Fälldin announced the names of his cabinet members and presented the new cabinet's program by the end of the week. In accordance with the new constitution, the role of the king was limited to his presiding at the new cabinet's first official meeting.

The three nonsocialist parties had declared their intention to form a coalition government well in advance of the election. Thus, the outcome was really never in doubt. Nonetheless, the negotiating among the three parties about ministerial posts and the contents of the government's program appears not to have been entirely frictionless. Meetings and bargaining continued virtually up to the last day of the breathing space provided by the constitution. As it worked out, ministerial posts were allotted on strictly proportional grounds among the three parties, with the exception that a former president of the Supreme Court without formal party affiliation was appointed minister of justice. Of the twenty cabinet members, eight belong to the Center party, five to the People's party, and six to the Conservatives. Apparently to stress that the new government is to have its center of gravity in the centrist parties, an entirely new position, deputy prime minister, was created for the People's party leader, Per Ahlmark, who will also be head of the important Labour Market Ministry. The old Ministry of Finance was divided: the Conservative leader, Gösta Bohman, became minister for economic affairs while the post of budget minister went to the People's party. The Center party, which has traditionally been seen to be especially close to the Social Democrats on foreign policy matters, made one of its members, Karin Söder, minister of foreign affairs. The somewhat surprising decision in the appointment of the minister of justice was apparently the result of a compromise between the centrist parties and the Conservatives, whose original candidate had a reputation for strictly conservative views on "law and order."

The new government's program (a comprehensive document of about 5,000 words) suggests that the coalition intends to modify, rather than reverse, the policies pursued by the Social Democrats.[17] Social welfare legislation planned during the previous period will be carried into effect with some modifications. As was expected, the government proposed to change the tax system so as to reduce the marginal tax for high-income earners, and the special taxes ("social fees") on employers and the self-employed are to be reduced.

On the most loudly debated question of the campaign, nuclear energy policy, the Center party was forced to yield to the standpoints taken by its two coalition partners, at least in the sense that no decisive, immediate action is being taken. In spite of the Center party's campaign pledge, a big new nuclear power plant which is nearing completion is being allowed to begin operating during the autumn. To satisfy the Center party, however, new measures to monitor and regulate this and other existing nuclear plants were to be enacted. Furthermore, the overall energy policy is to be reexamined, and a new program will be laid before the *Riksdag* in 1978. Meanwhile, no additional nuclear installations are to be put into operation, although work will continue on another major plant under construction. If even after this period of further investigations disagreement on the future expansion of nuclear energy production should persist, the coalition parties will consider the possibility of arranging a consultative referendum. The formula can be described as a compromise, but it is obvious that the Center party had to concede more than its coalition partners. The prime minister has already been bitterly accused of having betrayed his campaign pledge and of having misled the voters about his real intentions. Even his compromise, however, would inevitably result, at the very least, in the delaying of some new nuclear power plants. And energy policy is by no means defused as a political issue. When the coalition's long-term program comes up for decision in 1978, energy policy could become the stumbling block that causes the break-up of the tripartite coalition. Against that possibility weighs the overriding consideration that such a split could once again bring the Social Democrats into office, either alone or in a coalition government. The bourgeois parties now appear firmly determined to prove that they are able to govern the country.

---

[17] The full text of the government's program is published in the official journal *Från Riksdag & Departement*, no. 30 (1976). See also *Records of the Riksdag*, October 8, 1976.

In the coming period, the government will meet with a vigorous Social Democratic opposition under the leadership of Olof Palme, whose formidable political skills are generally acknowledged. There are no signs of disunity in his party. In contrast to their period of weakness in the 1950s, when the Social Democrats feared that they might permanently be forced into a minority position because of the growth of the white-collar strata, the party's experiences from the 1960s on have proved that it has a potential to attract enough support among white-collar employees to secure an electoral majority. Its strategy in opposition will certainly be to reconstruct that electoral base through policy initiatives on social services as well as management-employee relations intended to appeal to both white-collar and manual workers. The changes in the tax structure contemplated by the bourgeois government will also have consequences for next year's round of wages and salaries bargaining. The leadership of the manual workers' trade unions has already made it clear that it will seek compensation for any shift in real income distribution resulting from such changes by pressing harder for the wage demands of low-income groups. Obviously the unions could then count on the support of the Social Democratic party, just as the Social Democrats could hope to gain back their loss of electoral support in the working class under such circumstances. This is not to say that the next election period is bound to become a period of social strife or extreme political polarization. The consensus-seeking mechanisms are deeply embedded in the political culture and the organizational structure of Swedish society.

PART TWO
SOCIAL DISCONTENT AND THE MASS MEDIA

4

THE CHANGING BASIS OF RADICAL SOCIALISM IN SCANDINAVIA

Daniel Tarschys

Scandinavia has long been a showcase of political stability. Its history is filled with moderate statesmen—moderate conservatives, moderate liberals, and moderate socialists. Radical socialism never stood much of a chance here. The Marxist zeal of the early agitators had already subsided before the labor movement won a voice in national politics. After the Russian Revolution, the Scandinavian left was distinctly weaker than the right, and in Denmark and Sweden only minute factions followed the Bolshevik path. The Norwegian Labor party was a member of the Comintern for four years, but their partnership was later described as a mistake by both sides. The leadership of the International erred in its judgment of the Norwegian Labor party and the Norwegians had no intention of taking orders from Moscow. They withdrew from the Comintern in 1923, and adherents of piecemeal social engineering soon gained the upper hand in the party. Since then, a thoroughly reformist brand of social democracy has dominated the labor movements of all three Scandinavian countries. The high tide of Communist sympathies at the close of World War II was a brief interlude without lasting importance.

Against this background of historical weakness, the present ascendancy of radical socialism in all of the Scandinavian countries is notable. The Swedish Communist party won an all-time high of nineteen seats in the *Storting* in 1973. This is primarily due to the new electoral system enacted in 1969, but the popular vote of the Communists and the extreme left in the 1973 elections (5.9 percent) was also the highest they had received in any parliamentary election since 1948.[1] In Denmark the elections of 1973 and 1975 gave the

---

[1] Under the old electoral system in Sweden, many Communist votes were wasted because the party did not pass the constituency threshold for one seat in parlia-

three radical socialist parties (the Socialist People's party, the Danish Communist party, and the Left Socialists) over 11 percent of the vote. Although this is less than they won in 1971, it far exceeds the 4.2 percent that was the Communists' average share of the vote in the 1950s. In Norway, finally, many years of division on the left came to an end in 1973 with the creation of the Socialist Election Alliance, a large coalition that gained 11.2 percent of the vote and sixteen seats in parliament in the last election.[2] Compared with the one or two representatives usually returned by the Communists or the People's Socialist party in the past, this was a genuine breakthrough for Norway's left socialists.

For all its success, the radical left remains a peripheral force in the parliamentary arena. It has contributed to the erosion of Social Democratic support, especially in Denmark and Norway, but it is still very far from threatening the moderate socialists' traditional hold over the labor movement. At this stage it is an open question whether the present momentum of the radical left can be maintained. The major labor parties have had enemies on the left before, and they have fought them skillfully. Yet their new challengers have some significant assets and might well become more difficult to cope with than the Stalinists of the past.

. In assessing the outlook for the Scandinavian left, it is essential to take note of its changing social base. In this paper I shall argue that the present impact of the radical socialist movement in Scandinavia is largely a function of the new resources brought to it by the youth groups it attracted in the 1960s and early 1970s and that its future is to a large extent dependent on the views that these strata will hold in the future. I shall also suggest that a distinction between "institutional power" and "cultural power" is helpful for our appraisal of the movement's present influence on Scandinavian politics, which is less an effect of its numerical strength in representative bodies than of its impact on public opinion.

ment. Since 1970, seats have been apportioned as if the whole country were a single constituency. Each party receiving more than 4 percent of the national vote is guaranteed parliamentary representation proportional to its strength in the electorate.

[2] In March 1975 the Socialist Election Alliance was transformed into the Socialist Left party (*Sosialistisk Venstreparti*). The constituent parties have not been dissolved, however, and it remains to be seen whether there can be unity among the rather disparate members of this organization. The Socialist Left party bears some similarity to the Democratic League for the People of Finland, the "popular democratic" organization of the left. In Finland, however, the Communist party is the major constituent of the left coalition, while the Norwegian Communists are much weaker than the other forces on the Norwegian left.

Exit the Old Guard

Youthfulness, to be sure, is no new phenomenon in Scandinavian communism. The left-wingers who seceded from the Labor parties around or after the Russian Revolution (1917 in Sweden, 1919 in Denmark, 1923 in Norway) were also a youthful lot, largely products of the Social Democratic youth organizations in the various countries, but their revolt was soon stifled by the strategic rigidity of the Comintern. The upsurge of Communist sympathies in the mid-1940s also brought many young proselytes to the left-wing parties, but efforts in those years to rally the "democratic youth" around the Communist party in broad, progressive, but nonpartisan organizations never got off the ground. In the 1950s the movement was old and aging.[3]

It was also thoroughly proletarian. In contrast to some continental parties, the Scandinavian Communist parties in their first four decades never managed to attract a substantial number of intellectuals. There were left-leaning intellectual coteries of some importance (the groups associated with the magazines *Mot Dag* [Dawn] in Norway, *Clarté* [Light] in Sweden), but they were never firmly attached to the parties. The overwhelming majority of the Communist electorate was always working class. Two groups dominated the movement, one urban and one peripheral. The Danish CP had its strength in the most developed and industrialized parts of the country. Its voters were urban workers, to a large extent in the higher income brackets. In Sweden, there were Communists among the dockers, the shipyard workers on the west coast, the metal workers, the construction workers, the typographers, and the miners. Outside the two major urban centers, Stockholm and Göteborg, the party's strongholds were remote areas of central Sweden and above all the far north, where the socialist daily newspaper, *Norrskensflamman* (Northern flame), and the entire province organization of the Labor party had espoused the Communists in 1919. In this region, the radical left was strong in all working-class groups and also among

---

[3] *Femtio år i kamp. Norges kommunistiske parti 1923-1973* [Fifty years in struggle: the Norwegian Communist party, 1923-1973] (Oslo: A.s. All-trykk, 1973); Trond Gilberg, *The Soviet Communist Party and Scandinavian Communism: The Norwegian Case* (Oslo: Universitetsforlaget, 1973); Åke Sparring, *Från Höglund till Hermansson* [From Höglund to Hermansson] (Stockholm: Bonniers, 1967); Åke Sparring et al., *Kommunismen i Norden* [Communism in the Nordic countries] (Lund: Aldus, 1965); Henry Valen and Daniel Katz, *Political Parties in Norway* (Oslo: Universitetsforlaget, 1964); *Vänsterpartiet kommunisterna: Bidrag till partihistoria* [The Left party, Communists: toward a party history], Brev 1-5, 3 vols. (Göteborg: Västan Tryckeri AB, 1972).

the small freeholders. These people were separated from the rest of the nation not only by distance but also, frequently, by language and culture. In a large part of the northern province of Norrbotten, Finnish is still the language of the countryside, and radical-puritan religious movements have left their mark on the community.[4]

In schematic terms, then, the old Communist rank and file were either "working-class aristocrats" or victims of isolation and relative deprivation. They were also few. The leaders' stubborn loyalty to Moscow was costly for the three parties, and under the impact of the cold war they all lost ground to the Social Democrats. International developments have always affected the ups and downs of Scandinavian Communism, and in the period after 1948 it was mainly a matter of downs. The parties suffered severe losses after the consolidation of Soviet hegemony in Eastern Europe and after the 1956 revolt in Hungary. Together with Khrushchev's revelations at the Twentieth Party Congress of the Soviet Communist party, this event provoked great ferment inside the movement. In the following years, the attempt to chart an independent national course split the Danish and Norwegian parties, while the Swedish CP managed to preserve its unity by carrying out a cautious program of modernization from within.

The developments in Denmark were the most dramatic. From 1956 to 1958, the veteran party leader Aksel Larsen tried to give the Danish CP a more democratic image but met with fierce opposition from the old Stalinists. The hard core of the party leadership prevented him from publishing an article critical of the Soviets' arrest of Imre Nagy and attacked him for being less than enthusiastic about the Moscow Declaration of the Communist parties of 1957. A year later, Larsen was deposed by the party congress in the presence of Pyotr Pospelov, a deputy member of the CPSU presidium, and soon after was excluded from the central committee and the party. This was one of the last grand purges of a Western European Communist party, a mild and very Danish version of the classic ceremony.

Larsen's ouster proved disastrous for the party. In the following elections, the Communist vote went down to 27,298, or 1.1 percent of the electorate, while Larsen's new Socialist People's party gathered 149,440 votes, 6.1 percent, and won eleven seats in the *Folketing*. Obviously, a large number of Communist voters had followed their

---

[4] Leif Lewin, Bo Jansson and Dag Sörbom, *The Swedish Electorate 1887-1968* (Uppsala: Almqvist & Wiksell, 1972); Sven Rydenfeldt, *Kommunismen i Sverige: En samhällsvetenskaplig studie* [Communism in Sweden: a social science study] (Lund: Gleerups, 1954).

old leader. The new party also drew support from the left wing of the Social Democratic electorate and from young people active in the campaign against nuclear weapons.[5]

This electoral success was an important stimulus for the foundation of a similar organization in Norway, which grew out of conflicts on security and foreign policy within the ruling Labor party. In 1961, a Labor party congress declared that party membership was incompatible with membership on the editorial board of *Orientering* [Orientation], a magazine critical of Norway's commitment to NATO. The Socialist People's party was established shortly after this decision. Unlike its Danish counterpart, the Norwegian Socialist People's party was led chiefly by old Social Democrats or independent socialists. Nevertheless, the Socialist People's party was an attractive alternative on the left and soon cut into the traditional base of the Communist party, winning over both cadres and voters. It was supported primarily by workers, but its modern and undogmatic image also earned it some sympathy among socialist intellectuals.

The Swedish Communists saw the writing on the wall. To avoid a split, it would obviously be necessary to adapt the party to the new currents. A young faction wanted to cleanse the movement thoroughly of its alien rhetoric and old submissiveness to the Soviet Union, but the leaders around party chief Hilding Hagberg, many of whom had been staunch Stalinists since the 1920s, were not prone to disown the past. After a severe setback in the 1962 elections, however, where the Communists polled a dismal 3.8 percent after having defended the erection of the Berlin Wall, the hard-liners' position had clearly become untenable. As Hagberg's base of support shrank, the old guard agreed to his resignation, but on condition that the chief candidate of the "modernizers" not be nominated to assume the leadership. Instead, C. H. Hermansson, editor-in-chief of the main party organ, *Ny Dag* [New day], was launched as a candidate acceptable to both sides. An economist who had joined the party in 1941, Hermansson was old enough to be trusted by the executive committee but young enough to be attractive to the modernizers. He was elected unanimously at the Twentieth Congress of the Swedish Communist party in 1964.

The choice proved felicitous. Soft-spoken and reasonable, the new leader made a very good impression on television audiences and became a popular figure in Swedish politics. The party gathered

---

[5] Ursula Schmiederer, *Die Sozialistische Volkspartei Dänemarks: Eine Partei der neuen Linken* [The Socialist People's party of Denmark: a new left party] (Frankfurt: Verlag Neue Kritik, 1969).

momentum. In the parliamentary elections of 1964, it collected 5.2 percent of the vote, and in the communal elections of 1966, 6.4 percent. Though many members of the old guard remained in powerful positions in the party, resistance to the new line was weak. Without an abrupt break with the past, Hermansson took policy stands rather similar to those of Aksel Larsen and Finn Gustavsen, the leaders of the Socialist People's parties in Denmark and Norway. By 1967, when the modernization effort reached its peak with the adoption of a new party program, the Swedish CP had accepted the "rules of the game" of the Swedish system and had unambiguously declared its support for the parliamentary road to power.

The main part of the Scandinavian Communist movement, then, withdrew from the monocentrist internationalism of the Stalinist era and set out to shape credible national alternatives to the reformism of the Social Democrats. The shrinking pro-Soviet parties were wiped out of parliament in Denmark and Norway. In Sweden the orthodox minority fared better by staying within the Communist party, where it retained control of the newspaper and district organization of Norrbotten. But it could not threaten the new majority. For the Swedish CP as for the Danish and Norwegian Socialist People's parties, the strategic problem in the decade after 1956 was to shed the stigma of past loyalties and chart an independent radical course.

Enter the New Left

The modernization of radical socialism in Denmark, Norway, and Sweden brought modest gains at the expense of the left wing of the Social Democrats. What really changed the political climate, however, was the emergence of a vigorous New Left.[6] More influential in Scandinavia than in most other areas, this movement profoundly affected intellectual attitudes in the middle and late 1960s and made politics a central concern of large groups that had previously been passive. The explosive growth of secondary and higher education and the increased opportunity to travel in this period made Scandinavians more internationally minded, and television brought the misery and conflicts of the Third World into their living rooms. For large segments of the student generation, the response was an acute sense of awakening, and many liberal intellectuals joined them in their drift to the left. Confronted with a sharper exposure of Western

---

[6] Göran Therborn, *En ny vänster* [A new left] (Stockholm: Rabén & Sjögren, 1965); Daniel Tarschys and Carl Tham, *Den nygamla vänstern* [The new-old left], 2d ed. (Stockholm: Aldus, 1969).

colonial warfare and oppression than the media had ever presented before, they lost their faith in the liberal-democratic system and took refuge in visions of socialism with a human face.

The small stream of youths who were attracted to the People's Socialists and to the Swedish Communists in the late 1950s and early 1960s were to a large extent veterans of the pacifist and ban-the-bomb campaigns of these years. The Norwegian and Danish Socialist People's parties, with their vocal opposition to NATO, were particularly attractive to these groups. Toward the mid-1960s, however, the pacifist mood was gradually dispelled and succeeded by a more militant temper. Aroused by the war in Vietnam and the now widely publicized liberation struggles in different parts of the world, the young left moved toward a reevaluation of political violence. The pacifist ideals of the recent past, which were incompatible with the active support of a just war, they repudiated as humanitarian illusions.

The New Left arose outside of the established parties and remained largely unorganized for several years. Hostility to political machines was part of the movement's creed: the young militants wanted to work in a lively, spontaneous, and amorphous community without the constraint of any organizational structure. Thus, between 1965 and 1968 innumerable short-lived groups, ad hoc committees, and loose associations, often without formal structure, responsible functionaries, or the capacity to survive past the first few months of enthusiasm, emerged.

The authorities of the New Left were militants and radical theorists throughout the world: Frantz Fanon, Che Guevara, Ho Chi Minh, André Gorz, Herbert Marcuse. The movement had an "extrovert" character, and for a long time it gave foreign problems priority over domestic concerns. Of the activities of the Swedish New Left none was carried out more diligently than the solidarity work for the National Liberation Front in Vietnam. In Norway Vietnam activities were far less conspicuous.

The third-world orientation of the New Left created a generation of "disloyal Europeans." Scandinavian corporate capitalism, Scandinavian governments, and the Scandinavian labor movement were denounced by the New Left for their cooperation with the West and for their participation in the exploitation of the poor nations. The radicals were hostile to military, economic, and political integration with the West, but they viewed Eastern Europe with great suspicion, too. The ossified Soviet model appealed far less to the young socialists than the still vital revolutionary regimes of Cuba, China, and North Vietnam.

In its analysis of the class struggle at home, the New Left emphasized the cultural aspects of capitalist domination—what Antonio Gramsci had called the "hegemony" of the bourgeoisie, as opposed to its political dictatorship. The methodical criticism and unmasking of hidden structures of control was therefore an essential socialist pursuit. Much energy was expended on a radical scrutiny of art, literature, language, advertising, journalism, and education; and indoctrination and stabilization of the prevailing economic system were exposed as the hidden functions of all of them. While some radical critics went to ludicrous extremes, the whole enterprise spawned a new awareness of the ideological dimensions of social phenomena.

A prime target of exposure was the reformist leadership of the trade unions and of the Social Democratic parties. With more than a shade of fundamentalism, the New Left argued that the labor movement had abandoned its original ideals and had accommodated itself to its capitalist environment. The politics of compromise, according to this reasoning, was the politics of treason. The elite of the labor movement had become enmeshed with the corporate establishment in a vast network of negotiations and joint commissions and was now both prisoner and guardian of the system. This was essentially what the Communists had been saying for years and years, but the New Left's denunciation of the socialist-industrial complex was more imaginative and powerful than the old CP analysis. The great collusion at the top of the social pyramid became an important theme in theater, art, and fiction, all of which were heavily influenced by the new political vein.

The rapid diffusion of socialist ideas among the younger literary and artistic elite was one of the key factors behind the movement's impact on public opinion. In the 1950s, Scandinavian literature had been individualistic, introverted, and apolitical. Now it was opened to a wide range of social and economic problems, and many writers set out to discover the truth about "the system." The other creative and performing arts were similarly affected. The leftward turn of pop culture was both indicative of this development and important for the diffusion of the new values. In the early 1960s, the top-of-the-pops was almost always an English or American tune, though sometimes sung by a Scandinavian group. A few years later the hit songs were increasingly in Danish, Norwegian, and Swedish, and their lyrics were not only about sunny days and broken hearts but also about pollution, exploitation, and the struggle for liberation.

Cultural activism was part of the pattern. Independent theater groups mushroomed, almost all of them socialist. Exhibitions were organized. Films were made to reveal the secrets of the government-industrial complex. Study projects were carried out to lay bare the hidden ideological structures that shaped the everyday life of the welfare state. And while much of this was done awkwardly, the creative quality was often quite high. When the best talents of the New Left went at the establishment, they demonstrated both verve and marksmanship.

The party organizations played no great role in the evolution of this radical youth culture. But as they watched it happen, they also saw new opportunities for their own expansion. The People's Socialists were probably the most successful in gaining a foothold in the New Left during the early years, whereas the orthodox parties in Denmark and Norway initially made no headway at all. In Sweden, Hermansson tried to strike a balance between the anarchist extravagance of the students and the traditionalism of the old cadres. He also tried to establish himself as a spiritual leader of the new movement. In his book, *Vänsterns väg* [The road of the left], published in 1965, he offered some pungent criticism of past Communist errors and even raised the question of dissolving the Communist party in favor of a broader organization of the left. This courtship won him limited support from the young radicals, but in the parliamentary elections of 1968 any such gains were neutralized by the strong reaction against the Soviet invasion of Czechoslovakia. In spite of the four years the CP had spent modernizing and creating for itself the image of an independent national party, and in spite of Hermansson's explicit denunciation of the Soviet invasion, the Communist share of the vote in Sweden fell back to 3 percent, a record low since the war. As had so often happened before in Swedish electoral history, the prestige of world Communism determined the distribution of the vote between the two socialist parties.

1968 and Beyond

In the demonstrations and riots of May 1968 the New Left had its baptism of fire. Protests against bourgeois hegemony in higher education and pending university reforms were mingled with demands for the total liberation of society. The disturbances at the Scandinavian universities were pale and sometimes farcical reruns of the more spirited revolts taking place elsewhere, but they were sufficiently serious to deprive the rebels of several illusions. All appeals to the oppressed people had proved to be in vain. Not only had the workers refused to follow their self-appointed vanguard, but they had shown clear signs of resenting it. Students should study, not paint slogans on walls or bother the police: petty bourgeois or not, this had been the reaction of ordinary people, and it had to be reckoned with. It did not encourage further experiments in violent confrontation.

The conclusions drawn from this experience were many and varied, although long in gestation. 1968 became a watershed in the development of the new Scandinavian socialism. What stood out as the basic weakness of the student movement was its complete isolation from the rest of society. Hence, to a large number of militants, the main problem was to enlighten and mobilize the torpid majority, and this, many of them thought, could not be achieved from without. The left had to be reintegrated with the mainstream of the working class. What ensued was a genuine "going to the people" in the best Narodnik tradition, but in the course of it the movement split into a variety of ideological and strategic factions. The trends were somewhat different in the three countries, but some main lines of development can be distinguished.

A large segment recanted the romantic anarchism of the early New Left and set about to organize or joined existing organizations on the left. One stream, identified with the Chinese position in the Sino-Sovïet conflict, repudiated the revisionism of the domestic Communist and People's Socialist movements, and vowed to set up a new Communist party on a firm Marxist-Leninist foundation. In Sweden an orthodox group left the CP at the height of its internal modernization process with the view of setting up a new party, which they ultimately did in 1972. In the parliamentary elections of the following year this party captured 0.4 percent of the vote, while an even more radical offshoot collected 0.2 percent. Youth groups provided the bulk of the support for these organizations, the Swedish Communist party (*Sveriges kommunistiska parti*) and the Marxist-Leninist Communist League Revolutionaries (*Kommunistiska förbundet marxist-leninisterna, revolutionärerna*).

Several students on this militant fringe were quite serious about "going to the people." An appreciable number left their schools and universities to take up jobs in industry and agitate from within. Some groups went in for the radicalization of the trade unions, while others, deeming the unions irretrievably lost to the enemy, saw the only solution in the setting up of antiunion strike committees and so on. The effects of these activities remain modest, but the increase in the number of short wildcat strikes in recent years—particularly after the serious conflict in the Norrbotten mines in 1969–70 [7]—can be attributed partly to the efforts of the Marxist-Leninist youth.

Another part of the New Left aligned itself with the existing parties. The Communist party in Denmark obtained a new base and started to recover from its long period of weakness. In 1973 it won six seats in the *Folketing*, where it had not been represented since Aksel Larsen had whittled away its electoral support in 1960, and in the 1975 Danish election the Communist vote rose to 4.2 percent. Others joined the People's Socialists. In Sweden, the Communist party did very well among the young voters in the elections of 1970 and 1973, and an influx of educated youths slowly began to change the social profile of the party's rank and file. The most conspicuous change took place in the large urban centers, whereas Communist support in such districts as Norrbotten remained predominantly working class.

The far-reaching rejuvenation of the Swedish CP is easily detectable in survey data. The polls of the Swedish Public Opinion Research Institute (SIFO) from the first five months of 1974 indicate that the party then had 9.8 percent of the "manual" vote and 15.1 percent of the "nonmanual" vote in the age group between eighteen and twenty-four, but only 4.2 percent of the manuals and 2.9 percent of the non-manuals among forty to forty-nine year olds. Students were not included in this sample, so the actual proportion of Communists in the young generation was probably still larger. In the last two elections, the strongest wards of both Marxist-Leninists and Communists south of Norrbotten were the "student ghettos" close to university campuses.

In Norway, the New Left had not been as strong as in Denmark or Sweden, but in the early seventies a radical movement gathered momentum and upset the established party structure on the left of the political spectrum. This was primarily an effect of the great controversy over Norway's membership in the Common Market, which eventually led to a decisive "No" vote in the 1972 referendum and convulsed at least two political parties: the Liberals were split and almost disappeared from the parliamentary scene, and the Social Democratic party was severely damaged when its leaders became strong advocates of Norwegian entry. This led to serious conflicts

---

[7] The largest wildcat strike for many decades, the conflict in the state-owned Norrbotten iron-ore mines, disrupted the traditional peace on the Swedish labor market and posed a serious challenge to the government. While several left-wing groups were active in the strike, no single force dominated the controversy, which went on for more than a month.

inside the party and to an erosion of Social Democratic support, particularly in the rural and remote areas of the country. The victorious People's Campaign Against the Common Market gave the student radicals a natural link with the masses, and the peripheral sectors of the Norwegian electorate were welded together in opposition to the urban and technocratic center. The creation of the Socialist Election Alliance in 1973 was a logical extension of this campaign, and although the new party could not capture all of those hostile to Norwegian membership in the EEC, it made considerable dents in the traditional Social Democratic predominance on the left. In the 1973 *Storting* election, the Social Democratic vote went down from 46.5 percent to 35.3 percent of the vote, and most of this loss was absorbed by the Socialist Election Alliance.

As an ideological superstructure to the rejection of Europe by the periphery in Norway, there emerged a new brand of populism that contained both socialist and centrist-agrarian strands. Sometimes dubbed "green socialism," this creed emphasized the values of rural life, thrift, small-scale economy, traditional technology, autarchy, decentralization, and participatory democracy, while denouncing technocracy, economic integration, foreign trade, and economic growth. Populism gained a foothold in the Socialist Election Alliance, but it also spread to other parties and particularly to their youth organizations. This was not a counterculture; the "greening of Norway," unlike that of America as described by Roszak, Reich, and others, was a change in political attitudes rather than a revolution in life styles. But the main elements of its message were soon reflected in Norwegian fiction, theater, art, and journalism.

A less original and less powerful version of this populism appeared in the other countries as well. The thin intellectual edge of the ascendant Swedish Center party was quite receptive to the Norwegian ideas, and the youth league of this party evolved its own utopian vision of "the local community" as an alternative to the alleged centralism of the Social Democrats. The Marxist-Leninists, eager to reach out beyond the confines of the traditional proletariat, launched their own variant of populism, contrasting "the people's history" to "the history of the lords," "the people's arts" to the "fine arts" of the aristocracy and bourgeoisie, and so on. A magazine called *Folket i Bild/Kulturfront* [People in pictures/cultural front] became the foremost exponent of these ideas.

In Swedish politics, however, there was no issue that could give real leverage to the socialist left. The Swedish Social Democrats were more flexible than their Norwegian counterparts in their treatment of the Common Market question, as they had been previously in their approach to NATO and nuclear armament. As a result, they lost no votes on this issue and the Communists had no opportunity for a frontal assault.

The Danish predicament was more favorable to the left. Though the left was beaten in the referendum on the Common Market, the towering economic problems of the country kept discontent at a suitably high level. This favored a variety of populisms: the rightist taxpayers' protest movement sponsored by Glistrup, the alienated center of Jacobsen, and the three parties to the left of the Social Democrats (the Socialist People's party, the Communist party, and the Left Socialist party, an offshoot of the Socialist People's party). Here, as in the other countries, it was mostly the young age groups that moved to the left. The upsurge of radical socialism was a result of the new perspectives and values of Scandinavian youth.

The New Profile of the Scandinavian Left

In the early seventies the radical socialist parties were attracting large numbers of new members, most of them young. According to the Swedish election studies presented in Bo Särlvik's paper, the Communist share of the student vote, for example, increased from 5 to 18 percent between 1968 and 1973, while the number of Social Democratic supporters in this age group shrank from 34 to 18 percent.[8] Gallup and SIFO data for Sweden indicate a considerable influx of non-manual voters over the last decade (see Table 4–1). The Danish and Norwegian findings are similar. Ole Borre shows that the principal support of the Danish left wing in 1971 came from voters who were under forty. Henry Valen and Willy Martinussen report that younger voters with both low and high education—especially young Laborite voters—were more inclined than older ones to move to the far left (the Socialist Election Alliance) in 1973.[9]

As the radical parties grew, the homogeneous social composition of the old Communist parties was gradually replaced by a combination of young activists and traditional working-class supporters. Relations between the two groups were cordial in the early phase —new proselytes are welcome in any political movement—but the latent tensions were brought out when the newcomers became numer-

[8] See Särlvik, in this volume, Table 3-9.

[9] Borre, in this volume, Table 1-3; Valen and Martinussen, in this volume, Table 2-5. See also the same authors' *Velgere og politiske frontlinjer* [Voters and political front lines] (Oslo: Gyldendal, 1972), pp. 292, 336.

Table 4–1

THE EMERGING CLEAVAGE IN SWEDISH COMMUNISM

(in percentages)

	Occupational Class of Communist Sympathizers		
	Non-manual	Manual	**Total**
(1) Age of Communist sympathizers (farmers and students excluded), 1974			
Under 40	62	38	100
Over 40	25	75	100
(2) Period of survey (farmers and students included)			
1946–48	16	84	100
1974	50	50	100

Source: Compounded survey data from *SIFO Indicator*, February 1975 and Swedish Gallup for 1946-48, SIFO for 1974, as presented in a dissertation by John Stephens, *The Consequences of Social Structural Change for the Development of Socialism in Sweden*, Yale University, May 1976.

ous. A great deal of the recent controversy within the Scandinavian leftist parties can be attributed to the different backgrounds and attitudes of these two groups.

The cleavage is a complex one. In the first place, it is a question of social origin. A considerable number of the young radicals hail from working-class, often Social Democratic homes, but there is also an appreciable number of middle-class and upper-class youths in the new ranks. The urban milieu to which they are accustomed is quite remote from the rural setting of the Communist stronghold in Norrbotten. Second, there is an educational gap. This is a modern social phenomenon common to the Scandinavian countries, where, as in many other parts of the world, the young generation now receives far more education than their parents did. But certain groups are particularly vulnerable to the consequences of this development. The educational revolution will draw new sectors of the population into the culture of the upper and upper-middle class, but for the working class this process implies a growing cultural gap between young and old that may sharpen the sense of relative deprivation and social alienation among the old. When even the politics of the working class

146

is taken over by the adolescents from the universities, old socialist stalwarts can be expected to have mixed feelings.

Ideology and strategy are a third source of conflict between the two generations. On many issues, of course, the divergent views are not clearly related to age or social background, but on some they are. A few examples of questions hotly debated inside the Swedish Communist movement illustrate this attitudinal cleavage.

One highly controversial issue is the party's position on Communist parties in other countries. Since the leadership withdrew its unconditional support of the socialist regimes in Eastern Europe during the 1960s, it has voiced some cautious criticism of Soviet policies, particularly the treatment of dissenters and the invasion of Czechoslovakia, and it has tried to remain neutral on the Sino-Soviet split. This course, however, does not satisfy either wing of the party. Large segments of the old generation are still strongly attached to the Soviet Union, while many young militants are hostile toward its alleged revisionism and state capitalism. The Swedish Communist party is under pressure from its Marxist-Leninist competitors on the left to assume a more unambiguous stand on the Soviet Union, but such a move would be hazardous for party unity.

The movement's strategy vis-à-vis the Social Democrats is another moot issue. For a long time the Communist party followed the zigzag course of the Soviet leadership, with its abrupt shifts from advocacy of the popular front to denunciation of the Social Democrats as the vilest traitors of the proletariat. The last such change occurred around 1953, when the Swedish CP, like several others, dropped its more vehement attacks and began proposing close cooperation in a unified labor movement. During the last decade of Hilding Hagberg's chairmanship, the party conceived itself as the "friendly pusher" that would help drive the trade unions and the Social Democrats to the left.

The modernization process implied no ostensible break with this line. The CP continued to present itself as a loyal part of the Swedish labor movement and inched closer to the Social Democrats in several ways, notably by dropping its old jargon in favor of an idiom better adapted to the Swedish political environment. But this friendly line became less marked as the new converts began to win a voice in the party. Among the young there was a great deal of impatience with the emasculation of Communist militancy and with the party's soft attitude toward the Social Democrats. These groups wanted not to cooperate with the Social Democrats, but to intensify party propaganda designed to expose the passivity and defeatism of the labor leaders. They were prepared to make short work of the "modern" and "democratic" profile of the Communist party and advocated a return to the classical Marxist-Leninist analysis of the capitalist state.

Squeezed between the doctrinaire youth and the old generation, which was sympathetic both to the Soviet Union and to the Social Democrats, Hermansson took a few steps back from the "democratic" positions of the 1967 party program. A new program, passed only five years later, restored some of the traditional rhetoric and analyzed "the road to power" in more revolutionary terms. All references to Eastern Europe were dropped, no doubt as a concession to the veterans in Norrbotten and elsewhere, but there was no clear-cut denunciation of the Swedish political system, and the retreat from the modernist course was not made explicit.

So much for the Swedish case. Similar friction has frequently occurred in Denmark and Norway, both within and among the various parties on the left. In the early sixties, the orthodox Communist party in Norway stood firmly for "labor movement unity," while the People's Socialists contributed to the fall of the Social Democratic government by supporting a bourgeois vote of no-confidence on the so-called King's Bay affair (concerning the mismanagement of work safety in the accident-ridden coal mines on Spitsbergen). And from the early sixties until 1967, the Danish People's Socialists quarreled a great deal among themselves about the right stand towards the Social Democrats, with veteran leader Aksel Larsen taking the old soft line and the more contentious youth demanding an offensive strategy. This controversy ultimately led to a split in the party. The hard-liners left the Socialist People's party to form the Left Socialist party, which won four seats in the elections of 1975.

The Impact of Radical Socialism

Communists and People's Socialists have made headway in recent Scandinavian elections, but it is nonetheless clear that they are still very far from the commanding heights of the three political systems. While they have whittled away a part of the traditional Social Democratic base, the balance of power in the Scandinavian labor movement is still in favor of reformism. The trade unions are largely controlled by the Social Democrats, and no radical socialist has been a member of a Scandinavian government since the summer of 1945, when Aksel Larsen and another Communist had to leave the first Danish government formed after the liberation.

The left wing's influence in the parliamentary bodies is equally weak. It is true that the Norwegian and Swedish left-wing parties have sometimes held swing positions, but this has hardly been a boon to them. When the Norwegian People's Socialists brought down the Social Democratic government in 1964 they were punished by their voters in the subsequent election and were swept out of parliament. The memory of this defeat still hovers over radical socialist parliamentarians in Scandinavia. Even if some strategists on the left believe that a short spell of bourgeois rule would have the useful effect of accelerating political polarization, they are well aware of the voters' preference on this score. A Communist or People's Socialist party that opened the door to a nonsocialist government would have a very difficult time in its next encounter with the electorate.

The radical socialists, in other words, are prisoners of their position at one end of the political spectrum. They cannot do much bargaining with the Social Democrats since they have no way of putting a price on their support. Thus, Scandinavian labor governments as a rule have been able to count on the support of the socialist left on all important questions and have not felt compelled to make formal deals with them. This has been true of the Social Democratic governments in both Norway and Sweden.

Even if the Social Democratic governments make no formal deals with the left, however, they may take its positions into account when they frame their bills. It is hard to say whether and to what extent this happens, but it is probable that the Norwegian labor government, with its narrow parliamentary base—sixty-two seats in the *Storting* and 35.3 percent of the vote at present—is more inclined to do this than the government in Sweden, with its stronger electoral support and increasingly good contacts with its traditional adversaries on the right.

This is not to say that the parliamentary activity of the radical left is without importance. By giving vent to popular complaints and demands, the radical socialists can put the Social Democrats under pressure and restrict their freedom of action. They frequently try to articulate views that are widespread among the Social Democratic rank and file, and if such views are strong enough the Social Democratic leaders may have to move in order to forestall a leakage to the left. Similar actions can be effective in the trade unions, where the Communists consistently advocate a more militant line. So, while the socialist left is seldom given a chance to participate in the actual policy-making process, it may nevertheless exert a certain indirect influence on the decisions that are made.

In this context, the left wing of the Social Democratic parties acts as a kind of transmission belt. For its members, the persistent competition of the Communists and People's Socialists provides an expedient rationale for more resolute assaults on the capitalist structure of society, and they are constantly warning the Social Democratic leadership that votes will be lost unless radical positions are assumed. Whether such warnings are heeded depends greatly on the balance of political forces at any given time. In situations where the main danger appears to be a loss to the nonsocialist parties, the forebodings of the left-wingers do not receive much attention, but at times when the Communists or the People's Socialists appear to be dangerous competitors, the views of the left obviously cannot be neglected.

The mounting electoral support for the Communists and the People's Socialists has probably meant an increase in the indirect influence that they can exert on Social Democratic policy making. But the growing impact of the socialist left is due not only to quantitative change but also to the concomitant alteration of its social base. The leftward drift of a considerable section of the intellectual and artistic elite has given radical socialism some important assets that the Communist parties never possessed in the past. The Old Left, to exaggerate a bit, was a mute force in Scandinavian politics; the New Left is an articulate force, endowed with skills that make it an efficient communicator of political ideas. Ten miners are good to have in a political party, but ten schoolteachers or journalists may be more valuable in the long run.

The spread of radical socialism to members of the middle and upper classes has had paradoxical side effects in this respect. Communism, which was frightening to this segment of society two decades ago, has now gained a certain respectability. When the sons and daughters of the managerial and administrative elite return from their universities convinced Marxists, this is likely to have some impact on their parents, too; a certain radicalization of some parts of the bourgeoisie appears to have taken place over the dinner table. But other channels have also been important. The influx of socialists into the journalistic profession has left its mark on the handling of news, and it is likely that the Scandinavian image of the world has changed considerably in recent years.[10]

---

[10] See *Journalistkåren i Sverige* [Journalists in Sweden] (Stockholm: Almqvist & Wiksell, 1970) and *Stockholms-journalister* [Stockholm journalists] (Malmö: Förlagshuset Norden, 1971). A study of the changing Swedish "image of the world" is currently being carried out by Prof. Jörgen Westerståhl, University of Göteborg.

It would clearly be wide of the mark to attribute this influence at various levels to planned and concerted efforts. The Communist and Socialist People's parties in Scandinavia do not control much of anything, least of all the many left-wing intellectuals in the media and the universities. Yet the perspectives and concerns of the new communicators have to some extent been beneficial to the movement by creating a more sympathetic public understanding of its views.

In the universities, leftist activism was at its height in the late sixties and has now abated in most places. This may partly be due to a decline in left-wing sympathies, but it is also the effect of a basic reorientation of thought among Communist students. In the years around 1968, the schools and the universities were where the action was. If the revolution was ever to get off the ground, it should start right here, the students thought, through the exposure of capitalist society, the unmasking of reactionary professors, and the relentless pursuit of "critical studies." After the failure of the student movement, however, most left-wing organizations concluded that the action was elsewhere and began to work in proletarian milieus. Accordingly, there is now little unrest at universities. Nevertheless, Communist groups continue to capture some 20 to 30 percent in many student government elections, radical socialists are in power in the student institutions of several Scandinavian universities, such as those of Oslo and Umeå, and an old institution of Scandinavian academic cooperation, the Nordic Summer University (*Nordiska Sommaruniversitetet*), has turned increasingly Marxist.[11]

The radical left has a far greater impact on the creative and opinion-molding sectors of Scandinavian society than it does on the political structure. In assessing the influence of the radical left, it would therefore seem useful to distinguish between the movement's *institutional power*, which is insignificant, and its *cultural power*, which is sizable. In terms of formal decision making, the radical socialists can achieve little because of their peripheral position in the political spectrum and their weak bargaining power, but they do exercise a degree of influence on "the definition of the situation"— that is to say, on the general perception of political problems and the parameters of choice or, to borrow a concept from recent political theory, "the building of the agenda." The left's cultural power is largely a function of the political resources provided by its new supporters and sympathizers, whose votes every second or third year do

---

11 The Nordic Summer University is a series of seminars with participants from the Nordic universities, focusing on a variety of cross-disciplinary topics. The seminars are held at different places in Scandinavia.

not add up to much but whose activities between elections may mean a great deal. Unlike the old Communists, who had good backing in certain peripheral areas of Scandinavia, the new radicals are strongest in the very center—not the center of the economic or political system, perhaps, but the center of the cultural system.

The Future of Radical Socialism in Scandinavia

Prediction is always a risky venture, but if the past be any guide to the future, we should be able to make a few suggestions about the prospects of the Scandinavian socialist left. The radical socialist vote in Denmark, Norway, and Sweden has grown continuously since the fifties, and it is quite likely that this tendency will persist. The relative youth of the left-wing electorate is one ground for assuming that the Communists will do well in some future elections.

But it could also be argued that the trend discernible in the left's record at the polls is misleading. The vote of the radical left was artificially deflated in the fifties, one might say, when a Communist was an outcast. Now that the social stigma of Communism has largely worn off, the level of the Communist vote may have merely returned to a "normal" level.

The impact of the international environment adds a further element of uncertainty to the prognosis. The prestige of the Soviet Union has always had a strong effect on the Communist turnout in Scandinavian elections, and, as the Swedish Communist party discovered to its cost in 1968, public denunciation of the Soviet course is not sufficient to neutralize this influence. The memory of the party's historical ties with the Soviet Union was perhaps stronger in 1968 than it is now, but in the Scandinavian context it is nonetheless likely that Eastern Europe will always remain the principal showcase of far-reaching socialism. Whether they like it or not, this will be the burden of Danish, Swedish, and Norwegian Communists— and the comfort of the Social Democrats, who count on it to protect the main part of the electorate from Communist contagion.

The prestige of the opposite camp may also be of some importance. American foreign policy certainly affected Scandinavian public opinion in the sixties, and the opinion of youth in particular, but it is less evident whether it affected the distribution of votes among the parties. In Sweden, Palme deftly countered the Communist efforts to make Vietnam an important domestic issue, and in the other countries anti-Vietnam opinion was hardly strong enough to make much of a difference in national politics.

A second variable is the economic environment. Booms and recessions have not had any great impact on the radical socialist vote in the past, and it is even unclear whether the Communists fare better in good times or in bad. But recent Danish developments may be an indication of change in this respect. It is probable that the economic disarray in Denmark has made it easier for the three left-wing parties to rally support, and the indecisive leadership of Jørgensen has facilitated their efforts. But the recent gains may also be connected with the left's old opposition to the Common Market, which is now being blamed for all kinds of problems arising in the states that have recently joined.

Finally, we cannot yet foresee the long-range effects of the "cultural power" of the left. While it is likely to contribute to slow but inexorable change in political attitudes, it will not necessarily increase the drainage of votes toward the radical fringe. On the contrary, it may cause the Social Democrats to shift their platform in order to accommodate a new climate of opinion. Scandinavian political parties tend to be more jealous of their voters than of their ideals.

5

ON WELFARE, HAPPINESS, AND DISCONTENT IN THE SCANDINAVIAN COUNTRIES

Erik Allardt

The Scandinavian countries have recently been the focus of both excessively enthusiastic and excessively critical reports in the international press. As the richest and largest country in Scandinavia, Sweden has been the main target of the critics. Their case, essentially, is that, while there is a high level of well-being in Sweden or Scandinavia in general, there is also a high degree of alienation, passivity induced by a powerful bureaucracy, and unhappiness, to which high rates of suicide, of interest in pornography, and of other forms of deviant social behavior bear witness. This overall picture of Scandinavian society has been dubbed "the Eisenhower hypothesis," since President Eisenhower once publicly described Scandinavian society in this way.[1]

The purpose of this paper is to examine selected aspects of the relationship between welfare and discontent in Scandinavian societies. The analysis will draw on a large-scale comparative Scandinavian survey carried out in 1972, which focused on such welfare dimensions as standard of living, need satisfaction, and subjective attitudes toward welfare and happiness.[2] Using only some of the

---

[1] The views of President Eisenhower were subsequently refuted by Melvin Tumin in a paper explicitly referring to the Eisenhower hypothesis. See Melvin Tumin, "Velferdsstat og moral. En granskning av 'Eisenhower-hypotesen' " [Welfare state and morals. A scrutiny of the Eisenhower hypothesis], *Tidsskrift for samfunnsforskning* 2 (1961), pp. 1-16.

[2] This study was conducted by the Research Group for Comparative Sociology at the University of Helsinki and included Denmark, Finland, Norway, and Sweden. The field work of the survey was financed in each country by the National Social Science Research Council and, in Sweden, by the Centenary Fund of the Bank of Sweden. In each country a national probability sample of approximately 1000 persons between the ages of fifteen and sixty-four was interviewed. Finland will not be discussed here, although occasional references will be made where relevant.

survey's larger findings, we will demonstrate that the Eisenhower hypothesis and other sweeping statements of the same kind are too simple to convey an accurate picture of Scandinavian society. Phenomena such as alienation, satisfaction, and discontent are very different in kind. They are only marginally related to each other, and they are explained by different background factors.

Patterns of Alienation

If, as the Eisenhower hypothesis posits, welfare and discontent are related, Sweden, as the wealthiest Scandinavian country, should display the greatest degree of alienation. Let us examine this proposition.

What traditionally has been characterized as alienation can be gauged by the findings bearing on two components of the comparative Scandinavian survey, "insubstitutability" and "political resources."[3] The idea of insubstitutability has its basis in the view that the less substitutable a person is, the more he is a person and the less he is a thing. Political resources indicate to what extent people participate in decisions affecting their own lives.[4]

Four items in the survey questionnaire were designed to tap insubstitutability. Interviewees were asked whether: (1) only very few individuals could substitute for the respondent in his present job; (2) the respondent possessed special abilities needed in his job; (3) a group of friends would break up or considerably change if the respondent for one reason or another had to leave the group; and (4) the respondent had a position in an organization such that special organizational measures would be needed in order to fill his place. These items admittedly involve some particular difficulties; the distribution of survey respondents on the last two items turns out to

---

[3] These components in the comparative Scandinavian survey are "objective" measures of "welfare," as distinguished from "subjective" measures of "happiness." See the Methodological Note at the conclusion of this chapter for a brief introduction to the terms and conceptual framework of the larger survey study.

[4] In a large Norwegian study of political resources, Willy Martinussen rightly adopts a more comprehensive concept of political resources. He defines them as all those personal resources that enable the individual to participate in and to influence politics. These include factors such as income and education as well as some attitudinal tendencies. See Willy Martinussen, *Fjerndemokratiet* [The distant democracy] (Oslo: Gyldendal, 1973), pp. 18-23, and "The Development of Civic Competence: Socialization or Task Generalization," *Acta Sociologica* 15 (1972), pp. 213-27. The reason for not defining political resources in the same fashion as Martinussen is that our other components already contain the background factors included by Martinussen as political resources. (See Methodological Note at the end of this chapter.)

Table 5–1

DISTRIBUTION OF THE COMPONENT OF INSUBSTITUTABILITY
IN DENMARK, NORWAY, AND SWEDEN, 1972

(in percentages of respondents)

Substitutability	Denmark	Norway	Sweden
Substitutable according to all criteria	46	42	31
Insubstitutable according to one criterion	32	32	39
Insubstitutable according to two criteria	19	23	26
Insubstitutable according to three criteria	3	3	4
Insubstitutable according to all four criteria	0	0	1
	100	100	100
N	(1,000)	(1,005)	(1,005)
Mean	1.79	1.88	2.06
Median	1.12	1.24	1.50
Coefficient of variation	48%	47%	43%

Note: For criteria of insubstitutability, see p. 156.
Source: Comparative Scandinavian survey; see footnote 2.

be very skewed, and the answers are necessarily based on the perceptions of the respondents. Despite the shortcomings of the items, however, it seems permissible to construct a summated scale.[5] In the distributions presented in Table 5–1, it should be noted that the higher the mean score, the greater the degree of insubstitutability. Thus, if Sweden is to display the highest degree of alienation, it should have the lowest mean score. Yet as Table 5–1 indicates, Sweden has the highest score, Norway occupies the middle rank, and Denmark ranks lowest.

With respect to political resources, our second component of alienation, four items were designed for the survey questionnaire. Interviewees were asked whether: (1) the respondent had asked for

[5] In constructing summated scales, singular items have been dichotomized. Each scale groups the respondents into five classes, the lowest score being one and the highest score being five. Accordingly, the higher the mean, the greater the value realization. With respect to Table 5-1, it seems permissible to construct a summated scale for insubstitutability since the items correlate positively among themselves and with the summated scale.

Table 5–2

DISTRIBUTION OF THE COMPONENT OF POLITICAL
RESOURCES IN DENMARK, NORWAY, AND SWEDEN, 1972

(in percentages of respondents)

Political Resources	Denmark	Norway	Sweden
Lacks political resources according to all criteria	6	4	2
Has political resources according to one criterion	27	25	18
Has political resources according to two criteria	42	38	40
Has political resources according to three criteria	16	22	29
Has political resources according to all four criteria	9	11	11
	100	100	100
N	(1,000)	(1,005)	(1,005)
Mean	2.96	3.09	3.29
Median	2.41	2.54	2.75
Coefficient of variation	34%	33%	29%

Note: For criteria of political resources, see pp. 157-58.
Source: Comparative Scandinavian survey; see footnote 2.

the floor at public meetings; (2) the respondent had tried to influence a community or political decision by personally contacting a politician, an official, or a person in a decision-making capacity; (3) the respondent had voted in the last general election; or (4) the respondent felt that he had the possibility of influencing decisions concerning his personal life.

Once again it can be seen that the rank order as regards the value fulfillment of political resources is Sweden first, followed by Norway and Denmark.[6] In short, with respect to components related to alienation, Sweden tends to have a higher degree of value-fulfill-

[6] The data for Finland have not been included in Tables 5-1 and 5-2. Finland ranks right after Sweden on insubstitutability; it ranks last on political resources. Thus the rank order of all four countries varies somewhat for different components of alienation—both those included in the present study and others to be found in the comparative Scandinavian survey. Even so, Sweden is always first, while Denmark is either third or fourth. Indeed, Sweden is generally high in value fulfillment as regards all "objective" values. It is not always first, however. (For other basic "objective" values, see Methodological Note at the end of this chapter.)

ment and thus a lower degree of alienation than the other two countries. To be sure, it is not advisable to make bold inferences on the basis of the mean scores and the national distributions. However, if the Eisenhower hypothesis is taken to mean that there should be a particularly high number of alienated individuals in Swedish society, one can at least say that the data from the Scandinavian survey do not support it.

Alienation among Unskilled Workers and the Old Middle Class. Although the social class background of the patterns of alienation is very similar in the different countries, some distinctive patterns emerge when different social classes are compared as regards their scores on the components of insubstitutability and political resources. Since the two components give very similar results, it may suffice to analyze political resources only. In the following analysis, a division into six social classes has been used and an important distinction is made between the "old middle class," composed of artisans and shopkeepers, and the "new middle class," consisting of the members of other white-collar occupations.

The relationship between alienation and social class is by no means simple. It is to be noted that Table 5–3 makes a distinction between empirical and adjusted means, the latter controlling for factors such as income, age, and sex. In terms of this distinction, Table 5–3 reveals that Scandinavian farmers and the two categories of the working class have comparatively greater political resources according to the adjusted means than to the empirical means, whereas the contrary is true for the two middle-class categories. The unskilled workers have the lowest empirical mean in all countries, whereas the old middle class has the lowest adjusted mean. These findings reflect the fact that unskilled workers generally have a poor life situation and live in conditions that induce political passivity. The old middle class, on the other hand, generally lives in rather good conditions, but it has poorer political resources than others living under similar conditions.

It does not seem possible to pinpoint a single variable that alone could explain the differences between the empirical and adjusted means. The unskilled workers generally live in conditions that tend to be associated with a low degree of value-fulfillment. Together with the farmers they have the lowest average incomes, they have a much higher average age than skilled workers, and they more seldom live in the metropolitan region around the capital city than skilled workers. On an average, unskilled workers in all countries also have a lower

Table 5–3

EMPIRICAL MEANS, ADJUSTED MEANS, AND RANK ORDERS OF THE SOCIAL CLASSES AS REGARDS POLITICAL RESOURCES IN THE SCANDINAVIAN COUNTRIES

	Empirical Means			Adjusted Means		
Social Class	Denmark	Norway	Sweden	Denmark	Norway	Sweden
Upper class	3.53 (1)	3.67 (1)	3.73 (1)	3.08 (2)	3.25 (2)	3.37 (2)
Old middle class	2.91 (4)	2.93 (4)	3.27 (4)	2.67 (6)	2.75 (6)	2.98 (6)
New middle class	2.94 (2)	3.13 (2)	3.30 (3)	2.74 (5)	2.95 (5)	3.16 (4)
Farmers	2.93 (3)	3.08 (3)	3.40 (2)	3.16 (1)	3.30 (1)	3.55 (1)
Skilled workers	2.76 (5)	2.65 (6)	3.00 (5)	2.86 (3)	3.06 (3)	3.20 (3)
Unskilled workers	2.49 (6)	2.78 (5)	2.84 (6)	2.75 (4)	2.96 (4)	3.05 (5)

Note: Rank orders are in parentheses. Adjusted means are obtained by controlling for the effects of income, migration, age, sex, urban-rural continuum, region, and social mobility. By using MCA-analysis (a form of qualitative regression analysis, in which the independent variables do not have to be quantitative) in the group comparisons, it has been possible to obtain both empirical and adjusted means in a convenient fashion. For MCA-analysis, see Frank Andrews, James Morgan, and John Sonquist, *Multiple Classification Analysis*, mimeographed (Ann Arbor: University of Michigan, 1971).

Source: Author's analysis of data from comparative Scandinavian survey; see footnote 2.

level of education, a lower rate of employment, and poorer health than the other social classes.

The old middle class provides a telling contrast. In many respects it represents the average level of value-fulfillment. It is quite evenly distributed among the income categories, it represents an average as regards rate of migration and position on the urban-rural continuum, and on an average it has a higher level of education than the working class and a lower level of education than the new middle class. Its average age is somewhat higher than the national average, but both the farmers and the unskilled workers have a higher average age than the old middle class.

Thus, the political poverty among the unskilled workers is a reflection of their general life situation. By contrast, the lack of political resources in the old middle class is a specific and more isolated trait. The members of the old middle class have weaker political resources than members of other classes living in similar conditions. Compared with other groups, the old middle class is removed from organized political activities, stands outside the political system, and feels like a forgotten class. These findings are hardly startling. Indeed, they correspond very well with other observations that reveal the old middle class to feel itself threatened and useless during a period of monopolization, politicization, and bureaucratization. All over Scandinavia new populist credos, protests against taxation, and opposition to the state bureaucracy have gained support from the old middle class.

The position of the old middle class is highlighted by comparison with the position of farmers and skilled workers. The latter rise above their general life conditions in their political resources: farmers and skilled workers have better political resources than members of other classes living in similar conditions. It is well known that they are located at the very center of the political life of the Scandinavian countries. In this sense they hardly constitute the forgotten classes of their societies.

Satisfaction and Happiness

Unlike insubstitutability and political resources, which refer to behavior and social relationships, satisfaction and happiness are assumed to refer to perceptions and subjective experiences. Satisfaction and happiness cannot be measured by observation; they can only be revealed by the extent to which people deem themselves happy. Accordingly, the items in the survey questionnaire that deal with satisfaction and happiness ask directly whether people perceive themselves to be happy or unhappy and whether they are satisfied or not with the fulfillment of their social needs.

Interestingly, the results of the survey questionnaire on satisfaction and happiness are not very different from one Scandinavian country to another. This finding is partly due to the fact that the questionnaire items give very skewed distributions. Over 90 percent of the respondents in all the countries say, for example, that they do not feel lonesome. According to this finding, *individual* happiness and feelings of need satisfaction are quite prevalent in all the Scandinavian countries. Voices of discontent are heard only when subjects of a political nature, related not to personal life but to societal conditions, are broached.

The results of the questionnaire on satisfaction and happiness also raise some interesting theoretical problems. Satisfaction, for example, has hardly any relationship at all with objective measures of the standard of living, such as income or housing conditions, or with attitudes of dissatisfaction, such as perceptions of cleavages in society or perceived patterns of social discrimination. In other words, attitudes of satisfaction appear to be independent of material conditions and of attitudes of dissatisfaction. The oft-held assumption that an increase in the standard of living will have an impact on other aspects of well-being, such as personal satisfaction and happiness, is only minimally supported by the data.

On the other hand, in all Scandinavian countries satisfaction does have some positive correlation with people's relations with each other and with the existence of companionship and social cohesion.[7] To explain this correlation, it may be hypothesized that satisfaction attitudes are verbal in nature since they almost entirely depend on people's ability to articulate their feelings. Similarly, social relations always contain a strong verbal element. In a sense, social relations exist in the language. They presuppose, for example, mutual expectations that are understood and interpreted verbally by the participants.

According to this interpretation, the material and symbolic environments are rather independent of each other. Although well-being can relate to both types of environment, material well-being and symbolic well-being are more or less independent of each other. Quite clearly, this theoretical issue, which is not restricted in its application to the special circumstances of the Scandinavian countries, deserves to be explored further.

Dissatisfaction

Attitudes of dissatisfaction, like attitudes of satisfaction and happiness, refer to perceptions and subjective experiences. They are nevertheless measured differently in the survey questionnaire. Instead of asking directly whether people are unhappy, the items on the questionnaire deal with perceptions regarding cleavages in society, unjust privilege, discrimination, and the existence of groups with too much power and income.

The most interesting finding of the survey questionnaire on dissatisfaction attitudes is that there is a rather clear change in the rank order of the Scandinavian countries. Now Denmark ranks first as the country with the least dissatisfaction. Norway, although closer to

---

[7] Companionship and cohesion are values included under the category of Loving in the comparative Scandinavian survey. See Methodological Note at the end of this chapter.

Denmark, once again occupies the middle position. Sweden displays the highest amount of dissatisfaction. At first glance these results appear odd considering the instability of Danish politics and the stability of Swedish politics. But the items measuring dissatisfaction in the survey questionnaire are phrased so as to relate to traditional class conflicts and to the fundamental left-right cleavage rather than to the recent vicissitudes of party politics. These basic conflicts seem to be much more alive in Sweden than in Norway or particularly in Denmark.[8]

Two scales in particular illustrate the findings of the survey on attitudes of dissatisfaction: they deal with perceptions of political cleavages and perceptions of unjust privileges. The data for the first of these scales were obtained in response to the following:

> It is often said that there are conflicts of interest between different groups in Danish (Norwegian, Swedish) society, for instance, conflicts between political groups or between sexes. These conflicts, however, are not equally strong. Try to tell whether the conflicts listed below, in your opinion, are very strong, quite strong, or rather weak, or whether there are no conflicts at all. (The respondent is handed a card listing several cleavages.)

The data for the different countries are at first glance very similar. The conflict between capitalists and workers is most often perceived as strong, whereas the conflict between rural and urban people is most seldom perceived as strong. Indeed, though the rural-urban conflict is still referred to in public debates, its actual role is relatively insignificant. Like other geographical factors, including regional differences, the rural-urban cleavage seems to have had almost no effect on the variation in either welfare values or attitudes of dissatisfaction, compared with social class, political party, or age.

In any case, the perceptions of social cleavages are very similar in the three countries. In Denmark the conflict between more educated and less educated, in Norway the conflict between young and old, and in Sweden the conflict between manual and white-collar workers are only slightly more pronounced than in the other countries. These differences, however, are recognizable in terms of the actual politics of the three countries. Thus, at the time of the survey,

---

[8] Finland ranks last, with Sweden. This position is less startling than the findings for Sweden. Finnish society has a tradition of class conflict, which culminated in a bitter civil war in 1918. The strength of dissatisfaction voiced among the Swedish respondents is more interesting considering Sweden's high degree of political stability, high standard of living, and the fairly high level of political resources in Swedish society.

in Sweden a hotly debated national strike among university-trained employees had strained relations between manual and white-collar workers, while in Denmark the academically trained, the civil servants, and the teachers had been under strong attack from populist quarters. In Norway several new developments had produced cleavages between young and old within, for example, the important working-class party, the social democratic Labor party.

In all countries the perceptions of the different cleavages are positively and significantly correlated, and the correlation matrices for the different countries are on the whole very similar. There is a slight tendency for differences to appear between Denmark and Norway on the one hand, and Sweden on the other, as regards items related to traditional class conflicts. They are more strongly correlated in Sweden than in Norway or Denmark. The correlation, for example, between the perception of strong cleavages between employers and employees, on the one hand, and between capitalists and workers, on the other, is .31 in Denmark, .42 in Norway, and .50 in Sweden. A similar pattern is obtained for the correlation between the capitalist/worker cleavage and the manual/white-collar cleavage. The coefficient of correlation is .25 in Denmark, .23 in Norway, and .40 in Sweden. On the whole there appears to be a stronger clustering of attitudes in the Swedish data related to traditional class conflicts. In Sweden, too, the cleavages are more often perceived as strong than in the other two countries.

When the items listed in Table 5–4 are combined into a summated scale as the measures of alienation were earlier, Denmark has a mean score of 3.16, Norway a mean score of 3.15, and Sweden a mean score of 2.89. As before, the higher the score, the weaker the perception of conflicts.

Similar results are obtained for perceptions of unjust privileges. These were measured by two simple questions: (1) Are there in Denmark (Norway, Sweden) in your opinion persons or groups whose incomes are too high? and (2) Are there in Denmark (Norway, Sweden) in your opinion persons or groups with too much power? The replies to such questions are not based on any thorough social analysis on the part of respondents. A great variety of groups were mentioned, ranging from politicians, business elites, and royalty to students, pop stars, and drug addicts. Despite many variations, some consistent patterns can be discerned in the results. Some national peculiarities also emerge. The Danish respondents mention business executives and economic leaders much less frequently than the Norwegian and Swedish respondents, but they mention civil servants

Table 5–4

PERCEPTION OF SOCIAL CLEAVAGES IN DENMARK, NORWAY, AND SWEDEN, 1972

Social Cleavage	Percentage of Respondents Viewing Cleavage as Strong		
	Denmark	Norway	Sweden
Rural vs. urban people	42 (10)	43 (10)	34 (10)
More educated vs. less educated people	80 (2)	59 (5.5)	71 (4)
Agricultural producers vs. consumers	49 (8)	48 (8)	54 (8)
Rich vs. poor	73 (4)	67 (2)	75 (2)
Young vs. old	58 (5)	62 (3)	49 (9)
Religious vs nonreligious people	55 (6)	59 (5.5)	56 (7)
Manual workers vs. white-collar workers	44 (9)	45 (9)	62 (5)
Employers vs. employees	50 (7)	55 (7)	61 (6)
Politicians vs. ordinary citizens	76 (3)	60 (4)	73 (3)
Capitalists vs. workers	83 (1)	79 (1)	83 (1)

Note: The rank orders of the different cleavages are indicated in parentheses; (1) indicates the cleavage most often mentioned as strong in each country, (10) that least often mentioned as strong. For survey question, see text.

Source: Comparative Scandinavian survey; see footnote 2.

and teachers much more often. As many as 12 percent of the Danish respondents specifically mention university and school teachers, whereas only 1 percent of the Norwegians and 3 percent of the Swedes think of teachers as having excessively high incomes. The findings about power reveal similar tendencies. The Danes more often think that teachers, students, and representatives of the mass media hold too much power. In Sweden there is a stronger tendency than in the other countries to locate persons with too much power in the field of politics. In the Swedish sample, 26 percent of the respondents locate the groups with too much power in the political structure, while the corresponding figures are 14 percent in Denmark and 10 percent in Norway. Still, only a minority in any of the three countries think that any social groups hold too much power.

According to Table 5–5, perceptions of unjust privilege are most common in Sweden and least common in Norway. It can be noted that far fewer Norwegians think that there are groups with excessive income than do Danes or Swedes, a result that may reflect the comparatively even income distribution in Norwegian society. It should also be noted that the Danes are keener on identifying persons with too much income than persons with too much power. This may reflect the more privatized character of Danish politics, which has been colored less by traditions of class conflict and ideology than by more mundane concerns for bread and butter. There is a much greater concern with income than with power in Denmark, and the groups assumed to have too much income *and* too much power are often not groups that are traditionally assumed to be power holders, but instead highly visible groups such as teachers, students, and jour-

Table 5–5
PERCEPTION OF UNJUST PRIVILEGES IN DENMARK, NORWAY, AND SWEDEN, 1972
(in percentages of respondents)

	Denmark	Norway	Sweden
Responses to Questionnaire Items			
Agreed that the incomes of some groups or persons are too high	56	41	60
Agreed that some groups or persons have too much power	28	31	46
Summated Scale			
Perceived unjust privileges in terms of both income and power	28	19	33
Perceived unjust privileges in terms of either income or power	38	34	40
Did not perceive unjust privileges in terms of either income or power	34	47	27
	100	100	100
N	(1,000)	(1,005)	(1,005)
Mean	3.06	3.28	2.94
Median	2.58	2.91	2.43
Coefficient of variation	26%	23%	26%

Note: The correlations between the replies to the two questions are around .25 in all three countries.

Source: Comparative Scandinavian survey; see footnote 2.

nalists. At the same time, there is in Danish society less overall dissatisfaction of the kind related to the traditional left-right antagonisms than in Swedish society. For these reasons, one might say that Denmark is a more privatized and Sweden a more politicized society. In a privatized society people do not relate their difficulties and hardships to structural conditions or to their own class position, whereas in a politicized society they are inclined to explain social phenomena in terms of class politics.

The high Swedish scores in the scales of dissatisfaction, however, demand further explanation. After all, Swedish political life has been stable. Change has been gradual. Moreover, according to our survey findings, the Swedes on the average have more political resources than other Scandinavians. Yet these traits of Swedish politics may not really be in contradiction with Swedish attitudes of dissatisfaction. They may rather provide the basis for an explanation of that dissatisfaction. The Social Democrats have been in political power since 1932, a circumstance that presumably has implied continuous stress in Swedish politics on cleavages related to social class. The very stability of the political system has conditioned the reactions of the electorate to social phenomena—including their perception of cleavages. This interpretation is supported by an analysis of background factors related to attitudes of dissatisfaction such as income, social class, and age.

The Political Background of Dissatisfaction. At first glance, attitudes of dissatisfaction do not seem to be clearly related to any other variables. Their correlations with objective welfare values such as standard of living, social relationships, and personal achievement are all around zero.[9] They are also unrelated to background variables such as income, social class, region, and age. But they correlate positively among themselves. Not only are the items of the singular scales correlated but the separate scales measuring dissatisfaction are also positively correlated. Still, the most important fact is that attitudes of dissatisfaction do not seem to be related to observable levels of welfare.

A closer scrutiny reveals, however, that there are two background factors of importance. By treating all the Scandinavian countries as one unit—that is, by combining the national samples—it is possible to study whether the national differences remain when the effects of

---

[9] According to the comparative Scandinavian survey, these values come under the categories of Having, Loving, and Being. See Methodological Note at the end of this chapter.

other variables are controlled for.[10] Even when income, social class, political affiliation, age, sex, migration, the urban-rural continuum, region, and social mobility are controlled for, national differences are sustained. In other words, there are national differences in the patterns of dissatisfaction that cannot be explained by the fact that some other variables are distributed differently in the Scandinavian countries. The only other factor of some explanatory value is political affiliation. Almost the only positive correlations between dissatisfaction attitudes and various background factors within each country are related to politics.

Taken together, these two pieces of information—the fact that the national differences cannot be reduced to variations in other variables and the fact that within the countries the only significant correlations are with political factors—indicate that the explanations of the variations in dissatisfaction can be found in the political climates of the countries. It has already been suggested that Danish society is more privatized and Swedish society more politicized.

The comparative Scandinavian survey unfortunately was conducted in the spring of 1972, before the crucial elections of 1973. The respondents were asked how they had voted in the last elections, which in Denmark had been held in September 1971, in Norway in September 1969, and in Sweden in October 1970. The distributions of those respondents reporting how they voted correspond very closely to the national distributions in the actual elections. There is every reason to believe that the results can be regarded as rather reliable. In order to ensure comparability, political party support has been divided into only four groups: left of the Social Democrats (the "outer" left), Social Democrats, the political center, and conservatives. Supporters of populist parties, such as Glistrup's party in Denmark, were classified with the center. However, it is to be noted that the supporters of the populist parties were very few in 1972 when the survey was conducted in comparison with their numbers in the election year of 1973. Apparently there was a very sudden increase in the popularity of the populist parties in 1973.

The political nature of dissatisfaction attitudes is clearly revealed when the adjusted means for groups of different political orientation are compared (see Table 5–6). As before, a high mean score indicates a small amount of dissatisfaction. The general pattern displayed in Table 5–6 is clear. There are more dissatisfied individuals in the outer

---

[10] The method is multiple classification analysis (MCA). See Frank Andrews, James Morgan, and John Sonquist, *Multiple Classification Analysis*, mimeographed (Ann Arbor: University of Michigan, 1971).

Table 5–6

PERCEPTION OF STRENGTH OF CLEAVAGES AND UNJUST PRIVILEGES, BY POLITICAL ORIENTATION, IN DENMARK, NORWAY, AND SWEDEN, 1972

(in adjusted means, M, and rank orders, R)

Political Orientation	Strength of Cleavages						Injustice of Privileges					
	Denmark		Norway		Sweden		Denmark		Norway		Sweden	
	M	R	M	R	M	R	M	R	M	R	M	R
Left of Social Democrats	3.06	3	2.59	4	2.37	4	2.49	4	2.89	4	2.84	4
Social Democrats	3.13	2	2.94	3	2.77	3	3.09	2	3.17	3	2.90	2
Center	2.96	4	3.27	1	2.92	2	3.05	3	3.24	2	2.85	3
Conservatives	3.14	1	3.21	2	3.13	1	3.11	1	3.56	1	3.00	1

Note: A high mean score (M) indicates a small amount of dissatisfaction. The rank order (R) of the highest mean is 1, of the lowest, 4.

Source: Author's analysis of data from comparative Scandinavian survey; see footnote 2.

left than in other groups and fewer among the conservatives. It should perhaps be pointed out that, while there is a correlation between political orientation and attitudes of dissatisfaction, the situation in the Scandinavian countries is by no means completely polarized. There are individuals both on the left and on the right who perceive strong conflicts and unjust privileges, as well as individuals who perceive none. Nevertheless, such perceptions tend to appear more often on the left than on the right. Considering that social class and income do not correlate with attitudes of dissatisfaction, it seems reasonable to state that attitudes of dissatisfaction are politically colored. They do not have any clear social background; rather, they emerge out of the political divisions and the political climate.

There are, however, some slight national differences. In Denmark the political group with the lowest mean score in the perception of conflicts—that is, the group among whom the greatest number of individuals perceive conflicts as strong—is the political center. This indicates that dissatisfaction in Denmark is common among those who tend to vote for center parties. There are other indications of the same kind. In Norway and Sweden dissatisfaction with income is clearly more common among the outer left and the Social Democrats than among the center and the conservatives. In Denmark, however, income dissatisfaction is clearly most common among those who voted for one of the center parties. It should be noted that there is a very low correlation between actual income and satisfaction with income. Like the other dissatisfaction measures, income satisfaction has more to do with politically colored attitudes than with external conditions.

Attitudes in the Scandinavian countries are never strongly polarized. Still, the fact that attitudes of dissatisfaction have a political color is further revealed by comparison of some of the reactions of the political party groupings.

As we have seen, no clear polarization exists; expressions of dissatisfaction can be found on both the left and the right. Nevertheless, attitudes of dissatisfaction have a political color in that the outer left generally is the most dissatisfied political group. And there are some national peculiarities. It is noticeable that few Social Democrats generally say that some people have too much power. In Sweden the conservatives are most likely to perceive some persons as having too much power, a reaction that presumably is directed against the Social Democrats.

In any case, in view of the fact that attitudes of dissatisfaction do not have any relationship with background variables such as social class, income, or region, but do correlate with political orientations, we are almost bound to conclude that they are mainly expressions of ideological persuasion.

The Scandinavian party systems have by tradition been strongly based on social class. Voting patterns in Norway and Sweden have been the most class-based in the world.[11] This pattern is, of course, very understandable in view of the fact that cleavages related to race, language, and religion have been absent. The lack of criss-crossing cleavages has also made for a heavy politicization of the Scandinavian countries. The traditional class-based voting patterns were still quite prevalent when the survey was conducted in 1972, as can be inferred from a comparison of the social composition of the different political groupings.

It is evident that there is a much larger representation of the higher social classes and income groups in the outer left than among

---

[11] See, for example, Gerhard Lenski, *Human Societies. A Macrolevel Introduction to Sociology* (New York: McGraw-Hill, 1970), p. 362; Erik Allardt, "The Radical Vote and the Social Context: Traditional and Emerging Radicalism," in S.N. Eisenstadt, ed., *Political Sociology* (New York and London: Basic Books, 1971), p. 491. Voting patterns in Finland have also been heavily class-based.

Table 5-7

SOURCES OF DISSATISFACTION CITED BY RESPONDENTS IN DENMARK, NORWAY, AND SWEDEN, BY POLITICAL ORIENTATION, 1971

(in percentages of respondents)

Source of Dissatisfaction	Political Orientation of Respondent											
	Denmark				Norway				Sweden			
	I	II	III	IV	I	II	III	IV	I	II	III	IV
Unjust Distribution of Income	88	64	54	40	61	47	43	18	74	67	58	42
Unjust Distribution of Power	62	31	44	47	54	31	36	27	50	40	52	60
Strong Social Cleavages:												
More educated vs. less educated	76	72	71	71	65	57	46	52	71	67	67	67
Rich vs. poor	82	72	62	63	77	64	57	59	79	75	70	65
Manual vs. white-collar	42	42	28	25	51	51	33	33	67	62	57	40
Employers vs. employees	54	42	36	38	73	52	44	34	63	61	51	41
Capitalists vs. workers	88	78	78	75	88	78	74	64	79	84	81	85
N	(71)	(269)	(252)	(149)	(43)	(314)	(227)	(137)	(24)	(364)	(307)	(76)

Note: I = left of the Social Democrats, II = Social Democrats, III = center, IV = conservatives.
Source: Author's analysis of data from comparative Scandinavian survey; see footnote 2.

Table 5–8

COMPOSITION OF POLITICAL GROUPINGS IN
DENMARK, NORWAY, AND SWEDEN, BY SOCIAL CLASS AND INCOME, 1972

(in percentages of respondents)

	Political Groupings											
	Denmark				Norway				Sweden			
Social Class	I	II	III	IV	I	II	III	IV	I	II	III	IV
Upper	13	0	12	17	16	3	8	35	8	4	13	21
Old middle	1	4	7	20	0	6	5	6	8	3	10	17
New middle	35	19	18	32	35	28	36	47	21	28	38	42
Farmers	0	2	46	18	2	3	33	3	4	1	10	3
Skilled workers	44	53	15	13	33	47	14	9	33	53	24	8
Unskilled workers	7	20	2	0	9	12	4	1	21	9	6	4
Unclassifiable	0	2	1	1	5	1	0	0	4	2	1	4
Total	100	100	100	100	100	100	100	100	100	100	100	100

Income

Highest	20	9	20	33	19	14	14	42	21	10	23	42
Next highest	25	22	17	11	26	19	20	23	13	25	17	15
Medium	25	23	12	14	21	25	20	7	29	24	17	5
Next lowest	11	24	18	15	7	25	18	10	13	22	19	12
Lowest	9	12	17	13	19	16	24	12	21	16	17	18
No information	10	10	16	13	9	2	4	6	4	3	6	8
Total	100	100	100	100	100	100	100	100	100	100	100	100
N	(71)	(269)	(252)	(149)	(43)	(314)	(227)	(137)	(24)	(364)	(307)	(76)

Note: I = left of the Social Democrats, II = Social Democrats, III = center, IV = conservatives. Columns may not add to 100 because of rounding.

Source: Author's analysis of data from the comparative Scandinavian survey; see footnote 2.

the Social Democrats. The outer left is much more an ideological grouping than the Social Democrats, who have a clear class base, namely the working class. The upper-class element within the outer left is strongest in Denmark. The data also show that 14 percent of the Danish upper class voted for parties left of the Social Democrats, while only 2 percent voted for the Social Democrats. In Norway 9 percent and in Sweden only 3 percent of the upper class voted for groups left of the Social Democrats. As we have seen, the outer left contains the highest proportion of the dissatisfied on almost all counts, and on most counts the supporters of the left differ clearly from the Social Democrats. This is another indication of the strongly ideological nature of the dissatisfaction attitudes measured here.

One other aspect of Table 5–8 deserves special mention. It will be noted that the new middle class tends to have a rather large representation in all political groups. In other words, the new middle class is politically divided and does not have a political home of its own. Considering our conclusions about the alienation of the old middle class, it would seem that the entire middle class constitutes an unstable and strategic group within the Scandinavian party system. Given the importance of political party affiliation demonstrated in this paper, the middle class is the group within which attitudes of dissatisfaction are most likely to spread.

Summary and Discussion

(1) Our first important finding is that an increase or improvement in the standard of living has only a very small impact on the quality of family and social relations or on the level of individual achievement and self-realization. Although it is often assumed that welfare values or welfare goods are highly convertible resources by which other resources and goods can be obtained, the convertibles in the comparative Scandinavian survey are of negligible magnitude.[12] When studying by different kinds of multivariate techniques the extent to which each welfare value is explained by other welfare values, it seems possible to explain only a part of the variation. This unaccountability is common in social research, and the situation doubtless calls for hard-minded methodological research.[13] As regards wel-

---

[12] See, for example, James S. Coleman, *Resources for Social Change* (New York: Wiley, 1971).

[13] See Gösta Carlsson, *Individual and System Response*, forthcoming.

fare, however, the pattern of unaccountability has quite serious implications. If the standard of living and the quality of social relations and individual achievement are largely independent of each other, then it appears that the welfare state as an institutional pattern is not of the all-encompassing nature that has been envisaged both by its friends and by its "Eisenhower hypothesis" foes.

It should, however, be remembered that we have focused here on highly developed societies. It is possible that the convertibilities are much higher in less developed societies and that convertibility tends to decrease with increasing social differentiation.

(2) This study has also demonstrated that phenomena such as alienation, satisfaction, and discontent are very different in kind and lead to different rank orderings among the Scandinavian countries. From our study of welfare values related to self-realization and the absence of alienation (insubstitutability and political resources), it appears that the Swedes display the highest amount of value realization and the least alienation, followed by Norway and Denmark. Alienation, both in terms of weak feelings of personal importance and of inability to influence politics, is more common in Denmark than in the other countries.

On the other hand, in terms of attitudes of satisfaction, it is not possible to discriminate between the Scandinavian countries. An overwhelming majority in all three countries declare that they are happy, that life is interesting, that they are not lonesome, and so on. Discontent, however, can be detected in their attitudes of a more political nature, that is, attitudes toward cleavages in society and toward privilege and discrimination. On these counts the Swedes are more dissatisfied than the Norwegians and the Danes. Attempting to interpret the apparent paradox that Sweden, characterized by a high standard of living and political stability, is the most dissatisfied of the Scandinavian countries, we have speculated that the very stability of the system may provide the explanation. The continuous rule of the Social Democrats since 1932 has made for stability in class-related attitudes. And it is in terms of these attitudes that Swedish respondents react to the problems of their society.[14]

(3) In terms of the social class background of alienation and dissatisfaction in the different countries, the middle class occupies a special position. The old middle class, because it lacks, above all,

[14] Swedish class-related attitudes may also be due to the structure and influence of the mass media which have not been studied here. (Editor's note: see chapter 6 in this volume.)

political resources commensurate with its education and income, reveals a high degree of alienation. Only unskilled workers have a comparable degree of alienation, and in their case it is associated with a low degree of well-being on almost all indices. But it is not only the old middle class, it is also the new middle class that occupies a special position. A study of the relationship between social class background, political party affiliation, and attitudes of dissatisfaction reveals the new middle class to be the most divided politically, and not clearly associated with any distinct political tendency or political grouping. Along with the old middle class, the new middle class constitutes an unstable and strategic group in the Scandinavian political party systems.

(4) Attempting to explain the differences among the Scandinavian countries, especially in the matter of dissatisfaction, we have been struck by the fact that there is a clearer cluster of class-related attitudes in the Swedish data than in the Norwegian and Danish data. The Danes are less prone to formulate their dissatisfaction in terms of generalized class antagonisms. In the light of the attitudinal data, Danish society appears to be a more privatized, Sweden a more politicized, society. Norwegian society, which in this study has rather consistently occupied a middle position, might be characterized as "consensual." [15] The Norwegians are unusually concerned about preserving the local community and regard both the EEC and the oil boom as possible threats to community life. The Norwegians also have the highest value fulfillment with respect to community cohesion, family cohesion, and friendship patterns in Scandinavia. Moreover, they are unique in their integrative relations, according to all available criteria from the field of so-called moral statistics. Norway has much lower suicide and divorce rates and a higher fertility rate than Denmark, Finland, or Sweden.[16]

(5) Ultimately, it is national differences and political party orientations within each country that correlate with attitudes of dissatisfaction. No other variables help explain the phenomenon. It is the supporters of parties, and above all the supporters of parties left of the Social Democrats—Communists, left socialists, and so on— who more often than others display attitudes of discontent and dissatisfaction. In all three countries the supporters of these parties have

[15] As used here, the word "consensual" is related to consensus in Norwegian society as discussed by Harry Eckstein. See Harry Eckstein, *Division and Cohesion in a Democracy. A Study of Norway* (Princeton, Princeton University Press, 1966), pp. 111-20.

[16] *Yearbook of Nordic Statistics*, published annually since 1962.

on the average higher social backgrounds and higher incomes than the Social Democrats, who clearly gain their main strength from the skilled workers. From this perspective attitudes of dissatisfaction in Scandinavia seem to be a function of the purely ideological orientations of the supporters of specific political parties.

Methodological Note

The term *welfare state* is used in at least two senses. It is most commonly used to characterize a society with a high level of public expenditures in the fields of social security, education, and health. But the term is also used to focus on the actual level and state of social security, economic well-being, health, and so on, in a national population. It is in the latter sense that welfare state and welfare are understood in the comparative Scandinavian survey on which this paper is based.

In this sense, welfare is still a multifaceted phenomenon. Two basic distinctions help to define it:

(1) *Welfare* versus *happiness*. Welfare is based on needs: the amount of welfare is defined by the degree of need satisfaction. Happiness, on the other hand, refers to perceptions and subjective experiences: the amount of happiness is defined by the extent to which people feel themselves to be happy. The welfare of a society is studied by observing and gauging behavior and social relationships, whereas happiness is studied by measuring attitudes and perceptions.

(2) *Standard of living* versus *quality of life*. The standard-of-living concept as it is used here is based on those needs for which the level of satisfaction is defined by the material and impersonal resources individuals can command and master, such as income, housing, and employment. The quality-of-life concept refers to needs such as the need for love and self-actualization. These are not defined by the material resources an individual can command but by the nature of his relationships with other people and with society. Although the quality-of-life concept is often used to cover subjective evaluations and perceptions in contradistinction to the material standard of living, the point of departure here is that both standard of living and quality of life can be assessed by objective and external approaches in addition to subjective ones.

177

The implictions of the two conceptual distinctions are highlighted by the following four-fold table:

	Welfare	*Happiness*
Standard of living	Needs for which satisfaction is defined by having or mastering material and impersonal resources	Subjective evaluations and perceptions; how satisfied an individual considers himself as regards his material living conditions
Quality of life	Needs for which satisfaction is defined by human relations or by the individual's relationship with other people and with society	Subjective evaluations and perceptions; how satisfied an individual considers himself as regards his human and social relations

In order to distinguish between different objective components of welfare, basic needs have been classified in three simple categories: needs defined by the material or impersonal resources an individual has and can master (*having*); needs related to love, companionship, and solidarity (*loving*); and needs denoting self-actualization and the obverse of alienation (*being*). The needs of *having* refer to standard of living; the needs of *loving* and *being* refer to quality of life.

In the survey questionnaire the three need categories, having, loving, and being, are further subdivided into twelve components.[17] Although our aim has been to measure actual conditions and overt behavior, it has not been possible to be entirely consistent on this point. The twelve components are the following:

(1) *Having*

        income
        housing conditions
        employment
        health
        education

[17] For the operationalization of these twelve components along with the questionnaire and national percentage distributions, see Erik Allardt, "About Dimensions of Welfare. An Exploratory Analysis of a Comparative Survey," *Research Reports*, no. 1 (Helsinki: Research Group for Comparative Sociology, 1973), pp. 81-128.

(2) *Loving*
>   community cohesion
>   family cohesion
>   friendship patterns

(3) *Being*
>   personal prestige
>   insubstitutability
>   political resources
>   interesting things to do (doing)

In order to distinguish between the subjective components of happiness, a distinction is made between *satisfaction* and *dissatisfaction attitudes*. These are not simply the extremes of one and the same dimension, but qualitatively different attitudes. Satisfaction attitudes denote subjective experiences of happiness, need satisfaction, and so on. Dissatisfaction attitudes describe reactions to conditions in society.

In the survey questionnaire, satisfaction and dissatisfaction attitudes are further subdivided into the following six measures:

(4) *Satisfaction attitudes*
>   perceived feeling of happiness
>   perceived satisfaction of social needs

(5) *Dissatisfaction attitudes*
>   perceptions of the strength of cleavages
>   and antagonisms in the society
>   perceptions of discrimination
>   perceptions of unjust privileges
>   satisfaction and dissatisfaction with income

It should be noted that in the comparative Scandinavian survey there was originally a heavier stress on objective measures than on perception-centered ones, but measures of both types were used in the survey. It is, in fact, through the simultaneous use of both types of measures that it becomes possible to reach comparative conclusions. In the actual analysis there was a heavier emphasis on attitudes and perception-centered measures than had been planned at the outset of the study.

It should be noted that the findings concerning the material standard of living, in other words, the welfare values related to having, are not reported in this chapter. The findings clearly show that as regards the standard-of-living components, the differences within countries are generally greater than the differences between countries. At present, large-scale studies of the standard of living and especially of low-income groups are being conducted in all Scandinavian countries. Far fewer studies of other aspects of welfare and of subjective attitudes are being pursued. For a discussion of large-scale studies of the standard of living, see Stein Ringen, "Welfare Studies in Scandinavia," *Scandinavian Political Studies,* vol. 9 (1974), pp. 187–96.

6

THE POLITICAL ROLE OF MASS COMMUNICATION IN SCANDINAVIA

Steen Sauerberg
Niels Thomsen

This chapter assembles important evidence of the differences and changes in the communication systems of Denmark, Norway, and Sweden, especially from the 1950s to the present, in an attempt to illuminate one aspect of the background to political change in the area.[1] Important differences between the three countries have evolved over time. Some features have, of course, been identical, especially the breakthrough of television in the late 1950s and early 1960s, creating a new major leisure activity and primary source of information. But there are important differences in the ways in which the electronic media are controlled as well as in the remaining communication structure: party organizations, tabloids, the party press, and the professional autonomy of journalists. Public policy has played a role in this, but so have the autonomous developments inside the media.

The second part of the chapter is a case study of the role of mass communications in the Danish general elections of 1971 and 1973. The study confirms the overwhelming importance of television, but it also shows that large-scale radical changes seem to be accompanied, if not actually conditioned, by the availability of supplementary means of communication—either media or personal exchange. Moreover, the "floating vote"—when it goes to new or less established parties—comes from the more, rather than the less, politically interested voters. Thus the existence and character of alternative carriers of information remain important in the age of television.

During the decades when the Scandinavian countries were noted for the stability of their politics, their communication systems were

---

[1] This paper does not include Finland within the scope of its analysis. When especially relevant, however, references will be made to the Finnish experience.

intimately connected with their party systems, and the two reinforced one another. In recent years, potentially far-reaching changes in both the traditional political party systems and the traditional communication systems of the three countries have emerged. Whatever the cause-and-effect relationship, it is demonstrable that the earlier congruence no longer exists and that in each country a new set of interrelationships between mass communication and the party system is developing.

The Changing Structure of Political Communications in Scandinavia

The Traditional System. Parliamentary democracy based on universal suffrage and full civil liberties developed in Scandinavia between 1870 and 1920. The fight over the extension of rights and influence to new groups was totally peaceful, but intense and lengthy. The contending parties, which were gradually coopted into a plural elite system, mobilized their electorates by appeals to nationalism, religion, and prohibition, as well as to more sophisticated ideologies. But most of all they identified with sociocultural groups or classes, which during the same period were being organized in local and national professional associations, trade unions, cooperatives, savings banks, and so on. The farmers and small-holders, who remained passive and backward in most other European countries, constituted a highly organized and participating segment of the population. And Scandinavian labor movements mobilized a vast majority of urban workers well before World War I.

As a consequence, political participation was high and the recruitment of elites rather broad. Just before World War I, when all adult men had finally been enfranchised, some 70 to 75 percent of them actually voted. Voter turnout tended to increase until the 1940s, and during these decades the gap between men and women (the latter were enfranchised between 1906 and 1921) gradually closed. In addition to voting, some 25 percent of the active electorate were dues-paying members of major political parties. Many more—a large majority of all male citizens—belonged to economic and cultural organizations that were linked to the parties. To a large degree the basis of politics was the semicorporative organization of each class or group.

The support base of the first mass medium, the daily newspaper, to which most homes subscribed before 1914, was built up along the same lines. Cities and most middle-sized towns had three or four newspapers, each supporting one political party and relying on one social group for subscribers and advertising support.[2] Except for a few sensational sheets and highly specialized papers in the capitals, nearly every Scandinavian daily newspaper was more or less closely tied to one of the four or five established party or class movements, coordinated and, when necessary, financially supported by it. Daily newspapers were the dominant medium of political mass communication; trade papers were the only other medium concerned with politics, and these were oriented toward distinct classes rather than toward the mass of voters. The weekly magazines were almost totally apolitical, designed primarily to entertain.

The advent of radio in about 1925 caused some unrest in the press. The characteristic Scandinavian solution was to create a national monopoly under parliamentary control in order to keep programming "neutral," "cultural," and "educational" (as well as to prevent the loss of national advertising revenues by the press). The newspapers—adopting Anglo-Saxon editorial techniques by now, but remaining political party organs—managed to retain their role as the paramount vehicle for political information and debate. Not only did the newspapers set the tone for the broadcast news, in some cases they actually controlled it.

World War II naturally meant the suspension of freedom of the press (particularly in Denmark and Norway) and created problems for the established parties as well as for the media supporting them.

---

[2] For further information on the party press, see: Stig Hadenius and Lennart Weibull, *Press Radio TV*, 2d ed. (Stockholm: Aldus-Bonnier, 1973), part III; Svennik Høyer, "Pressen som massemedium" [The press as mass medium], mimeographed (Oslo: University of Oslo Institute for Press Research, 1971); Niels Thomsen, *Dagbladskonkurrencen 1870-1970* [Newspaper competition 1870-1970], 2 vols. (Copenhagen: Universitetsforlaget, 1972); Stig Hadenius, Jan-Olof Seveborg, and Lennart Weibull, *Socialdemokratisk press och presspolitik 1899-1909* [Social Democratic press and press policy 1899-1909] (Stockholm: Tiden, 1968) and *Parti-press. Socialdemokratisk press och presspolitik 1910-1920* [Party press: Social Democratic press and press policy 1910-1920] (Stockholm: Rabén & Sjögren, 1970); Torbjörn Vallinder, "Political Parties and Newspapers in Sweden 1900-1970," mimeographed, European Consortium for Political Research (ECPR) seminar, 1974; Anders Y. Pers, *The Swedish Press* (Stockholm: Swedish Institute, 1966); Svend Thorsen, *Newspapers in Denmark* (Copenhagen: Danske Selskab, 1953); articles by Stig Hadenius et al., Svennik Høyer, and Nils Thomsen in *Scandinavian Political Studies*, vol. 3 (1968), part II "Rise and Structure of the Party Press"; and Svennik Høyer, Stig Hadenius, and Lennart Weibull, *The Politics and Economics of the Press: A Developmental Perspective* (Beverly Hills: Sage Publications, 1975). For the subsequent discussion of the role of the radio, see: Hans Fredrik Dahl, *Hallo-Hallo! Kringkastingen i Norge 1920-1940* [Hello, Hello! broadcasting in Norway 1920-1940] (Oslo: Cappelen, 1975), chaps. 6-7; Roar Skovmand, ed., *DR 50* (Copenhagen: 1975), especially pp. 11-114, 195-280, 319-74, and summary in English.

But the political and communication systems reemerged after 1945, undamaged and in full control. The authoritarian movements on the left and on the right had gained some support during the crisis of the 1930s. But not even the Communists—who scored 11 to 13 percent of the votes in all three countries in 1945–46—could seriously challenge the traditional system. Their electoral support declined quickly after 1946, and the circulation of their few newspapers fell sharply.

Around 1950 the typical Scandinavian household had one radio receiver and received one daily newspaper. Eighty to 100 percent of the households paid the license fees demanded from owners of radio receivers, and others listened illegally or collectively. Only a very few persons, mainly the young or the socially isolated, did not have regular access to the radio. Adults spent an average of two to three hours a day listening to eight to nine different program items. The ten- to twenty-minute newscasts in the morning, at noon, and especially in the evening were top scorers, received in 60 to 80 percent of all homes.[3]

Also around 1950, the sales of the daily press on weekdays corresponded to 110 to 130 percent of the number of households. Generalizing from a Swedish survey (1963) and from circulation figures in all three countries, it seems that nearly all homes in the biggest cities subscribed to a morning paper and that half of them acquired a supplementary evening or morning paper later in the day. In small cities and in the countryside some 80 to 90 percent of all homes subscribed to a local morning or evening paper, and 20 to 30 percent received or bought one more paper, usually a national morning paper. Taking into account collective access through libraries, restaurants,

[3] The statistics for this paragraph and the next two paragraphs are drawn from: for radio, Rune Sjödén, *Etermediernas publik* [Radio and TV audience] (Stockholm: Sveriges Radio, 1967), pp. 26-32; Theodore J. Geiger and Torben Agersnap, *Kortfattet rapport vedr. Radioundersøgelsen* [Brief report concerning radio research] (Copenhagen: 1952); Per Torsvik, *Mediaforskning* [Media research] (Oslo: Universitetsforlaget, 1972), pp. 27ff; for the press, "Dagspressens ekonomiska villkor" [The economic condition of the daily press], *Statens Offentliga Utredningar* (SOU) [Official state investigations] 1965 vol. 22, pp. 11-18; Jørgen Westerståhl and Carl-Gunnar Janson, *Politisk press* [The political press] (Göteborg: Statsvetenskapliga institutionen, 1958), pp. 58ff; "Stat og Presse" [Report from the Commission of the Press, Norway], *Instilling om tiltak for å opprettholde en differensiert dagspresse* [Recommendations on how to keep a differentiated press] (Orkanger: 1967); "Dagspressen og samfundet" [Daily press and society], Betaenkning: 536 [Official investigation 536] (Copenhagen: 1969), pp. 13ff; for other media, see national yearbooks of statistics, Audit Bureau of Circulation figures (U.S.), and some readership surveys on the biggest magazines in *Eberlins bladliste 1948* and subsequent annual editions.

and so on, probably less than 5 percent of adults did not read or see a daily newspaper regularly.

Other media were important for entertainment and advertising. Most households bought two or three of the big family or women's magazines every week, but they received practically no information on political questions from these sources. Apart from a number of free, purely local, advertising circulars, and trade and professional papers distributed to organization members, other periodicals were small or extremely specialized. Book sales and the use of the well-developed public library systems were high by comparison to those in other parts of the world. Still, book reading was confined to a minority and the reading of nonfiction books to a very small minority—presumably some 10 percent or less of adults.

In summary, then, political mass communication around 1950 was dominated by newspapers and state-operated radio. Both were strongly tied to the traditional major parties and both largely reflected their views.

The Changing Use of the Mass Media. Television came to Denmark in 1954, to Sweden in 1956, and to Norway in 1960. Within a few years the introduction of regular television broadcasting revolutionized media habits. Not only did television create a major new leisure activity, it also provided a primary source of information.

The expansion of the new medium is charted in Table 6–1. Judging from license statistics, which lag about a year behind and underestimate actual usage, television coverage extended to more than 50 percent of all households in Denmark and Sweden by 1961 and in Norway, with its hostile topography, by 1968. By the late 1960s the vast majority of any segment of Scandinavian society, with the exception of the populations living north of the Arctic Circle (less than 5 percent of the Scandinavian population), had access to television in their homes. Some 50 to 70 percent of the population watched for one or two hours per day. One of the most popular programs, the thirty-minute newscast in the early evening, was followed by nearly half the population.[4]

Since the late 1960s there has been some slight change in the patterns of television usage. This has notably been the case in Sweden where an alternative channel was introduced in December 1969: news-

---

[4] The discussion is drawn from Sjödén, *Etermediernas publik*, pp. 91-114; Natalie R. Ramsöy, ed., *Det norske samfunn* [Norwegian society] (Oslo: Gyldendal Norsk Forlag, 1968), pp. 368-76; Skovmand, *DR 50*, pp. 339-67; P. H. Kühl et al., *Fritidsvaner i Danmark* [Leisure activities in Denmark] (Copenhagen: Teknisk Forlag, 1966).

Table 6–1

MEDIA SUPPLY IN SCANDINAVIA, 1955–73
(per 1000 inhabitants)

Country	Newspaper Copies Sold (Weekdays)			Radio Licenses			Television Licenses			House-holds	
	1955	1966	1973	1955	1966	1973	1955	1966	1973	1960	1970
Denmark	364	354	365	304	306	317	1	229	287	336	365
Norway	374	379	409	277	295	316	0	152	248	317	335
Sweden	446	529	535	339	380	371	1	268	339	344	378

Note: Certain questions of definition that affect the decimals for newspaper figures are ignored here. Figures for radio and television licenses probably underestimate the numbers of radios and televisions actually in use, perhaps by as much as 10 percent. The figures for radio coverage in Denmark and Sweden in 1973 include combined licenses for radio and television as well as special radio licenses; these figures too are probably underestimates.

Source: *Nordisk Statistisk årbog* [Yearbook of Nordic statistics], 1974 and 1967; *Statistisk årbog* [Yearbook of statistics (Denmark) 1957], based on information compiled by UNESCO.

casts and other programs of "social relevance" have lost ground to entertainment. Viewers have become more selective, but their preference does not appear to be for informative programs. Since the early 1970s, there has been a slight drop in the average television viewing time per day,[5] though television broadcasting time is still expanding. Thus, the early period of intense preoccupation with a novel medium seems to have come to an end.

Radio listening has definitely decreased, though how much is unclear. Survey data for radio listening are difficult to interpret because of the problem of distinguishing between main and accompanying activities when auditors are listening to the radio while driving, eating, working, and so on. At the very least, it can be said that prime evening time has been taken over by television, and radio has increasingly found its public through daytime pop music programs. These were introduced in Sweden and Denmark in the early 1960s to counter illegal competition from "pirate stations" on the high seas, and they quickly outdistanced the more traditional programs in audience fig-

[5] Ulf Berg et al., *Hur valde publiken?* [How did the audience choose?], Sveriges Radio, Publik och programforskning [Swedish Radio, audience and program research], SR/PUB 113/73, mimeographed; *Att informeras med radio och TV* [To be informed through radio and TV], SR/PUB 204/72, mimeographed.

ures. The brief, very factual radio newscasts, however, remain high in public favor.[6]

As for the use of the daily press the trend has differed from country to country. In Sweden the proportion of adults who read more than one newspaper grew from 48 percent in 1953 to 51 percent in 1964 and remained at about that level in 1974. A dominant and increasing share of this double coverage falls on the metropolitan evening papers—street sale tabloids—which have expanded their role as supplementary papers in the small cities.[7] In Denmark double newspaper consumption was 26 percent in 1965. Most people in Copenhagen read only one paper now, and about half of them— mainly the younger and/or less-educated groups—have stopped subscribing to the morning paper and buy a tabloid instead. In the provinces the tabloids have also grown, mainly by replacing the metropolitan morning papers; they have only marginally affected the circulation of local evening and morning papers.[8] Finally, in Norway, double readership was slightly higher than in Denmark in 1964; more recent data are not at hand, but the increase in circulation must have caused this figure to rise slightly despite the delayed expansion of tabloids.

The decline of the daily press should not be exaggerated. Only 7 to 9 percent of adults in Denmark and Norway do not read newspapers, and in Sweden the figure is 4 percent at most. Average reading time per day is estimated in all three countries at about thirty minutes.[9] Furthermore, some of the decline of the daily press may be due to the growth of other periodicals. While general entertainment magazines, including photo and women's magazines, have not expanded their circulation since the early 1960s, there has been a profuse growth of more specialized magazines and of the trade and technical press.[10] There has also been a marked growth in the num-

---

[6] For evidence, see J. Schulman, "Radiopubliken" [Radio audience], in *Radio och TV möter publiken* [Radio and TV meeting the public] (Stockholm: SR/PUB, 1972), and the findings of regular audience studies carried out by Sveriges Radio and Danmarks Radio.

[7] SOU 1975 vol. 79, p. 134.

[8] Kühl, *Fritidsvaner*, pp. 188ff; *Dansk Media Index* [Index of Danish media] (Copenhagen: 1961 and subsequent annual volumes); Betaenkning 536, pp. 13ff.

[9] For Denmark, see note 8; for Norway, Per Torsvik, "Massemedia i Norge," in Ramsöy, ed., *Norske samfunn*; and for Sweden, SOU 1965 vol. 22, p. 14, SOU 1968 vol. 48, and SOU 1975 vol. 79, pp. 135 and 158.

[10] Erik Hjortkaer Andersen et al., *Massekommunikation som erhverv* [Mass communication as an industry] (Copenhagen: Erhvervökonomisk Forlag, 1973), pp. 51ff and 72ff; Torsvik, "Massemedia," pp. 360-64; Hadenius and Weibull, *Press Radio TV*, pp. 142ff; SOU 1975 vol. 79, pp. 237-57.

Table 6–2

MEDIA PREFERENCES IN SWEDEN, 1965

(in percentages of responses)

	Newspapers		Tele-vision	Radio	Other	Don't Know	Total
	Morn.	Tabloid					
"Best medium"							
Foreign news	17	4	71	8	0	—	100
Swedish news	27	8	52	13	0	—	100
Local news	68	10	10	12	0	—	100
Culture	22	1	57	17	3	—	100
Social problems	29	5	43	22	2	—	100
N = 278–293							
"Most reliable medium"							
Parliament	16		64	11	2	7	100
Social problems	38		43	10	1	8	100
Disaster and crime	51		32	10	1	6	100

Source: For "best medium": Dan Lundberg and Olof Hultén, *Individen och massmedia* [The individual and the mass media] (Stockholm: Norstedt, 1968), p. 178; for "most reliable": SOU 1968 vol. 48.

ber and circulation of free weeklies, which bring advertising and community news to all households in a restricted area. In Denmark the total circulation of free weeklies is now 3.5 million. This figure has doubled in ten years, hurting the advertising and readership of the dailies, which sell at high prices compared to those in other countries. The development of local nondaily papers in Sweden and Norway has been slower, and bi-weeklies, which—unlike most of the free weeklies in Denmark—also deal with national politics, have tended to predominate.

Recent surveys about the relative merits of the news media show that a large majority of the general public now give prime place to television, except for purely local news (see Table 6–2). Television in Sweden has a solid "credibility" lead over newspapers, particularly in the area of political information. This lead is much larger than in the United States. Other surveys confirm these preferences for all three countries.[11] They also hold true for campaign situations, with

[11] Paul Hammerich and Bent A. Koch, eds., *Madsen og medierne* [Mr. Madsen and the media] (Copenhagen: Kristeligt Dagblad, 1970), pp. 172-76; and Per Torsvik, "Television and Information," *Scandinavian Political Studies*, vol. 7 (1972), p. 223. See also SOU 1975 vol. 78, p. 58.

the modification that television's lead seems to increase as election day approaches. Before the start of the Danish 1971 election campaign, 42 percent of the respondents said that television was their most important source of political information, while 8 percent indicated radio and 31 percent, newspapers. During the campaign, television's lead increased to 64 percent over 22 percent for newspapers and 8 percent for radio. Illustrated magazines, pamphlets, posters, public meetings, and so on, ranked far behind the three major news media.[12] By all reports, however, respondents with some higher education and political opinion leaders have as much confidence in newspapers as in television and tend to use them more than television news as a basis for discussion.[13]

The overall picture, therefore, is that in all three Scandinavian countries television has come to dominate the mass media, in terms of both the number of people it reaches and its reputation as a source of political information. Although the extent of the decline of radio listening is unclear, there is no question that radio is no longer a dominant medium for the public at large, as it was before the advent of television. As for the daily press, the Scandinavian record is uneven. In Sweden and by inference in Norway, newspaper consumption has actually been increasing. In Denmark, on the other hand, it has been declining slightly, but the time spent on newspaper reading and the importance of newspapers as a source of political information seem to be roughly the same in the three countries.

Changes in Mass Organizations since 1950. A survey of changes in the traditional communication systems of Scandinavia should not omit developments within the mass organizations. The traditional party organizations and their affiliates for special groups, such as women or youth, or devoted to special activities like education maintain branch units or clubs in every constituency and municipality. During campaigns they communicate with the local public through open meetings, pamphlets, and posters. In nonelection periods they arrange discussions and publish periodicals for members. Along with trade organizations, such as trade unions and employers' organiza-

---

[12] Steen Sauerberg, "Kommunikation til vaelgere—og mellem vaelgere" [Communication with and among the voters] in O. Borre, H. J. Nielsen, S. Sauerberg, and T. Worre, *Vaelgere i 70 'erne* [The voters in the 1970s] (Copenhagen: 1976).
[13] Rune Sjödén, *Sveriges första TV—val* [The first TV elections in Sweden] (Uddevalla: Sveriges Radio, 1964); Dan Lundberg and Olof Hultén, *Individen och massmedia* [The individual and the mass media] (Stockholm: Norstedt, 1968), p. 179; Torsvik, "Television and Information," p. 225; Hammerich and Koch, *Madsen og medierne*, pp. 172 and 175.

tions, mass organizations are therefore prime sources of political media content and important factors in media control and support. They even constitute independent channels through which information and propaganda reach the public.

Unfortunately, despite the importance of this aspect of communication systems, information about the mass organizations is scarce and unsystematic. Early surveys indicate, for example, that 21 percent of Swedish voters attended election meetings in 1950. By 1956 the percentage had declined to 16 percent, and figures for the 1960s range between 5 and 10 percent; in the area of Stavanger, in Norway, 9 percent of voters attended election meetings in 1965 and 1969. In the case of Denmark, the figure is 5 percent for 1971.[14] Admittedly, participation in the day-to-day activities of political parties has always been restricted to a minority, even among party members. Still, it is generally believed that attendance at party meetings has been declining, so that local efforts have become less important than the increasing sums of money that are now spent from central headquarters on advertising and handbills. This development has meant that party propaganda relies less and less on reports and comments in local newspapers or on local organizational activities and that the deliberate news policies of national headquarters and the mass appeals launched by top party spokesmen have gained in importance.

In 1950, 20 to 30 percent of the active voters were members of political parties. This ratio seems to have been declining during the last decades. As Table 6–3 indicates, however, the differences from country to country are very striking.[15] The percentage of voters who are party members has declined only slightly in Sweden, but it has dropped dramatically in Denmark. This trend in Denmark was noticeable before the massive breakthrough of new parties, which invariably have very low memberships. In Denmark, moreover, support for the

---

[14] Svensk Gallup A-B [Swedish Gallup Poll, Inc.], *Radions insats i valkampanjen 1950* [The contribution of radio in the election campaign of 1950], mimeographed, 1950; Jørgen Westerstahl and Bo Särlvik, *Svensk Valrörelse; Arbetsrapport* [The Swedish election movement, working report] (Göteborg: Statsvetenskapliga institutionen, 1955); Henry Valen and Willy Martinussen, *Velgerne og politiske frontlinjer* [Voters and political front lines] (Oslo: Gyldendal Norsk Forlag, 1972), p. 22.

[15] Danish youth organizations officially had 130,000 members in 1948 and 100,000 in 1953; the biggest youth organization had 5,000 members in 1972, a reduction of 89 percent over twenty years. See sources for Denmark in Table 5-3; also a 1974 pamphlet, *Venstre i dansk politik* [The Liberals in Danish politics]. For the age of party members in 1971, see Hans Jörgen Nielsen, *Det politiske system i Danmark* [The political system in Denmark] (Copenhagen: 1974), p. 42.

Table 6–3

VOTER MEMBERSHIP IN SCANDINAVIAN POLITICAL PARTIES, SELECTED YEARS SINCE 1950

Country and Year	Communist	Social Democrat	Liberal (Radical)	Center (Agrarian)	Conservative	Other	Active Voters	Electorate
Party								
Sweden								
1952	12	42	12	44	23	—	31	25
1962	16	40	15	33	31	—	33	26
1970	6	39	16	18	22	?	26	23
Norway								
1957	10	18	16	38	28	16	21	16
1969	?	20	15	30?	30	?	19	16
Denmark								
1953	21	32	21	37	24	15	29	23
1966	?	23	15	31	27	2	21	19
1973	?	17	7	30	33	3	13	12

Note: Entries are percentages of voters for the stated party or in the stated group ("active voters" or "electorate") who are party members. Most of these figures were reported by party officials and may be somewhat exaggerated. Also it should be noted that the lowering of the voting age (from twenty-three or twenty-one to twenty or nineteen) has tended to lower the percentages. In Norway and Sweden 60 percent and 70 percent, respectively, of the Social Democratic membership are accounted for by the collective membership of local labor unions.

Source: Sweden: Pär-Erik Back, *Det Svenska Partiväsen* [The Swedish party system] (Stockholm: Almqvist & Wiksell, 1967); Kay-Vilhelm Winquist et al., *Svenska Parti Apparater* [Swedish party organizations] (Stockholm: Aldus-Bonnier, 1972). Norway: Henry Valen and Daniel Katz, *Political Parties in Norway* (Oslo: Universitetsforlaget, 1965), p. 70; Stanley Henig, ed., *European Political Parties* (New York: Praeger, 1970); Willy Martinussen, *Fjerndemokratiet* [The distant democracy] (Oslo: Gyldendal Norsk Forlag, 1973). Denmark: Niels Thomsen, unprinted 1953 data in private possession; K. Gedde, ed., *De Politiske Partier* [Political parties] (Copenhagen: Danske Forlag, 1949); Erik Rasmussen, *Komparativ Politik I* [Comparative politics I], 2d ed. (Copenhagen: Gyldendal Norsk Forlag, 1971), chapter 5; *Kristeligt Dagblad* [Christian daily post], December 20, 1974.

traditional political youth organizations has dwindled, and the average age of party members is now over fifty.

By way of explanation for the disparity between Sweden and Denmark, it may be relevant to note that Sweden has subsidized party organizations since 1967, distributing to them some $6 million a year in proportion to their voting strength. In Norway political parties receive in government aid less than half the amount per voter that those in Sweden receive, and in Denmark government support is insignificant. Sweden also permits municipal councils to support the parties and subsidizes the party press. While public finance has at least doubled party revenue in Sweden, Danish parties still get about half their income from members and half from trade unions, employers' associations, and business firms.

There has been a general growth of professional organizations in all three countries. For most people membership is indispensable or even obligatory. By 1970, the three national labor federations in Denmark, Norway, and Sweden together counted over 3 million members, covering 80 to 90 percent of all workers. Fifty to 70 percent of civil servants and clerical workers have more recently been organized, partly in the national labor federations and partly in independent unions. Another 450,000 people are members of farmers' organizations and cooperative organizations, and some 150,000 employers in trade and industry are organized. In all, at least 5 million individuals are members of major interest organizations. Ignoring the possibility that some individuals are members of more than one organization, the figure corresponds to 81 percent of the number of Scandinavian households—63 percent in Norway, 78 percent in Denmark, and 90 percent in Sweden.[16]

Even considering the fact that some households account for more than one membership, it is safe to conclude that trade papers, circulars, and so on from interest organizations reach most families. During 1974, trade unions in Sweden, for example, distributed 49 million copies of their journals to their 1,863,000 members, and public servants' organizations sent out another 15 million copies of their publications.[17] These communications are channels for political debate in that they focus on political issues which are of direct interest to organization members. Given their source, moreover, the credibility of their content is likely to be high. In 1969, 46 percent of a Norwegian sample considered professional organizations the best guardians of their interests, while 27 percent pointed to the politicians and 11 percent to parties.[18]

Organizations for employers and farmers have long provided funds for conservative, liberal, or center party activities, including

[16] Ingemar Lindblad, Krister Wahlbäck, and Claes Wiklund, *Politik i Norden* [Politics in the Nordic countries] (Stockholm: Aldus-Bonnier, 1972), chapter 3; *Nordisk Statistisk årbog 1974* [Yearbook of Nordic statistics 1974].

[17] SOU 1975 vol. 79, pp. 244ff. Annual figures on most trade and union papers from 1963 on can be found in *Media Scandinavia 63* (Copenhagen: 1963) and subsequent editions.

[18] Willy Martinussen, *Fjerndemokratiet* [The distant democracy] (Oslo: Glydendal Norsk Forlag, 1973), p. 174.

the daily press. In turn these parties have recruited leaders from the organization ranks. The relationship between party and organization used to be relatively permanent, consistent with a kind of corporatist thinking. But changes have taken place since 1950. In Denmark important interest organizations, such as the employers' organization, have tended to avoid alliances with particular parties. Instead, their support is divided between sympathetic parties on an ad hoc basis. In the long run, the new policy implies a loss of moral support and propaganda strength for certain traditional parties.

For historical and other reasons, manifest party politics have been more fully and more openly embraced by the regular trade unions than by other organizations. With some brief and partial exceptions during periods of strong Communist influence in the aftermath of both world wars, Social Democrats have been in full and uncontested control of all large unions and the national federations since the 1880s. The parties have been able to rely on the powerful union structure not only for campaign and press funds, but also for support of the party line in union declarations, trade journals, and meetings, as well as at the level of the individual union or federation member. In return, the trade union movement has had an actual influence on recruitment and policy making at all party levels. Its public policy positions and declarations have usually been made in agreement or in loyal interplay with the party.[19]

This harmonious division of functions is less secure than it was. Faced with wildcat strikes and persistent pressure from leftist minority groups, several Danish trade unions have taken stands on general political problems in defiance of the party line. This was especially the case during the campaign leading up to Denmark's entry into the European Economic Community in 1972. The EEC referendum in Norway the same year provoked similar widespread confrontations. By way of contrast, the Swedish trade union federation and its more efficiently organized substructure seem rather safely allied with the Social Democratic party.

As this survey has indicated, the contrast between the solid Swedish political system and the deeply disrupted Danish system— with the Norwegian system somewhere in between—has its counterpart in the quite different patterns of development among the communication systems of the countries' mass organizations. Whatever causal relationship links developments in these two systems is difficult to assess, since mass organizations are themselves to some degree

---

[19] Further discussions of trade unions and the Social Democratic parties can be found in Walter Galenson's chapter in this volume.

part of the political system. Yet at the very least it can be noted that the declining number of voters who are party members and the increasing divorce between parties and professional organizations in Denmark correlate very well with the apparent confusion and instability of Danish electoral behavior.

Public Control of the Electronic Media. In recent years, three issues have dominated discussion of public policy toward television and radio in Scandinavia. First, problems have arisen with respect to the structure of public control and the extent of partisan political influence. Second, debate has arisen over programming, more specifically the criteria of objectivity to be applied in presenting news broadcasts and treating controversial issues of public policy. Finally, there has been the issue of access, the extent to which new and minor political parties are to be provided equal time with established major parties on television and radio. On each of these issues, Denmark, Norway, and Sweden reveal some rather interesting differences in policy and in practice.

Radio and television in all Scandinavian countries are run by national monopolies which have the "sole and exclusive rights to broadcast."[20] In Denmark and Norway the monopoly is exercised by independent public institutions. In Sweden, it is controlled by a corporation, operating on a ten-year charter granted by parliament; 60 percent of the capital in the corporation is owned by different social and cultural organizations, 20 percent by newspapers, and 20 percent by private firms. The basic situation is nevertheless similar to that in Denmark and Norway, since parliament in all three cases lays down the basic goals, organizational structure, and public policy of radio and television and exercises budgetary control, approving changes in the license fees which are practically the only income of the companies. Despite this basic similarity, however, the degree and kind of public influence on the electronic media are very different.

Danmarks Radio is ruled by a Radio Council which has supreme authority over program policy. From 1926 to 1959 different popular

---

[20] For relevant legislation, see "Norsk Rikskringkasting, Organisasjon og ansettelsesvilkår" [The Norwegian state broadcasting system, organization, and operating conditions], NOU 1972 vol. 25 (Oslo: 1972), which includes the text of the Radio Act and regulations. For Danish Radio, see *Lov nr. 421 af 15. Juni 1973 om radio-og fjernsynsvirksomhed* [Statute law number 421 of June 15, 1973, on the activity of radio and television]; see also Skovmand, *DR 50* for a discussion of control problems. For Sweden, see Sveriges Radio, *Laws and Basic Regulations* (Stockholm: 1970); earlier structure is described in F. Johansson and T. Carlsson, *Kan vi lita på TV* [Can we trust TV?] (Stockholm: 1966). For Norway, see M. Berg, ed., *Massemedier i Norge* [Mass media in Norway] (Oslo: 1975), pp. 180ff.

radio organizations had considerable representation on the council, but now parliament appoints twenty-two of its twenty-seven members. With advice from the Radio Council, the government appoints a director general who is responsible to the Radio Council for appointments and daily operations. While party politicians have increasingly dominated the body, which in principle determines program policies, this trend has been paradoxically counterbalanced by the increasing difficulty of implementing the council's decisions in an institution of rapidly growing size and complexity. The means of controlling program content were reduced when prior censorship, which had grown burdensome, was finally abolished in 1964, and even more when a version of editorial democracy was sanctioned in 1971. Under these conditions little effective control was exercised by the busy political appointees who shun committee work and are tempted to use the Radio Council more as a propaganda platform than as an administrative organ. Over the years this has led to ever more open conflicts between the "radio politicians" and the staff, presumably weakening public confidence in both groups.

The Norwegian government appoints a responsible director general, five governors, and other top officials who are in charge of programming and the daily administration of *Norsk Rikskringkasting* (NRK). The government also appoints eleven members of the Norwegian Radio Council. Parliament appoints the remaining twelve members of that body, but active politicians are not usually considered for the positions. The Radio Council discusses program policy in general; its function is mainly advisory. In effect, the government has influenced policy only through its choice of appointees, and program control has been vested in the civil servants of NRK. Until recently, tensions were kept at a low level, but since the early seventies the role of party politics seems to have been increasing.

In Sweden the corporation's shareholders can influence the program policy of *Sveriges Radio* (SR) only through their right to appoint five members of the radio board. Till 1973 all remaining members—six including the chairman—were appointed by the government; two of the shareholders' representatives were always Social Democrats, so that party had a safe majority. In 1973 the inclusion on the board of two members chosen by the staff of SR complicated the situation. The board appoints the director general, but otherwise it has rather limited functions. Responsibility for programming is largely delegated to six autonomous units within SR, which are supposed to "establish a climate of liberty, independence, variety and stimulating rivalry in the creation of ideas and the shaping of programmes."

Furthermore, inside these units the formal structure of the organization guarantees a wide delegation of powers to the individual producers. The major nonprofessional check on programming lies in a special radio/television tribunal (*radionämnden*) consisting of seven members, who are appointed by the government to broadly reflect party strength in parliament. But neither through the verdicts of this tribunal nor in other ways do considerations of party politics directly enter into policy making. Nonprofessional influence on programs has been channelled through the broad social and cultural organizations and by governmental departments represented in the two elected bodies—not by party politicians. Controversy over programs has not been frequent and rarely has centered on issues of party politics.

In brief, direct control over *Danmarks Radio* by members of parliament has produced polarization along party political lines. The civil servant version in Norway and the Swedish combination of delegated powers and social consensus control have proved far less controversial.

Not surprisingly, the controversy in Denmark over the structure of public control has spilled over into the issue of programming. In radio laws and charters, all Scandinavian parliaments have laid down certain summary instructions for programming. As subsequently codified, the basic rules require that information be truthful, objective, balanced, and reflective of varied viewpoints. Radio and television, because they have been entrusted to a state monopoly within a democratic society, must be bound by law to meet high standards of reliability, impartiality, and relevance.

In the late 1960s these BBC-inspired "middle of the road and consensus principles" were strongly challenged by groups of professional journalists and intellectuals. They felt that so-called objective newscasting and balanced programming prevented any vigorous discussion of public policy issues. The general public was receiving a homogenized and unrealistic view of society, they claimed, one that actually worked to the benefit of the social and political establishment. Information, these groups believed, should be "messages which are likely to change the world view of the recipient to a more realistic one." It was better to promote social reform, they said, than to pay lip service to an unattainable or even nonexistent objectivity.

These views were at first most cogently expressed by a group of journalists and researchers in Finland, where they were put into practice to some extent during the period 1965–70.[21] The Finnish

---

[21] For the Finnish experience, see Kaarle Nordenstreng, ed., *Informational Mass Communication*, mimeographed (Tampere: 1973), pp. 29 and 31. For discussion in this and subsequent paragraphs, see *Journalistkåren i Sverige* [The journalistic

experience had considerable influence in the other Scandinavian countries, especially on the younger generation of journalists. It has been repeatedly shown that young journalists today subscribe to a much more activist and leftist ideology than their elders. The growth of personnel, which accompanied the expansion of programs during the 1960s, meant that radio and television recruited heavily from the generation which had a natural sympathy for the "youth revolt" of the late sixties. At the same time the vogue for participation gave rank-and-file staffers in radio and television a say in most decisions and weakened editorial control. The result was an upsurge of socially committed and leftist reporting, vigorous attacks on the establishment, and increased coverage of social unrest and the merits of political minorities.

In Denmark after 1970, right-wing politicians made repeated attacks on the "red hirelings" of Danish radio. The right-wing Social Democrat, Erhard Jacobsen, meanwhile organized "vigilance committees" all over the country to decry leftist outrages on radio and television. After Jacobsen broke away from the Social Democrats and founded his own party (the Center Democrats) in November 1973, the issue of leftist influence in the media received even greater attention. Radio Council meetings became regular party battles, eagerly reported in the newspapers. Since the 1973 election, the general tone of Danish broadcasting has been somewhat more cautious. The feeling is growing, however, that the problems of controlling the electronic media can only be solved by the creation of alternative radio and television stations, independent of the national *Danmarks Radio* and possibly financed at least in part by advertising. Up to 1973, only the Conservatives advocated this solution, but now more and more parties are questioning the wisdom of preserving the monopoly of *Danmarks Radio*. The Social Democrats, caught in the middle, are trying to take the pressure off by implementing a geographical decentralization of programming.

The Norwegian and the Swedish broadcasting corporations have also been decentralizing in recent years. So far radio has been chiefly affected, but television, especially cable television, is likely to be involved in the future. In Norway and Sweden, however, the question of decentralization has not been directly linked to controversies over

corps in Sweden], research report from the School of Journalism, Stockholm (Stockholm: 1970); *Iagttagelser* [Observation] no. 1, mimeographed (Stockholm: 1974); Nils Thomsen in *Pressens årbog 1975* [Yearbook of the press, 1975] (Copenhagen: 1975), pp. 24ff; Jørgen Westerståhl, *Objektiv nyhetsförmedling* [Objective news coverage] (Stockholm: Läromedelsförlagen, 1972); and Lars Furhoff, *Makten över medierne* [Power over the media] (Solna: Seelig, 1974).

program policy, which on the whole have been far less intense than those in Denmark and Finland.

It must be underlined that the problems mentioned have had considerably less impact on newscasts and political broadcasts than on cultural, educational, and general feature programs. The daily thirty-minute news commentaries on all television stations rely heavily on ordinary wire copy from national and other Western (mainly British and American) news agencies, and the private coverage of local events, as well as the activities of eight to twenty-five correspondents abroad, tend to conform to the norms of Western journalism. Such criticism as arises comes mostly from supporters of "engaged" journalism and radical observers who detect a Western, capitalistic bias in the sources and criteria of news reporting.

There may be little doubt that the existing professional standards in news reporting favor the bigger parties, particularly the party in government. Government politicians can rely on their "news value" and their "natural" connections with the political reporters to bring their activities to the attention of the public. However, the same standards also imply intense coverage of unorthodox and entertaining political personalities—like Glistrup and Jacobsen in the Danish shock-election of 1973. Generally speaking, the official requirement of balanced presentation, of due respect for "variability" and "many-sidedness," is applied to newscasts as well as to debate programs and treatments of topics of general political interest. Above all, during election campaigns, the criterion of balanced presentation and "variability" is interpreted rather rigorously to mean "equal time for all parties."

Compared with other Nordic countries, Denmark interprets the equal-time rule most strictly, to the benefit of new and small parties. Until the late 1950s, the equal-time rule was basically interpreted as meaning equal time for the four old parties. However, in 1959—precisely one year before the first televised national election campaign—the Danish Supreme Court adopted a wider interpretation, ordering that fully equal time be given to all parties, even those not (yet) represented in parliament. The principle is even extended to ordinary broadcasts during campaign periods (including referendum campaigns, according to a 1963 ombudsman decision): no candidate for parliament or member of the government is allowed to participate in any program other than news programs or approved campaign programs. The parties may choose either to use the production facilities of Danmarks Radio free of charge, or to produce their programs independently with grants from the station.

In Norway, the new and small parties' access to the broadcast media is limited in two ways. The party must have a nationwide organization and must normally have been formally recognized at least six months before the election to allow necessary time for "program planning." All parties that fulfill these requirements are granted equal time in which to present and discuss their ideas. In political debates, all representatives are allowed exactly equal time on the air, though the government and "a clear opposition" are favored by an extra representative each. Like that in Denmark, the system is frustrating for the participants as well as for the audience and has often been described as democracy carried to the extreme. The time limit itself becomes a tactical device: one candidate exhausts his opponent's talking time by forcing him to discuss intriguing but minor problems, another refuses to answer a question on grounds of insufficient time and thus saves time for his final comments, and so on. In Norway, one of the political parties appealed to the ombudsman to secure a change in the equal-time rule, but the ombudsman refused to take a stand, claiming that the *Norsk Rigskringkasting* has sovereignty over decisions concerning campaign broadcasts.

In Sweden, the equal-time rule has been more limited in its application and does not benefit new and smaller parties to quite the same degree. New and minor parties are allowed less time on the air than the four big ones, and of these the Social Democrats have rather more broadcast time since they are the party in government and have to defend themselves against several different parties in opposition. The Social Democrats' time advantage is slight, however, and only applied in political debate programs. The Swedes have avoided the rigid application of the time rule that, in Denmark and Norway, prevents the appropriate use of debating time. Reporters and staff may refer to "journalistic criteria" in determining how to conduct a debate. Thus, an equal-time principle has been adopted in all three countries, but it has been applied with some discrimination in Sweden, and even in Norway, whereas Denmark has applied the rule to the letter.

Quite apart from its specific controversial applications, the equal-time rule raises a deeper political question, the question of whether new and small parties are receiving excessive advantages at the expense of the large and established parties. It can be argued, of course, that the ability to voice criticism is vital for the proper functioning of a democracy. On the other hand, television has achieved an extremely important position in the Scandinavian political communication system at a time when the countervailing effects of a differentiated press are no longer present. Before the advent of television, the electorate took its political bearings by the daily press and the mass organizations. Today this is no longer true. Television, by giving exposure to the ideas of new parties, by dramatizing politics, and possibly by encouraging greater voter turnout, may be contributing to the greater mobility of the electorate and thus to the instability of the political party system.

The Concentration of the Press and Tabloids. The conditions and character of the Scandinavian daily press have changed profoundly since the 1940s.[22] Circulations have risen only slightly, but prices have been kept so high that sales income has increased considerably. Advertising income has risen even more because of the general economic expansion and the fact that the electronic media do not carry advertising. But despite a doubling of total newspaper income between 1955 and 1965 and again between 1965 and 1973, the daily press has been troubled by low profits—averaging about 5 percent of gross income—and by recurrent crises. No major productivity gains have been able to offset the steep rise in expenses. These stem only in part from wage increases. Equally important have been staff increases as the newspapers have grown in response to strenuous competition.

These are general trends which have varied in degree in the three Scandinavian countries. Owing to more positive circulation trends and, as we shall see, to state subsidies, the Swedish dailies do slightly better, for example, than the Danish. Even so, a systematic profit squeeze automatically leads to concentration. This has been happening in Scandinavia since 1950, though at different rates in the different countries, depending possibly on their transportation systems and geography. The number of daily newspapers in Denmark declined between 1950 and 1975 from 112 to 50 (by 55 percent), in Sweden, from 133 to 89 (by 33 percent), and in Norway, from 191 to 152 (by 20 percent). Generally the pattern has been the elimination of competition within given local markets, so that only the biggest cities retain more than one local paper. Metropolitan morning papers have not made any headway in the small-town areas of the provinces, and the gains of the newer tabloids are largely due to supplementary sales. As a result, increasing portions of the populations of Denmark and Sweden now live in areas where local news and advertising are

---

[22] See SOU 1965 vol. 22, chapter 3, and appendix 1; SOU 1975 vol. 79, chapter 9, and appendix 3; annual surveys of developments in the Scandinavian daily press by Niels Thomsen in *Pressehistorisk årbog* [Historical yearbook of the press], annual issues, 1968-72; similar surveys for each of the four countries in *Pressens årbog 1975* (Copenhagen: 1975); and T. Høyem, "Tabloidetik i Norden" [Ethics of tabloids in Scandinavia] in *Pressens årbog 1976*, pp. 151ff.

transmitted by "monopoly" dailies. The traditional structure—three or four local papers each representing one major party and relying mainly on one sociocultural group—tends to be replaced by "community papers" which abolish or play down their traditional party line.

At the same time, the metropolitan press, printed in Oslo, Copenhagen, Stockholm, Göteborg, and Malmö, has changed in structure. A few of the five to ten papers formerly printed in each of these cities have ceased publication, but most of them have been able to maintain their separate identities and distinctive styles, ideologies, or subject matters. However, the mass audiences in the cities and a considerable number of the double readers outside them have been increasingly attracted to the sensational, illustrated, popular tabloids. In Stockholm, the circulation of *Expressen* [Express] grew steadily from zero to 600,000 during the period 1944–70; *Aftonbladet* [Evening post], taken over by the trade unions in 1958, tripled its circulation to almost 500,000 during the 1960s. In Copenhagen, *B.T.* doubled its circulation during the 1950s, and *Ekstrabladet* [Special post] did the same from 1965 to 1970; their growth has continued, and each now has a circulation of close to 250,000. Norway entered the tabloid market somewhat later. In 1968 *Verdens Gang* [Way of the world] (now *V.G.*), in Oslo, adopted the new tabloid style and tripled its circulation during the next five years. Soon, if somewhat reluctantly, it was followed by the more traditional *Dagbladet* [Daily post], which now has sales of 120,000.

These tabloids—apparently patterned after the London *Daily Mirror* of the 1940s—are very different from the morning and evening papers that were read by all city dwellers twenty years ago. The choice of subjects they cover as well as their style and presentation are much less serious and comprehensive, much more sensational and human interest oriented than those of the morning papers. Indeed, the morning papers have to some extent been contaminated by their more successful offspring. To some degree, the less exacting style of the tabloids has probably stimulated interest in political and social subjects—rather as television has. At the same time, their reckless and phony crusading and their chronic lack of balance and perspective may encourage cynicism and contentiousness, thereby weakening respect for established authority.

There are important differences in content and function between Danish and Swedish tabloids; their Norwegian counterparts fall in between, though closer to the Swedish version. In Copenhagen, *Ekstrabladet* and *B.T.* have largely supplanted the morning papers as sole reading for less serious-minded people, particularly the young and less educated blue- and white-collar workers. These tabloids have carried the neglect of traditional informative newspaper functions to extremes, ignoring conventional press ethics in their coverage of debates, reports, and foreign dispatches. Both papers are now completely independent of party politics and ideology, taking strong stands rather randomly and pandering to the popular mood.

By way of contrast, the Swedish *Expressen* (liberal) and *Aftonbladet* (Social Democrat), although they have some of the common characteristics of tabloids and cannot be described as party organs, have nevertheless maintained some party loyalty and political coherence. Their information content is generally much higher, the choice of subjects less trivial. Furthermore, very few people in Sweden read these papers alone—fewer than 5 percent in Stockholm as against 30 to 40 percent in Copenhagen—and the level of political interest among their readership seems to be above average.

Along with the rise of tabloids and the concentration of the press, another change that has occurred among Scandinavian newspapers is the increasing tendency to avoid affiliation with a political party or association with a particular point of view. Until recently the political background of most papers could be easily identified by simple content analysis.[23] The traditional party press inevitably, indeed openly, printed biased commentary and even biased political reporting. But the ties between party and newspaper took many forms. In some cases, as with the Socialist or Communist press, the party or affiliated professional organizations were owners or patrons. In most other cases, the link between party and paper was based on tradition or on the presumed expectations of the readership. Another factor, which had considerable weight for many small papers, was the advantage of cooperation with fellow party papers in such matters as joint editorial agencies.[24]

---

[23] SOU 1975 vol. 75, pp. 140ff, 158ff, and 161; Lundberg and Hultén, *Individen och massmedia*, part III; Lars Furhoff and Hans Hederberg, *Dagspressen i Sverige* [The daily press in Sweden] (Stockholm: Aldus-Bonnier, 1965), pp. 109ff and 126ff; Hadenius and Weibull, *Press Radio TV*, chapter 8; Westerståhl and Janson, *Politisk press*; Stig Hadenius, "Riksdagen i pressen" [Parliament in the press], SOU 1972 vol. 17; Westerståhl, *Objektiv nyhetsförmedling*, chapter 5; Niels Thomsen, *Partipressen* [The party press] (Århus: Institut for Presseforskning og Samtidshistorie, 1965); Høyer, *Pressen som massemedium*, chap. 6.

[24] Hadenius and Weibull, *Press Radio TV*, pp. 195ff; P. Hémanus in *Pressehistorisk årbog 1972*, pp. 22ff; E. Lund and Niels Thomsen in *Pressens årbog 1974*, pp. 121ff; Torbjörn Vallinder, *Press och politik* [Press and politics] (Lund: Gleerup, 1970), chapter 5; Kai Kronvall et al., *Partipressen idag* [The party press today] (Lund: Studentlitteratur, 1971), *passim*.

Today it is difficult to discover any party identification, not only in most tabloids, but in other big papers as well. Some of the big morning and provincial papers have formally declared their independence from any party allegiance and tend to define their editorial stand from issue to issue, though, to be sure, they still manifest a basic preference for certain political principles and styles. Thus *Dagens Nyheter* [Daily news] (Stockholm), *Politiken* [Politics] (Copenhagen), and *Dagbladet* (Oslo) have ceased to be organs of the Liberal party in their respective countries, and *Sydsvenska Dagbladet* [Southern Swedish daily post] (Malmö) and *Berlingske Tidende* [Berling's times] (Copenhagen) have stopped automatically supporting the Conservatives. This trend brings the Scandinavian press closer to the patterns that prevail in the rest of Western Europe. It also makes statistical surveys more difficult or less meaningful. The figures in Table 6–4, which shows the political structure of the Scandinavian press, must be interpreted with the understanding that a nonaligned paper's position on the left or right of center is not always officially acknowledged by the paper itself.[25]

In Table 6–4, net circulations are related to population to give a general view of total press coverage. As the table shows, the concentration of the press, the expansion of tabloids, and the weakening of partisan loyalties have sharply altered the political profile of the press in all three countries, especially during the last decade. Denmark's traditional party press has been supplanted by mostly independent papers, leaning to the right or left of center, but without declared loyalties. The Danish Conservatives lost their press support by the defection of seven or eight big newspapers. The Radical Liberals suffered the defection of two papers, while the Social Democrats had to close all their local newspapers except two very small ones. Only the Liberal party, the *Venstre*, still has a full party press —interestingly, however, entirely outside Copenhagen.

In Sweden and Norway, where local monopolies are still not the rule, the changes have been less spectacular. In Sweden five formerly conservative and liberal papers have gone independent to the right of center—one big group in Malmö after an abortive venture with a new party (1964–66). In contrast, Sweden's biggest morning paper, *Dagens Nyheter*, has gone to the left of center, while the flourishing evening tabloid, *Expressen*, remains liberal. The Social Democrats managed to increase their support when the trade unions bought out a big liberal publishing group in Stockholm in 1956. They

---

[25] Changes in major newspapers are recorded in the annual reports of *Pressens årbog*.

Table 6-4

POLITICAL STRUCTURE OF THE SCANDINAVIAN PRESS
(in copies sold daily per 1,000 inhabitants)

Political Tendency of Newspapers	Denmark 1950	Denmark 1964	Denmark 1974	Norway 1950	Norway 1965	Norway 1974	Sweden 1950	Sweden 1964	Sweden 1974
All Newspapers									
Conservative	123	121	—	151	150	139	110	124	74
Center, agrarian	{ 104	108	{ 100	25	17	16	21	18	23
Liberal, moderate	{	58	{	{ 103	105	{ 86	{ 242	{ 249	{ 203
Liberal, radical	77		11	{		{	{	{	{
Independent, right	18	15	143	{ 77	36	52	—	5	68
Independent, nonaligned	23	11	5	{	46	79	25	17	28
Independent, left	—	—	74	—	—	30	—	—	55
Social Democratic	47	35	17	101	108	113	87	120	113
People's Socialist	—	—	1	—	—	—	1	—	—
Communist	5	1.5	2	6	2	(2)[a]	9	3	2
Newspaper total	396	348	353	463	464	480	496	536	567
Tabloids only									
Conservative	17	35	—	—	—	—	6	8	—
Liberal	22	17	—	—	—	—	51	68	81
Independent, right	—	—	47	—	—	35	—	—	15
Independent, nonaligned	10	—	—	—	—	—	—	—	—

Independent, left	—	—	47	—	—	—	(30)[b]	—	—
Social Democratic	—	—	—	—	—	—	13	38	58
Tabloid total	49	52	94	—	—	65	70	114	154
Population, in thousands	4,270	4,722	5,055	3,265	3,724	3,973	7,010	7,661	8,170
Households per 1000	308	341	364	c.300	320	335	331	357	390

[a] Not regular daily.

[b] Typology ambiguous (*Dagbladet*).

Note: The independent papers are classified summarily after the following criteria: "Left" covers the newspapers generally advocating parliamentary decisions in accordance or cooperation with the Social Democrats; "Right" covers those preferring government formation, and so on, without that party.

Source: *Nordisk Statistisk årbog, Statistisk årbog* (Copenhagen); publishers' trade papers, *Dansk Presse* [Danish press], *Dagspressen* [Daily press], *Pressens Tidning* [Press news]; *Statens Offentliga Utredningar* (SOU) [Official state investigations] 1965 vol. 22; "Stat og presse" [Report from Commission of the Press, Norway], *Instilling om tiltak for å opprettholde en differensiert dagspresse* [Recommendations on how to keep a differentiated press] (Orkanger: 1967); Niels Thomsen, *Dagbladskonkurrencen 1870-1970* [Newspaper competition 1870-1970], vol. 2, appendix.

had to bury their morning paper in 1966, but the evening tabloid, *Aftonbladet*, enjoyed a real sales boom thereafter.

In Norway, concentration has been proceeding slowly and most papers have remained affiliated with parties. The split of the Liberal party over the EEC in 1972 provoked a similar split in the Liberal press; the largest paper, the tabloid *Dagbladet*, broke with the party entirely. The main organ of the Social Democrats, *Arbeiderbladet*, is losing ground. No doubt its working-class clientele is now turning to the tabloids. On the other hand, the party's provincial press is doing rather well in most of the country.

The relationship between press support and voting strength has been studied repeatedly since about 1960 in all three countries.[26] The main result, as would be expected by students familiar with studies in other countries, is that even the dedicated newspaper that dominates a particular locality is not an automatic vote catcher. It seems clear that newspaper support in itself has nowhere been able to prevent changes in voter affiliation. At most, papers can delay voting changes. Beyond that, research has indicated that a party press can have a reinforcing effect; it can intensify existing partisanship among already committed groups. And, through the agenda-setting function of the press, it can alert its readers to the issues that are deemed significant by the party.

Whatever the important functions of the traditional press may have been, politicians grew more skeptical about the role of the press in the 1960s. Relying more on television, they found it increasingly hard to finance the growing deficits of declining party papers. Subventions continued to some extent, but even the trade unions grew more discriminating. Instead, interest was aroused in the possibility of public financing of the press, and after investigations of press concentration, legislation designed to check it was passed in all Scandinavian countries. The publishers' associations, opposed to radical reform, were eager to obtain more public advertising, reduced rates of postal and teleservices, and easy credit for investments. The Social Democrats and the trade unions, more interested in radical reform, wanted to be relieved of the heavy burden of supporting their press. In the end, substantial legislation to prevent further concentration of

---

[26] For further discussion of this problem, see Hadenius and Weibull, *Press Radio TV*, pp. 210ff; Westerståhl and Janson, *Politisk press, passim*; Vallinder, *Press och politik*, pp. 120-24; Niels Thomsen, "The Danish Political Press," *Scandinavian Political Studies*, vol. 3 (1968), pp. 144-64; Thomsen, *Dagbladskonkurrencen*, vol. 1, p. 531 and vol. 2, p. 1,052; Stein Rokkan and Per Torsvik, "The Voter, the Reader and the Party Press," in Stein Rokkan et al., *Citizens, Elections, Parties* (New York: David McKay Co., 1970), pp. 397-416.

the press was passed in Sweden. In Norway the legislation was not as far-reaching, and in Denmark it was extremely weak.

According to the Swedish legislation started in 1969, a tax of 6 percent is levied on newspaper advertising and a tax of 10 percent on advertising in all other media. A newspaper with smaller circulation than a local competitor receives up to $3 million a year if it is a "national" morning paper and up to $1 million if it is local. Even excluding exemption from the general turnover tax, Swedish newspapers in 1974 received a sum approaching $40 million in aid, half of which was distributed to Social Democratic papers. The trend toward concentration seems to have been almost halted, though by no means reversed, by these measures.

It should be noted that the monopolies that are emerging through the elimination of local competition have not been checked by the growth of tabloids. In the large cities the fact that almost all of the tabloids are owned by big publishing houses built around the big morning papers has emphasized the problem of press monopoly. Three major family concerns—Berlingske in Denmark, Schibsted in Norway, and Bonniers in Sweden—each control about 25 percent of total circulation in their respective countries, and they also have important interests in books, magazines, local weeklies, and so on. Not surprisingly, the legitimacy of such concentration of power has been questioned, and various solutions have been discussed. One is to make each firm a self-owning, nonprofit institution. This is being done now to *Politiken/Ekstrabladet* and four other major Danish papers. Another solution is to leave editorial decisions, including hiring, to the editors or to the editorial staff at large. A modified version of this "editorial democracy" has recently been introduced into some of the biggest Danish and Swedish newspapers. Inspired by discussions and reforms in West Germany and France, "editorial democracy" is another version of "industrial democracy," the principle embodied in Social Democratic legislative proposals that would give all employees a voice in the decision making of their place of employment. Obviously, the effects of such legislation would depend on the distribution of power and functions it established. But the important thing is that many people are trying to find solutions to the problem of media control in terms of delegation of authority to professionals. It is possible, therefore, that the same problems will develop in the printed media that have already appeared in state radio and television.

In any event, the Scandinavian press has moved quite far from its traditional support of particular political parties. Many newspapers have not only played down their own party line; they have also played down politics as a whole. As we have seen, one reason has been that most surviving newspapers have less need than papers did two decades ago for the party press agencies and for the economic subventions by which the parties and the economic interest groups behind them supported and integrated their press systems. Another reason, no doubt, has been the professionalization of journalism. The pressure of the more successful media, especially television, has induced the daily press to focus on very concrete local news and/or trivial sensations. The newspapers have largely abandoned their classical role as collective propagators and organizers of democratic party politics.

The Danish General Election of 1973

Broadcasting and the Press: The Supply of Political Mass Communication. In the literature of political communication, the limited impact of campaigns on the formation of electoral opinion has become something of a truism. Yet not only did one-third of the Danish voters change party in the Danish election of 1973 and only slightly fewer in 1975,[27] but one-third of the voters decided which party to vote for during the campaign. Indeed, one-fifth to one-sixth stated that they had made up their minds "in the last days" before the election.

This evidence of the increased importance of campaigns appeared at a time when the structure of the mass media had changed radically. The shift in media consumption from radio and traditional (omnibus) morning papers to television and tabloids had been on its way since the 1950s. Its full impact on media content did not appear until several years later. That something important was happening in journalism became clear when, in the middle 1960s, the extremely aggressive and uninhibited tabloid, *Ekstrabladet*, took the lead over its more benign competitor, *B.T.* About the same time television gradually developed a style more its own than the modified version of radio journalism it had begun with, treating news in a freer and more selective way. From the late sixties on, the media, new and old alike, seemed to favor controversy and personalization much more than they ever had before.

The new style of communication came fully into its own in the election campaign of 1973. Two of the new parties were the creations

---

[27] Data and analysis on the Danish election can be found in Ole Borre's chapter in this volume.

of colorful, well-known personalities who were acting under highly dramatic circumstances that placed their personal positions at stake. Glistrup, whose Progress party gained 16 percent of the votes, was the most important tax lawyer in the country when he challenged the authorities in 1971, boasting of his intention and ability to escape the unjust income tax system. His successful debate with the minister of finance was broadcast on television, and when legal investigations of his activities were started, making him a hero and martyr to many tax evaders and taxpayers, the media covered the affair closely. Though nearly all journalists and publishers disliked him intensely and said so, they all gave enormous publicity to his witty and unorthodox remarks, thereby adding to the steep rise of his popularity in the opinion polls in the spring of 1973. In the same way, when Erhard Jacobsen, a very popular suburban mayor, broke away from the Social Democrats and caused the downfall of the government, he caught and kept the attention of the whole country for a week or two. Jacobsen had always been widely publicized in radio, television, and the tabloids by the very journalists whom he was constantly and vigorously attacking for their leftist bias and general unreliability.

In short, Jacobsen and Glistrup both benefited from intensive media coverage before the election. Then, during the election campaign when "normal" media coverage was no longer possible, they were able to benefit from the equal-time rule, and their parties took their places, alongside the larger established parties, in the picture of the political world that was presented to the electorate by the media. For voters who were not strong identifiers with other, chiefly older parties, the media coverage given to the newer and smaller parties expanded the range of available choices.

Very clearly, in 1973 television was the dominant source of political information for all groups of voters, as it has been in Danish politics since 1960. Even though there seems to have been a slight revival of voters' meetings in 1973, this means of communication was only a minor source of political information for the voters. More significant was a clear tendency for the more involved voters to look with greater frequency to the newspapers for political information (see Table 6–5). The correlation between a higher level of political involvement and greater attention to newspapers as sources of political information is unquestionably due in part to the fact that print media are used more by persons with high status and high education and that there is a higher proportion of politically involved people in high status groups than in other groups.

Table 6–5

CORRELATION BETWEEN INDICATORS OF POLITICAL INVOLVEMENT AND PREFERRED NEWS MEDIUM, DANISH ELECTIONS, 1971 AND 1975

(in Pearson correlation coefficients)

Preferred News Medium	High Interest		Great Discussion Activity		Political Self-confidence	
	1971	1975	1971	1975	1971	1975
Newspaper	.42	.45	.35	.34	.31	.30
Television	.26	.29	.16	.11	.15	.09
Radio	.15	.28	.05	.11	.10	.16

Note: N = 1,302, 1971; N = 1,047, 1975; DK/NA between 4 and 15 percent. The same results were obtained in 1973. The data collected then, however, were based on a smaller and slightly less representative sample.

Source: O. Borre, H. J. Nielsen, S. Sauerberg, T. Worre: *Vaelgere i 70'erne* [The voters in the 1970s] (Copenhagen: 1976), p. 223.

Mass Communication Consumption and Voting Behavior. Based on their research into U.S. presidential and British parliamentary campaigns, Converse, and Blumler and McQuail have concluded that middle-interest voters are the ones most likely to change party and to be influenced by the mass media.[28] The most apathetic voters either do not vote or vote generally in a very stable way. The more interested voters follow campaigns because they have already made up their minds; people seldom go to church to be converted. For such individuals, the function of mass communication may be to reinforce existing attitudes and beliefs, rather than to change them. A well-established line of reasoning would be the reduction of dissonance: the politically aware try to be well-informed in order to better defend —to themselves and to others—the decisions they have already made. When some aspects of the chosen party's program are in conflict with the general attitudes of such voters, they turn to the media for more information on the party and its program as a way of minimizing, if not removing, such conflicts.

Danish election surveys carried out from 1960 generally confirm these patterns, though the high participation compared to that in

[28] Philip E. Converse, "Information Flow and the Stability of Partisan Attitudes," in Angus Campbell et al., *Elections and the Political Order* (New York: John Wiley & Sons, 1966), pp. 136-57; Jay G. Blumler and Denis McQuail, *Television in Politics: Its Uses and Influence* (London: Faber, 1968); also Joseph T. Klapper, *The Effects of Mass Communication* (Glencoe, Ill.: Free Press, 1960).

Anglo-Saxon countries means that the apathetic group is rather marginal. Political interest, high media use, and stability in voting are closely related. The data in the surveys from the elections in 1971 and 1975 support the proposition reported above by showing that convinced partisans change party less the more they follow the media, while voters who are more loosely attached to the parties change party more frequently the more they follow the campaign. In other words, it seems that nonpartisans use the media to change their vote, whereas partisans use them for reinforcement.

For the 1973 election, which saw sweeping and unparalleled changes in the Danish party system, the evidence was, however, quite different in important respects. For one thing, it turned out that there was little relationship between the voters' following of the campaign and their tendency to shift parties. Similarly, the highly politically interested voter was as likely to shift party as anybody else.

But more interesting are the findings with respect to the differences between voters who changed between old established parties ("traditional" changers) and those changing between an old established party and a small or new party ("unorthodox" changers). As Table 6–6 indicates, the more a voter followed the mass media, the more likely he was to be an unorthodox changer and the less likely to be a traditional changer. Thus, traditional changers were more likely to have used the media infrequently. Unorthodox changers, on the contrary, were more likely to have used the media to a greater extent than the average voter.

For 1973, as for the elections of the 1960s, it is difficult to say whether or not the media were the actual cause of vote changes. At the very least, they were considered important by voters who were deciding which party to support. One other finding of the 1973 survey should be mentioned, however. It appears that the unorthodox voters did not limit themselves to television usage. The conclusion that changers from old to new or small parties were the greater media users emerges only when *both* press and television broadcasting are considered. In other words, unorthodox voters seem to have been unwilling to rely on a single source. They were greater media users not only in terms of the amount of time spent on the media but also in terms of the number of different media consulted.

Looking back on the two earlier elections in the sixties when major changes took place, the one in 1960 and the one in 1968, the picture is much less clear because of lack of specific survey data and because the changes were less sweeping than in 1973. There is, however, some evidence which may support the 1973 pattern. In

Table 6–6

PARTY SWITCHING, 1971–73, BY MASS MEDIA
CONSUMPTION DURING 1973 CAMPAIGN

Change, 1971-73	Level of Media Consumption			
	Low	Middle	High	Total
Switched parties				
Percentage	42	37	45	40
N	(64)	(259)	(113)	(463)
Switched between old parties[a]				
Percentage	27	17	15	18
N	(44)	(187)	(72)	(320)
Switched from old party to new or minor one[b]				
Percentage	19	26	35	28
N	(57)	(250)	(111)	(444)

[a] $\chi^2 = 3.199$, df $= 2\chi^2 = 5.99$.
[b] $\chi^2 = 6.346$, df $= 2$; significant difference.
Note: NA/DK is not included, hence the figures do not add vertically.
Source: O. Borre, H. J. Nielsen, S. Sauerberg, and T. Worre, *Vaelgerskreddet 1971-73* [Electoral landslide, 1971-73] (Copenhagen: 1974), p. 178.

1960 a new party, the Socialist People's party, sprang up from zero to 6 percent of the votes. In 1968 the Radical Liberal party after years of stagnation jumped from 7 to 15 percent, gaining ground in entirely new groups and areas. In both cases the party was led by a politician, who functioned very well with the new medium. In general, of course, the well-known pattern of selective exposure means that campaign party broadcasts on television attract audiences in proportion to the party's size. But the programs of the People's Socialist party in 1960 and the Radical Liberal party in 1968 were watched by quite disproportionately large audiences. It seems likely, then, that many voters looked eagerly to television for information about the party they were considering and that the performance of the main spokesman had some influence on their decision. From this point of view the media in general, and today television in particular, may be thought of as catalysts for vote changing, so far as new or relatively unknown parties are concerned.

The Voters' Use of Mass Media. In the 1973 Danish survey, respondents were asked to indicate their most important reason for using the mass communication media during the election campaign (see Table 6–7). With respect to both television and the press in 1973, the most important function of the media for the voters—that which they themselves mentioned most frequently—was to provide a basis for discussion. This was true for television, but also for the daily press, though people attached less importance to the press for all uses. Furthermore, details not reported in the table seem to indicate that the discussion function of television and the vote-guidance function of the press will rise with increasing media use.

The frequent use of television as a basis for discussion is easily explained by the high probability that one's friend or colleague has seen yesterday's broadcast, while he may have read a different newspaper. Consequently, it may be reasonable to consider television an important source of subjects for discussion—with subsequent alterations of issue saliency for the voters. The 1971 survey reveals that

Table 6–7
VOTERS' REASONS FOR MEDIA USE, 1973 DANISH CAMPAIGN
(in percentages of respondents)

Reason for Following Campaign	Television	Press
Basis for Discussion "Do you find it important to watch the election campaign on television / read about it in the newspapers to be able to take part in discussions?"	69	50
Entertainment "Do you find it entertaining to watch the election campaign on television / read about it in the newspapers?"	58	41
Habit "Would you have watched television anyway at the time the election broadcast was on?"	39	—
Vote Guidance "Have you watched the election broadcasts / read the newspapers to help you find out which party you should vote for?"	31	23

Note: N = 533; DK/NA between 11 and 18 percent. Similar results were obtained in 1975, "vote guidance," however, being the only reason reported clearly less often than the other reasons.
Source: O. Borre, H. J. Nielsen, S. Sauerberg, T. Worre: *Vaelgerskreddet 1971-73*, p. 184.

the issue saliency as perceived by voters was changed during the campaign to correspond much more closely to their importance as reflected in television and radio coverage (see Table 6–8). Of course, the table offers no final proof that television and radio determine issue saliency for the voters. The voters' perceptions of issue saliency always change during election campaigns, and television and radio coverage may be just a reflection of these trends. On the other hand,

Table 6–8
ISSUE SALIENCY IN MEDIA COMPARED WITH CHANGE IN VOTERS' PERCEPTIONS, 1971 CAMPAIGN
(in percentages)

Issue	Issue Saliency Among Voters		Issue Saliency in Radio and TV
	Before the election, Aug. 1971	After the election, Oct. 1971	Sept. 1971
Change in voters' perceptions correlates with issue saliency in media			
Saliency declined			
Social problems	29	16	11
Housing	16	13	7
Environment	11	8	1
Saliency increased			
Economy	12	20	16
Taxes	9	11	18
EEC	7	19	19
Trade	2	5	4
Change in voters' perceptions does not correlate with issue saliency in media			
Wages and conditions on labor market	6	5	14
Education and culture	8	4	10
Total	100	100	100

Note: The voters' answers concerning most salient issues are reduced for double answers; DK/NA are not included. The saliency of issues in the campaign on radio and television is computed from results of a content analysis excluding other categories; thus the index adds up to 100.

Source: For data and further discussion, see Ole Borre and Karen Siune, "Setting the Agenda for a Danish Election," *Journal of Communication*, Winter 1975.

the responses of the most interested and active voters regarding issue saliency do not differ significantly from those of other voters at any period of the campaign. It is clear, then, that the changes in saliency do not simply reflect the success of what are usually called the horizontal opinion leaders in convincing their followers of their own priorities. It seems likely that the media—and especially television—did function as agenda-setters via discussions between voters. These discussions seem to be very close to the core of voting decision. Discussion activity was high in 1971, rose steeply in 1973, and declined somewhat in 1975—thus closely reflecting the different degrees of voter mobility. Furthermore, at all three elections there was a close correlation between change of party and discussion activity at the individual level. The kind of party change experienced at recent Danish elections does not take place in silence or isolation, but after discussions, for which the mass media are decisive purveyors of material. This person-to-person communication seems to be the decisive black box between media influence and voting behavior.

Concluding Remarks

As we have seen, changes in technology, media economics, and life styles have led to profound changes in the traditional Scandinavian communication systems. The quasi-corporatist linkage of political parties, mass organizations, the press, and socioeconomic groups has given way in greater or lesser degree to a more disparate and less integrated pattern of relationships. Instead of a self-evident and assumed communication policy that was based on free speech, free competition for the printed media, and public regulation of the electronic media to avoid partisan advantage, the Scandinavians have had to devise new policies to deal with highly controversial problems—problems such as the concentration of the press, the institutional structure of the publicly controlled media, and appropriate criteria for the presentation of news and contending viewpoints. In the process, several viewpoints and interests have clashed: the professionalist ideology of the journalists has clashed with the group and consensus goals of political and social elites, consumers' choice with social responsibility, print media with electronic media, social radicalism with liberalism, and participation with more traditional forms of hierarchical control.

Thus far, few of the problems have been fully resolved, few of the clashing viewpoints reconciled. It is clear, however, that the

Social Democrats in Sweden have decided on a broad policy aimed at sustaining at all costs certain basic pillars of the traditional communication system: the parties, the party press, and noncommercial state television. At the same time, there has been some movement towards greater journalistic professionalism and towards somewhat freer programming in radio and television. As for Norway, its political leaders seem so far to have been moving in the same direction as the leaders of Sweden, though more slowly. The leaders of Denmark, on the other hand, seem to be overwhelmed by contradictory goals—expressive participation, equal access to the media, individualistic nonconformity, responsiveness to group interests—that have led them into heated controversy and zigzagging policy decisions.

The different reactions of the Scandinavian countries to the problems of their communication systems can be related to the changes in the voting patterns of their electorates. The downfall of party organizations and newspapers, primary elements of a political culture, and the dominance of television and tabloids seem to correlate with the increasing confusion and instability of electoral behavior in Denmark. Conversely, in Sweden the policy of deliberately sustaining certain basic pillars of the traditional communication system correlates with the (so far) much greater stability of electoral behavior.

This conclusion from a general comparison between systems, which were extremely similar just ten years ago but have now diverged in important respects, warranted a closer look at communication patterns during the most dramatic electoral period in Scandinavia during the last fifty years: the Danish electoral upheaval in December 1973. The central finding here is that the customary typology of groups of voters seems to be invalid. The recent Danish experience provides no support for the theory that it is the partially interested, partially informed voters who become mobilized during periods of extensive electoral instability. Instead, it is precisely the politically interested voters, the greatest users of the communication media, who change from the established parties to the newer and smaller parties and thereby contribute to electoral instability. On this showing, the importance attributed to the impact of the mass media on the nature of political debate in Scandinavia during the last decade seems fully justified. The precise structure and role of television—but also the structures and roles of the press and (party) organizations—may very well become decisive factors in maintaining a reasonable degree of efficiency in the functioning of Scandinavian political institutions.

PART THREE

BUSINESS AND LABOR IN
THE WELFARE STATE

7

ECONOMIC DEVELOPMENT IN DENMARK, NORWAY, AND SWEDEN

C. G. Uhr

This essay focuses on economic growth and the major structural changes and problems it has generated in Denmark, Norway, and Sweden during the interwar and particularly the postwar decades. Throughout the interwar years from 1919 to 1939, these countries were governed by a succession of political parties and administrations. Conservative governments representing a combination of business and agrarian interests were at various times replaced by labor or social democratic regimes. In subsequent elections these gave way to bourgeois-liberal governments. The latter in their turn were replaced by liberal-labor or liberal-agrarian coalition governments.

The point is that no political party primarily representing the interests of labor, or business, or the farmers was able to dominate the politics of Denmark, Norway, or Sweden for very long. No party was sufficiently strong to remain at the helm long enough to impose its own long-run economic program on the nation as a whole. This, then, was a period of gradually shifting political alliances, a period more pluralistic than the period that followed in the sense that every significant economic interest had a distinctive role to play in the political arena and each had a positive share in the formulation of economic policy and the development of the institutional framework for policy action.

The postwar period has been quite different. In Sweden the Great Depression ushered in a Social Democratic government that has remained in power continuously (occasionally in coalition with some of the smaller parties—for example, during World War II) for forty-four years, ever since the fall of 1932. In Norway the Labor party governed continuously from 1945 to 1965. Then it was replaced by an agrarian-bourgeois coalition government that lasted until 1969, when Labor returned to power on a coalition basis. In Denmark the situation has been less clear-cut. A series of coalition governments has been in power since the beginning of the 1950s. In these governments, labor, though not united in one distinctive party but spread over several "left" political parties or factions, has several times been the strongest component; at other times it has been the strongest component of the opposition, facing a coalition government of several of the smaller conservative, liberal, and agrarian parties.

The extent to which a socioeconomic restructuring of a nation can be carried out depends largely on whether one major economic interest (in this case labor and its allies among small farmers and craft-shop entrepreneurs) can effectively dominate the political scene over a great number of years. Such domination gives it the opportunity to impose and to institutionalize its long-term program, that is, to create what may be called a laboristic society.

This political aspect of Scandinavian economic development—political stability under what were primarily labor governments in the postwar era—cannot be ignored. The fact that even the conservative parties in the Scandinavian countries no longer advocate a return to laissez faire is evidence of the abiding influence of this political stability. Neither do they urge any dismantling of the welfare state programs that their parliamentary representatives have participated, however grudgingly, in creating. Nowadays they concern themselves most of the time with such matters as reduction and reform of taxes, greater decentralization of the political decision-making process and of public administration, and criticism of the large and growing government bureaucracy.

Before the War, 1919-45

The relatively prosperous 1920s were characterized (1) by a moderate rate of economic growth (real GNP increased about 3 percent per annum), (2) by the continuation of trends in structural change that began in the 1870s, notably the drift of manpower and capital from agriculture, fishing, and forest work to manufacturing, mining, engineering products, and service-trade industries, and (3) by persistently high unemployment, which was considered to be chiefly of a technological rather than a cyclical origin and nature.[1]

---

[1] In order to minimize the detailed documentation of data, much of which may already be familiar to persons interested in economic conditions in Scandinavia, I shall indicate only the main sources I have used: Svend Aage Hansen, *Økonomisk vaekst i Danmark* [Economic growth in Denmark], vol. 2 (Copenhagen: Akade-

In Sweden unemployment averaged about 11 percent of the trade union membership in the 1920s. In Denmark, which at that time was still primarily an agricultural economy, unemployment was lower, 8 to 9 percent, while in Norway close to 15 percent of trade union members were out of work during the 1920s. These high rates of unemployment were attributed principally to two causes. An international decline in the prices of agricultural products made farming on the numerous small-scale family farms (five to fifteen acres) unprofitable and produced an increasing flight of labor to the urban industries. The expanding manufacturing industries were characterized by high and rising capital intensity of production and could only make limited use of the inflow of relatively unskilled labor from the rural areas.

Svend Aage Hansen regards this decade in Denmark as characterized by a power struggle between domestic-market-oriented manufacturing industries and export-oriented agriculture, a struggle that would be won by industry in the 1930s.[2] Agriculture was losing ground in two directions at the same time. In the European market Danish agricultural exports encountered intensive competition and rising tariff barriers and import quotas. In the domestic market Denmark's large agricultural sector encountered terms of trade that declined progressively in relation to those of industries in the non-agricultural sector. The urban industries as a rule operated under tariff protection and in much less competitive (oligopolistic) market conditions than did agriculture.

In Norway and Sweden the situation of agriculture was similar but less pronounced. From the turn of the century on, in Norway the importance of agriculture as a source of national income declined, while the importance of merchant shipping and fishing was rising. In the 1920s the leading position of these industries was being challenged by the country's chemical and mining industries, which expanded rapidly as a result of the development of abundant hydroelectric energy resources that had begun before World War I.

In Sweden industrialization started considerably earlier than it did in Norway and Denmark, and by the 1920s the industrial revolution had already passed through its secondary and into its tertiary

misk Forlag, 1974), pp. 22-89, and the appendix of statistical tables, pp. 201ff; T. K. Derry, *A History of Modern Norway 1814-1972* (Oxford: Clarendon Press, 1973), pp. 298-333; Erik Lundberg, *Business Cycles and Economic Policy* (London: G. Allen and Unwin, 1957), pp. 1-123; Erik Westerlind and Rune Beckman, *Sveriges ekonomi* [Sweden's economy], seventh revised edition (Stockholm: Bokförlaget Prisma, 1973), pp. 7-126.

2 Hansen, *Økonomisk vaekst*, pp. 51ff.

stage. From producing essentially an exportable output of raw materials, such as ores, timber, and semifabricated articles (such as bar-iron and steel), Swedish industry had turned primarily to producing finished engineering industry products, machinery, consumer durables and appliances, and finished forest products (paper, pulp, veneers, and so on). At the same time, while employment in agriculture declined, the productivity of farms increased as more and more agricultural operations were mechanized and many family farms too small to remain viable were consolidated in larger production units.

The Great Depression retarded but did not reverse these changes in Scandinavian economic structure, although unemployment rose dramatically to about 30 percent of the urban labor force, and bank-ruptcies and poverty spread alarmingly among the rural population. The combined effects of the depression forced the authorities first to abandon the gold standard and then, under the shield of devaluation and freely floating exchange rates, to launch a series of recovery policies. These consisted of a variety of measures—easy money policy, deficit-financed public works programs, subsidies or premiums for certain exports, and farm subsidies and price regulations for the domestic sale of several major agricultural products designed to provide a floor against further decline of the incomes of the numerous small farmers. These measures of the early 1930s were the beginnings of the basic welfare state and of the continuous expansion (up to now, at any rate) of the public sector at the expense of the private sector, for which the Scandinavian economies are noted the world over.

The recovery of 1934–36, initiated by a rise in demand for Scandinavian exports, occurred in a period of rising international tensions and autarkically restricted channels and volume of international trade. Recovery was followed by a period of international armaments buildup, especially in Germany, preparatory to the outbreak of World War II. But the war brought special problems and hardships. Shortages of raw materials vital for production led to direct allocation of available supplies to industrial users according to a scale of priorities determined by the authorities; during the occupation these were German authorities in Denmark and Norway. Production allocations in turn necessitated rationing and price control of a host of commodities at the consumer level. In this period real income and the standard of living declined considerably in all three countries. This decline was less severe in Sweden than in Norway and Denmark. The Swedes managed to maintain a battered and compromised position of neutrality, and, more important, Sweden's resource base and the industries built on it provided a greater variety of output vital to the belligerents—and consequently gave the Swedes greater bargaining power than either Denmark or Norway had for obtaining the imports they needed from the German war machine.

Yet the war years were not entirely negative in their economic effects. Efforts to find substitutes for rubber, petrochemical products, and certain fibers led to the birth and development of the synthetics industries. In Norway the Germans forced through a further expansion of the country's hydroelectric power plants for the purpose of increasing the mining of pyrites and their reduction to copper, which had become extremely scarce.

At the end of the war, the three Scandinavian economies emerged essentially intact, though in Norway the Germans had applied a scorched-earth policy in the northern provinces as they retreated. But while most of the prewar capital stock remained intact, some of it had been depleted for lack of replacement, and most of it had of necessity been undermaintained. Furthermore, by 1946 much of the capital stock, built for the most part in the years before 1939, had become obsolescent. Consequently, rationing of consumer goods had to continue considerably beyond V-E Day to hold down consumption and thus provide more output capacity for the production of investment goods. In Sweden this reconversion and retooling process extended into 1948. In Norway and Denmark it was 1950 before most of the wartime controls could be lifted. In all three countries housing was not decontrolled until many years later, in the 1960s. Almost no additional housing had been built since 1939–40, while at the same time those industries that had been expanded and were operated on a three-shift basis during the war years—namely industries that had produced goods for export to the belligerents—attracted and absorbed many thousands of the formerly unemployed or underemployed from the rural areas into the already crowded urban centers. The result in the later 1940s and throughout the 1950s was an excess-demand gap for housing that kept rising, even though construction activities and the governments' support of special arrangements for financing construction of multiple-unit apartment complexes greatly expanded.

The Postwar Decades

The Reconversion Phase. A surprising feature of the early postwar years from 1945 to 1949 was that instead of producing the anticipated depression, they generated an aggregate demand that was on the whole large enough to yield practically full employment. This was especially the case in Norway, which faced a genuine reconstruction problem. It was also true of Sweden, where industries enjoyed a strong sellers' market as continental Europe and Great Britain began the task of rebuilding and repairing the damage wrought by the war. It was less true of Denmark, where the labor market remained slack compared with those of Norway and Sweden—though the level of employment in Denmark was nonetheless considerably higher than in the prewar years (about a 5 percent unemployment rate in 1945–49 compared with 10 percent and over in 1935–39). In fact, almost the entire postwar period up to the early 1970s (which brought stagflation) has been one of full and often overfull employment and inflation for Sweden and Norway; for Denmark this has been the case from 1958 onwards. There has been only one exception of any consequence, namely, the recession of 1957–58. The other shorter, milder setbacks that were noted internationally had only weak echoes on the Scandinavian scene.

In the first few postwar years, inflation was kept within bounds or even more or less suppressed by the continuation of several controls and regulations that had been applied during the war. Rationing of many varieties of consumer goods was continued into 1949. Wartime priorities in the allocation of the slowly increasing flow of investment goods were gradually modified. Later a loose priorities allocation was effected under special features of the taxation and credit policies that were applied until the achievement of a relatively free market in investment goods. As was expected, this occurred first among commodities traded internationally. The one large and enduring exception was agricultural products. Many Scandinavian agricultural products are exported and are to that extent subject to unpredictably changing world market prices. Yet the lion's share of Scandinavia's agricultural output is sold in the domestic markets of the three countries. Neither Sweden nor even less Norway is self-sufficient in food products; Denmark is more nearly so and is a significant net exporter of animal husbandry products, notably hams, bacon, poultry, and dairy products. In the domestic markets the agricultural products of Denmark, Norway, and Sweden have been subject to price supports and subsidies since the 1920s. These measures are intended to yield farmers incomes equal to those of the general run of industrial workers.

Economic Growth and Structural Change from the Early 1950s.
In order to provide an overview of the economic growth and structural changes that have occurred in Denmark, Norway, and Sweden from

the reconstruction and reconversion phase of the postwar era to date, we present four tables based on the national accounts statistics of the United Nations.

It is true that the national accounts statistics maintained by the United Nations often cannot be readily reconciled with the national economic accounts published by the individual member nations. The reason for this is that data reported by member countries have to be adjusted to fit the conceptual framework and classifications of economic accounts that the United Nations is able to apply to the great majority of member nations. The UN accounts are also usually much less complete than those of the individual countries. For instance, the UN data supply information on the GNP and its components for most countries in fairly great detail, but they provide very little parallel information on the allocation and utilization of manpower by the nations and by their industrial sector components.

Nonetheless, the UN accounts supply some important economic data on the three Scandinavian countries on a more uniform and commensurate basis than one finds in the official economic reports of the three countries. Between the 1950s and 1970s all three have modified and redefined their GDP concepts more than once. Inflation at rates ranging between 3 and 8 percent per year has affected the GDP figures reported in current market prices. Also the bases for GDP figures reported in constant prices have been changed. For the 1950s and early 1960s, the base years were 1954 in Norway and Denmark and 1956 in Sweden. For the later 1960s and early 1970s the base years were 1967 and 1970 respectively. Consequently the GDP figures shown in the leading columns in Tables 7–1 and 7–3 for Denmark, Norway, Sweden, and the United States for selected years from 1954 to 1973 do not possess vertical comparability in the sense that if the figure for 1973 is divided by one for 1954 for a given country, the quotient expresses the extent of real economic growth that has occurred since 1954. The GDP growth rates are shown separately in Tables 7–2 and 7–4.

However, to indicate the nature and extent of structural change that has occurred, vertical GDP comparability in Tables 7–1 and 7–3 is not essential. What matters is horizontal comparability of GDP components expressed as percentages for selected years shown and vertical comparability of these percentages between the years shown.

A few cross-checks against related data on GDP components and their variation over time since the 1950s, derived from detailed economic reports published by the three respective Scandinavian countries, indicate that the ratios expressed in the UN data by the GDP

Table 7–1

GROSS DOMESTIC PRODUCT AND ITS MAIN COMPONENTS,
DENMARK, NORWAY, SWEDEN, AND UNITED STATES,
SELECTED YEARS, 1954–73

Country and Year	GDP (in billions)	Main Components of GDP (in percentages)		
		Government consumption	Private consumption	Capital formation
Denmark				
1954	28.8 D.kr.	13	70	17
1960[a]	—	—	—	—
1961	45.3	13	66	25
1963	54.3	14	65	20
1970	116.8	20	60	21
1972	144.7	22	57	21
1973	166.0	22	56	23
Norway				
1954	26.1 N.kr.	13	60	27
1960	32.7	14	58	28
1961[a]	—	—	—	—
1963	41.5	15	53	30
1970	79.8	15	55	27
1972	97.3	16	55	28
1973	110.2	16	53	30
Sweden				
1954	42.0 Sw.kr.	16	63	21
1960	72.0	16	61	23
1963	91.6	17	59	23
1970	170.3	21	55	25
1971	182.9	23	54	21
1972	199.2	23	54	22
1973[a]	—	—	—	—
United States				
1954	$ 363.2	18	65	16
1960	509.0	19	64	17
1963	596.3	20	63	17
1970	983.2	20	63	17
1971[a]	—	—	—	—
1972	1,161.9	19	63	18
1973	1,297.5	19	62	18

[a] Data unavailable from UN sources.

Source: *U.N. Yearbook of National Accounts Statistics 1961,* pp. 74, 195, 242, and 271; *U.N. Statistical Yearbook 1974,* pp. 610, 615, 616, and 617.

Table 7–2

AVERAGE ANNUAL GROWTH RATES OF GDP AND
ITS MAIN COMPONENTS (CONSTANT PRICES),
DENMARK, NORWAY, SWEDEN, AND UNITED STATES,
SELECTED PERIODS, 1960–73

(in annual percentage increases)

Country and Period	GDP	Main Components of GDP		
		Government consumption	Private consumption	Capital formation
Denmark				
1961–70	4.7	6.3	4.1	6.6
1970–73	3.6	6.6	2.9	7.3
Norway				
1960–70	4.9	6.3	4.1	8.3
1970–73	4.6	6.0	2.9	7.9
Sweden				
1960–70	4.2	5.2	3.8	5.0
1970–72	1.3	2.2	0.9	2.2
United States				
1960–70	4.6	5.0	4.6	4.7
1970–73	4.1	1.1	5.2	7.4

Source: *U.N. Statistical Yearbook 1974*, pp. 634, 635, and 636.

components in Tables 7–1 and 7–3 for the several years are quite acceptable approximations to the real ratios. Hence they serve well as benchmarks of structural economic change.

As for the economic growth rates of GDP and its components shown in Tables 7–2 and 7–4, these are average annual growth rates computed by the United Nations from GDP data expressed in constant prices for the decade 1961–70 and also for the years 1970–73. As such, the rates for 1961–70 deviate only minimally from annual growth rates expressed in a number of governmental as well as private economic studies for the respective Scandinavian countries on the basis of time-series data covering almost the entire postwar period. Consequently the growth rates shown in Tables 7–2 and 7–4 for 1961–70 can be taken as representative of the economic growth of the three countries for most of the postwar period.

Table 7-3

GROSS DOMESTIC PRODUCT BY ECONOMIC ORIGIN, DENMARK, NORWAY, SWEDEN, AND UNITED STATES, SELECTED YEARS, 1954–73

(in percentages of GDP)

Country and Year	GDP (in billions)	Agri-culture, Forestry, Fishing	Mfg. and Allied Industries [a]	Construc-tion	Wholesale and Retail Trade	Transpor-tation and Communi-cations	All Other [b] (mainly services)
Denmark							
1954	28.3 D.kr.	19	29	7	15	9	20
1961	45.3	14	31	8	16	9	20
1970	116.8	7	29	9	14	9	24
1973	166.1	8	28	9	14	9	25
Norway							
1954	23.4 N.kr.	13	30	9	12	15	20
1960	32.7	9	29	8	18	16	19
1970	79.8	7	26	8	15	16	23
1973	110.2	6	25	8	15	15	25
Sweden							
1954 [c]	—	—	—	—	—	—	—
1960	72.0 Sw.kr.	7	31	7	10	7	26
1970	170.8	4	28	8	10	6	31
1972	199.2	4	28	8	10	6	33

United States

1954	$ 298.7	5	34	4	17	7	31
1960	509.0	4	33	4	17	6	34
1970	983.2	3	30	5	17	6	37
1972	1,297.5	4	29	5	17	6	27

a Includes the manufacturing industries, mining, and the utilities industries for electricity, gas, and water.
b Includes finance, insurance, real estate, business services, community services, social services, public administration, and defense.
c Figures unavailable from UN sources.
Source: *U.N. Yearbook of National Accounts Statistics 1961*, pp. 75, 196, and 272; *U.N. Statistical Yearbook 1974*, pp. 623, 628, 630, and 631.

Table 7-4

AVERAGE ANNUAL GROWTH RATES OF GDP BY SECTOR (CONSTANT PRICES), DENMARK, NORWAY, SWEDEN, AND UNITED STATES, SELECTED PERIODS, 1960–73

(in annual percentage increases)

Country and Period	GDP	Agriculture, Forestry, Fishing	Mfg. and Allied Industries	Construction	Wholesale and Retail Trade	Transportation and Communications	All Other (mainly services)
Denmark							
1961–70	4.7	0.8	5.6	5.5	4.5	5.2	4.4
1970–73	3.6	1.5	5.1	4.6	3.0	3.8	4.2
Norway							
1960–70	4.9	0.1	5.5	3.8	4.7	7.5	4.7
1970–73	4.6	1.9	4.3	3.2	2.4	6.0	6.4
Sweden							
1960–70	4.2	0.6	6.2	5.0	4.0	4.5	3.9
1970–72	1.3	1.6	2.4	0.8	0.2	2.6	2.9
United States							
1960–70	4.6	2.5	5.3	1.2	4.6	6.2	4.7
1970–73	4.1	3.7	7.0	3.3	5.2	6.3	2.8

Source: *U.N. Statistical Yearbook 1974*, pp. 634-36 and 638-41.

Table 7–1 shows the broad features of the structural economic change that has taken place in Scandinavia since the early 1950s. It is characterized by a persistent and fairly substantial expansion of the public sector at the expense of the private sector, indicated by the growth of government consumption as a ratio of GDP and the concomitant shrinkage of the private consumption percentage as well as by the growth of the capital formation rates.

In Denmark government consumption (defined as the purchase of goods by government and the provision of all manner of governmental or public services including defense) rose from 13 to 22 percent of GDP between 1959 and 1973. At the same time private consumption declined from 70 to 56 percent and capital formation rose from 17 to 23 percent. In Sweden the development was rather similar. Government consumption rose from 16 to 23 percent, private consumption declined from 63 to 54 percent, and capital formation rose slightly from an already high level of 21 to 23 percent of GDP. In Norway government consumption rose less, from 13 to 16 percent. Private consumption declined moderately from 60 to 53 percent of GDP, while capital formation rose from the already high ratio of 27 percent toward 30 percent of GDP. The situation in the United States was much less striking. Government consumption increased only slightly from 18 to 19 percent of GDP, while private consumption declined slightly from 65 to 62 percent, and capital formation rose a little from 16 to 18 percent.

Looking at rates of growth in Table 7–2, we find that GDP grew at an average annual rate of about 4.5 percent in the three Scandinavian countries during the decade 1961–70, while government consumption grew at about 6 percent per year. At the same time private consumption increased less rapidly than GDP at about 4 percent per year while capital formation increased slightly more than 6 percent per year, exceeding 8 percent only in Norway.

The growth rates shown for 1970–73 are of a short-run character and more erratic than those for the previous decade, hence less representative. In the case of Sweden they are affected by a fairly sharp, short recession in 1971–72. Something similar happened in Denmark but on a more moderate scale, while Norway was hardly affected at all by that downturn.

In many respects Table 7–3, which shows GDP by variety of economic activity, is a better gauge of structural change than Table 7–1. First of all, the table reveals the drastic decline in the economic role of agriculture and the allied pursuits of forestry and fishing (all three of which are classified as extractive industries). Until the 1920s (although the table does not show this) the extractive-industry sector dominated the Danish economy, but by 1954 it accounted for only about one-fifth of Denmark's GDP and by the early 1970s for less than one-tenth. In Norway and Sweden the decline of agriculture, forestry, and fishing was even greater, with those industries accounting only for about one-twentieth of GDP by the 1970s. But it must be borne in mind that in Norway agriculture had become secondary to merchant shipping and fishing already around the turn of the century, and in Sweden to the manufacturing and forest products industries in about the 1880s.

Until the 1930s the flight of manpower (much of it under-employed) from agriculture facilitated the expansion of Sweden's manufacturing and engineering products industries, which dominated the economy at that time. But since the later 1930s the tertiary and service industries have progressively expanded and now have come to play the major role in the Swedish economy. By the 1960s and early 1970s the manufacturing and allied industries, combined with the construction trades, accounted for only somewhat more than one-third of Sweden's GDP, while the combination of wholesale and retail trade, transportation and communications, and "all other" (mainly public and private services) industries accounted for about 50 percent of GDP.

The development in Norway is in one sense more dramatic, for there 55 percent of GDP in the early 1970s consisted of the combination wholesale and retail trade, transportation and communications, and "all other" industries. At the same time the construction and manufacturing industries accounted for 33 percent, and agriculture and allied pursuits for only 6 percent of Norway's GDP. But in Norway's case the growth of manufacturing was to a great extent delayed until the interwar period and the buildup of Norway's considerable hydroelectric energy resources. Still, manufacturing never came to play the dominant role in Norway's economy that it did earlier in Sweden. This development has apparently gone farther in the United States than in Scandinavia, for by the early 1970s U.S. agriculture produced only 4 percent of GDP, manufacturing and construction 34 percent, and the tertiary and service industry combination no less than 60 percent.

For the decade 1961–70 (shown in Table 7–4), the manufacturing and transportation-communications industry sectors show the highest rates of growth in Scandinavia, 5.5 to 6.0 percent annually. These compare favorably with the growth rates for wholesale and retail trade and for "other" (mainly services) industries of about 4.5 percent per annum. It would seem that if these relative growth rates were to persist, manufacturing might eventually assume the dominant role in the Scandinavian economies.

This is, however, rather unlikely, partly because, as the data for 1970–73 show, these industries are subject to considerable cyclical variation or fluctuation. Moreover, there are measurement problems involved here that may account for some of the difference in annual growth rates between the manufacturing and the service industries. It is much more difficult to ascertain and measure productivity (in the value-added sense) and aggregate output in the service industries than it is to measure them in the manufacturing industries.

While it is true of the three Scandinavian countries and also of the United States that consumption as a whole has declined and capital formation has increased, the continued growth of public or government consumption and the dramatic decline of private consumption represent for the most part a substitution of tax-financed public spending for consumer-financed private consumption. A case in point is the introduction of compulsory national health insurance in Sweden in 1955 and somewhat later in Denmark and Norway. Provision for supply and delivery of the bulk of health services was shifted from finance by private health insurance and fees paid by patients to finance by payroll taxes on employers and specified tax contributions levied on employees and on self-employed persons. At the same time the administration of the national health insurance system was readily set up by expanding and absorbing into the civil service the staffs of the former health insurance societies, now under the Ministry of Social Affairs. National health insurance made medical services available on terms easier than those that had obtained under the private schemes and extended medical services to a fairly large fraction of the population that had not opted for and might not have been able to obtain health insurance coverage when it was only available on a voluntary basis. One immediate result was that demand for medical services increased dramatically.

Then again, in some situations the distinction between private and governmental consumption is almost arbitrary. Rent allowances or subsidies extended to families with several children and to pensioners whose incomes do not exceed certain ceilings illustrate the difficulty of drawing this distinction. Families in the lower earnings brackets who have several children cannot as a rule afford to rent apartments sufficiently large so as to meet the "norm" of not more than 1.5 persons per room. To help them meet this social norm and avoid overcrowding, rent subsidies equal to the difference between the rent of sufficiently spacious housing and a specified percentage of the family's income are provided. A similar scheme applies to pensioners. The result of this arrangement is, of course, that a public consumption allotment is added to what is obtained from the income of the families or individuals involved insofar as they meet the qualifying conditions as to level of income and number of dependents. But, then, is housing that is rented under such subsidy arrangements public or private consumption? Obviously it is a little of both, but it is not certain that this distinction is maintained consistently in the social and economic accounts.

Moreover, while the data in Table 7-2 show that capital formation or gross investment has increased as a proportion of GDP, they do not reveal to what extent the increase comes from private or from government action. Normally, to be sure, one would be inclined to infer that the savings propensity of the people is greater in a country where gross investment is a high proportion (say, 30 percent) of GDP than in one where that proportion is low (say, 20 percent). But this is not necessarily a matter of free choice by individuals if a significant share of gross investment comes from the public sector and a corresponding share of gross savings is public sector savings resulting from the taxes and fiscal policy in force. By now each of the three Scandinavian countries has earnings-related national pensions systems in force in addition to basic national pensions independent of earnings. First introduced in Sweden in 1958 as a supplement to the basic pensions, the earnings-related pensions system accumulates premium reserve funds mainly from payroll taxes, rather as U.S. social security trust funds do. These pension reserves are growing rapidly and are scheduled to reach very large amounts in the early decades of the twenty-first century, after which the reserves will cease to grow.[3] However, these accumulations are the result of a significant rate of collective and forced saving, on which the individual can only exercise an indirect and relatively infrequent choice in the political arena. These collective savings are being invested in both the private and the public sectors of the various Scandinavian economies.

The foregoing four paragraphs indicate that it is necessary to supplement the information gleaned from UN national accounts statistics with data from the official economic reports of the individual countries in order to arrive at a clear perspective on the postwar structural changes in Scandinavia. Unfortunately, the data from the

---

[3] Carl G. Uhr, *Sweden's Social Security System*, Research Report No. 14, Social Security Administration (Washington, D.C.: U.S. Government Printing Office, 1966), pp. 49-66, 136-45.

respective countries featured below will usually not be uniform as between countries and for that reason will not lend themselves readily to intercountry comparisons. They are, however, what are available to us and what we must use in our analysis.

In terms of employment figures, Danish agriculture and allied pursuits show even more of a decline than they do as a proportion of GDP. In 1900 about 43 percent of the Danish labor force was engaged in agriculture. By 1939 that figure had shrunk to 28.6 percent, by 1950 to 22.8, by 1960 to 16.6, and by 1970 to 11.2 percent.[4] Many factors have contributed to this trend. One of them has been a progressive consolidation of farms too small to be economically viable (worthy of mechanization and modernization) into larger units. Thus, in 1960 the average size of Danish farms was sixteen hectares (about forty acres). By 1972 absorption of thousands of small units into larger ones had increased the average size of Danish farms to twenty-two hectares (or fifty-five acres).[5]

Because of its high productivity, Danish agriculture might readily have weathered the sale of its exports at falling prices. What made its situation precarious was that at the same time as world market prices of farm products were falling in several years during the 1950s and 1960s, costs of production were rapidly rising. This rise was mainly due to expansion of the manufacturing and service industries, which enjoyed a high income elasticity of demand for their output, compared with a much lower income elasticity of demand for food products.

As demand for labor by the manufacturing industries grew, this gave rise periodically to an increasing difference in earnings between urban industrial workers and self-employed farmers and workers in agriculture. This earnings differential in large measure accounts for the continuing flight of manpower from agriculture. In 1960, incomes of wage earners in the manufacturing industries were about seven percentage points higher than incomes of self-employed farmers, with the earnings of hired farm laborers still lower. By 1969 the earnings differential between self-employed farmers and industrial workers had increased to thirty-two percentage points.

In their efforts to arrest the economic decline of agriculture, the authorities found themselves forced to institutionalize or make permanent measures formerly applied only in emergencies (such as in

---

[4] Data for Denmark, Norway, and Sweden respectively were obtained from: *Perspektivplan-redegørelse 1972-1987* [Report of the perspective plan 1972-1987] (Copenhagen: Statens Tryckningskontor, 1973), pp. 415-17; *Økonomisk Utsyn Over Året 1973* [Economic survey 1973] (Oslo: Statistisk Sentralbyrå, 1974), pp. 85-92; Westerlind and Beckman, *Sveriges ekonomi*, p. 87.

[5] Hansen, *Økonomisk vaekst*, pp. 203-4, 223-24, 227-28, 231-32.

World War I and the Great Depression). These included price supports and subsidies for the major agricultural products sold on the domestic market. The result is that the prices of farm products in the domestic markets of Denmark, Norway, and Sweden are considerably higher than the world prices for exports of farm products. It is estimated that agricultural support schemes in Denmark accounted for 13 percent of the gross product of agriculture in 1972.

What has been said here about agriculture in Denmark applies in principle, but with differences in extent and timing, to agriculture in Norway and Sweden. Norway's agriculture supplies only about 39 percent of the country's food consumption, with the rest imported. The Norse agricultural system is decidedly one of small holders. Of some 200,000 farms in operation in 1970, only 130,000 had at least two hectares of arable land (five acres), and 85 percent of the farms had less than ten hectares (twenty-five acres) under cultivation. In 1900 about 34 percent of the labor force was engaged in agriculture, forestry, and fishing. By 1969 this ratio had declined to 15 percent. Wages in agriculture and allied pursuits were only 63 percent of those in manufacturing industries in Norway in 1969. Price supports and subsidies for Norway's farmers amounted to 32 percent of the gross product of agriculture in that year.[6]

Sweden's farms have also undergone a process of consolidation so that they are now on the average comparable in size to those of Denmark. At the turn of the century slightly more than half the country's labor force was engaged in agriculture, forest work, and fishing. The shift to the manufacturing and later the service industries, which began before the turn of the century and became significant during the 1920s, accelerated through the 1930s and 1940s into the 1950s. Between 1930 and 1962 the country's population increased by 1.44 million persons, but that of its metropolitan centers and towns increased by 1.64 million. By 1970 agriculture and allied pursuits employed only 9.4 percent of the labor force, and for 1975 this ratio is estimated to be lower still, some 8.0 percent.[7]

For the time being the foregoing sketch of structural economic change in Scandinavia must suffice. Some additional features of this

[6] Data relating to Norway's agriculture were obtained from Olan Borgan, Executive Director, Central Federation of Agricultural Cooperatives, *Norwegian Agriculture and its Organizations* (Oslo: Central Federation of Agricultural Cooperatives, 1972), pp. 7-41, and 69-71.

[7] Data on Sweden's agriculture and structural change were obtained from Uhr, *Sweden's Social Security System*, p. 22, and from Sekretariat för Ekonomisk Planering [Ministry of Finance], *Svensk ekonomi fram till 1977* [Sweden's economy projected to 1977] (Stockholm: Statens Offentliga Utredningar 1973:21, Esselte Tryck, 1973), pp. 101-2.

development will receive attention in the subsequent treatment. But at this stage it seems appropriate to consider, however briefly, some of the economic welfare implications of the transformation described above.

The Welfare Impact of Structural Change in the Scandinavian Economies

The structural change described above has taken place under conditions of almost continuously full employment in the postwar years and has given rise to an average annual growth rate of 4 to 5 percent in real income. Because demand for Scandinavian exports has remained strong and the thoroughly organized urban industrial labor markets in the three countries have remained tight, this economic growth has been accompanied by inflation at annual rates varying from 3 to 8 percent in practically all the postwar years.

One result of these developments is that in recent years Sweden has achieved and maintained the highest per capita income in Europe, second only to that of the United States. This fact has been widely publicized. Less familiar is the fact that in this respect Denmark and Norway are not far behind Sweden. Moreover, Norway may surpass Sweden when its North Sea oil deposits become available for effective exploitation in the next few years.

In this connection it seems necessary to point out that in the course of their postwar economic growth Denmark, Norway, and Sweden have developed comprehensive "cradle to grave" social security and public welfare systems. Major expansion and improvement of these systems began in the later 1940s and continued year by year into the 1960s.

Currently the main social security–welfare programs in Sweden begin with maternity and parenthood allowances of about $1,100 at the birth of each child. For the first sixteen years of each child's life, a child allowance of about $350 a year is payable to the parents. If the child continues schooling beyond sixteen, as most of them do nowadays, student cash allowances and a combination of grants and study loans are available. Throughout his life, every Swede is protected by health insurance which provides free hospitalization, cash sick benefits to adults, medical services at minimal fees at polyclinics, and many medicines at production cost or less. Unemployment insurance and industrial accident insurance, vocational retraining allowances, and related benefits are available to all persons who work for wages or salaries. As the adult reaches the pensionable age of sixty-five (lowered in 1975 from the traditional sixty-seven), he or she receives for the most part a combination of basic national pensions which are not related to earnings, and supplementary earnings-related pensions which are scheduled to bring the individual's total pension up to approximately 65 percent of his or her highest earnings (up to certain ceilings) averaged for the fifteen years of best earnings at work.[8] Comparable programs are in effect in Norway and Denmark.

The Scandinavian social security or welfare systems have made substantial progress over the years not only toward relieving but even toward gradually eliminating abject poverty by providing what is in essence a floor below which the individual's income may not decline, regardless of age, state of health, and ability, as well as opportunity for obtaining employment. Moreover, all this has been achieved by democratic processes, not by any harsh regime of intensive toil by workers, either voluntary or imposed. On the contrary, the work week has been reduced in a succession of steps from forty-eight hours in the first postwar decade to forty hours in 1972. At the same time annual paid vacations for blue- and white-collar workers alike were increased by legislation from two to four weeks per year in the 1960s.

These "successes" of the Scandinavian welfare states, which reflect the laboristic political outlook of the majority of the people, raise interesting questions to which there are no definite answers, but which, in part for that very reason, deserve contemplation. In the first place, we may ask, can the trends outlined above be expected to continue?

Technological progress notwithstanding, resource depletion may ultimately prevent the indefinite continuation of a positive growth trend. Moreover, a continuous increase at, say, 3 percent per annum of a per capita real income that has a high material commodity content might prove burdensome. At a growth rate of 3 percent per year over a century, an initial level of income increases nineteen-fold. An alternative would be for people to increase leisure time rather than real income. But there are limits to such choices, too. The four-day work week may become a reality in industry generally in the next decade or two. But once that were achieved, would a further advance toward a three-day and then a two-day work week seem desirable?

Be that as it may, there are two conditions that make it seem doubtful whether a 5 percent average annual economic growth rate,

---

[8] The Swedish Institute, *Social Benefits in Sweden 1974-75* (Stockholm: The Swedish Institute, 1975), pp. 1-12.

such as was experienced in Scandinavia in the 1960s, will be achieved in the decades immediately ahead. One of these conditions is demographic. Demographic trends seem likely to reduce the future growth rate of the Scandinavian labor force and of its man-hour input drastically, even from the modest rate of growth attained during the prewar decades. The other condition has to do with the progressive growth of the public sector at the expense of the private sector. To a certain extent these two conditions may be related. Both merit attention. In the interest of brevity they will be discussed with reference primarily to Sweden; the outlook for Norway and Denmark in these respects is essentially similar.

Demographic Constraints on Economic Growth. It is well known that the rate of population growth in Scandinavia has long been among the lowest in the world. The Scandinavian populations also include a larger proportion of elderly people than those of most other countries.

Sweden's population increased from 6.37 million in 1940 to 8.07 million in 1970 at an average annual rate of 0.795 percent. But the population of "active working age" (defined as between the ages of sixteen and sixty-four) increased during that same period at a slower rate of 0.57 percent per annum, while the rate of increase in the number of persons sixty-five and over was significantly higher, 2.8 percent per year.[9] Despite the fact that Sweden has been receiving additions to its labor force from adult immigration ever since the 1940s in numbers varying between 10,000 and 20,000 persons per year [10] and from the rising proportion of married women who work, the labor force has shown a declining rate of increase in recent years. While the labor force had increased at a rate of about 1.0 percent per year during the decades 1900–39, its annual rate of growth in the

[9] Data for this section were obtained from Westerlind and Beckman, *Sveriges ekonomi*, pp. 23-32; Sekretariat för Ekonomisk Planering, *The Swedish Economy 1971-75 and the General Outlook up to 1990: The 1970 Long-Term Survey, Main Report* (Stockholm: Government Official Report 1970:71, Esselte Tryck, 1971), pp. 66-74; and Sekretariat för Ekonomisk Planering, *Svensk ekonomi fram till 1977*, pp. 17-38.

[10] Most of the immigrants in Sweden's labor force are Finns, Danes, and Norwegians, many of whom settle permanently in Sweden and become Swedish citizens. In addition a more seasonal supply of immigrant labor is made up of Estonians, Latvians, Poles, Yugoslavs, Italians, Spaniards, Greeks, and Turks. According to the *Statistical Abstract for Sweden 1973* (Stockholm: Central Statistical Bureau, 1974), p. 45, there were 407,000 aliens out of 8.2 million people resident in Sweden in 1973. Of these 197,000 were Finns, 29,000 Danes, and 27,000 Norwegians. The remaining 175,000 were not Scandinavians, and of the 407,000 aliens approximately 200,000 were in the labor force.

period 1960–65 was 0.8 percent. The figure declined to 0.6 percent during 1965–70 and is estimated to be no greater than 0.4 percent for 1970–75.[11]

The effect of the dwindling labor force growth rate has been intensified by the considerable reduction in the number of man-hours worked per year, resulting from the gradual reduction of the work week and the increase in paid annual vacations. To this must be added a significant albeit varying degree of absenteeism from regularly scheduled working time, especially in years of overfull employment. The result is that, while the number of man-hours worked increased at an annual rate of 9.3 percent in 1960–65, during 1965–70 it decreased at an annual rate of 1.0 percent. This rate of decrease has also been projected for 1970–75. By 1973 this development had led to a downward revision of the long-term prognosis for the economy that had been issued by the Secretariat for Economic Planning of the Ministry of Finance in 1970. The revised prognosis or "indicative plan" used new data to extend the earlier survey from 1972 to 1977 and projected, instead of the earlier 4.0 percent economic growth rate, a growth rate of 3.4 percent per year for 1970–75.

The growth rate of an economy is, of course, a function of more variables than the growth rate of its labor force. It depends, notably, upon the ratio of investment or savings to GNP and on the rate of technological improvement affecting various industries and production processes. Yet with these variables given, in any two economies A and B identical except for the fact that A has a larger service-industry sector, including a larger public sector, than B, the growth rate observable in B is likely to be greater than that in A.

The growth rate in B would most likely be greater than that in A because production of commodities is more directly amenable to technological, organizational, and engineering improvements than production of services. Moreover, given the difficulties of measuring services output, the growth rate in A would be smaller than that in B because A's larger service sector contains a large proportion of public sector services. While most of the services produced in the private sector are directly subject to the market pricing mechanism and can to that extent be measured in value terms, very few of the public sector services receive quantification and valuation or prices by market processes.

Denmark, Norway, and Sweden have comparatively large public sectors, accounting for upwards of 40 percent of their GNP. Of the

---

11 The Sekretariat för Ekonomisk Planering, *The Swedish Economy 1971-1975 and the General Outlook up to 1990*, p. 69.

Table 7–5

SCOPE OF THE PUBLIC SECTOR IN THE SCANDINAVIAN ECONOMIES IN THE EARLY 1970s
(in percentages of GNP)

Country and Year	Public Expenditures, Including Social Transfer Payments (1)	Social Transfer Payments (2)	Public Sector Real Use of the Nation's Output (3)
Sweden, 1974	52.0	17.5	34.5
Norway, 1973	47.4	22.4	25.0
Denmark, 1971	49.4	20.4	29.0

Source: For Sweden, Konjunkturinstitutet, *Konjunkturläget Hösten 1974* [The business situation, fall 1974] (Stockholm: Business Institute, 1974), pp. 9, 69, 135, and 136; for Norway, Statistisk Sentralbyra [Central Statistical Bureau], *Økonomisk Utsyn over Året 1973* [Economic review of the year 1973] (Oslo: Statistisk Sentralbyra, 1973), p. 94; for Denmark, *Perspektivplan-redegørelse 1972-1977* [Report of the perspective plan for 1972-1977] (Copenhagen: Statens Tryckningskontor, 1973), pp. 395, 415.

three, the public sector of Sweden is the largest both in absolute and in relative terms. Its scope and prospects are worth looking into, however briefly.

The Public Sector. The real scope of the public sector for the three countries in three recent years is indicated by column 3 in Table 7–5. Except at times when public sector expenditures are in part deficit-financed, total direct and indirect taxes inclusive of social security and health insurance contributions must, of course, match the amounts implied by the percentages in column 1. In Sweden's case, 6.7 percent of the public sector outlays in 1974 were deficit-financed. Consequently, the total taxes of that year were 48.5 rather than 52.0 percent of GNP. In decreasing order of relative magnitude the social transfer payments to households and individuals consist mainly of (1) old age, invalidism, and widows' pensions, (2) child allowances and education grants for adolescents beyond age sixteen, (3) maternity allowances, (4) disability compensation or sick-benefits under the health insurance scheme, and (5) unemployment benefits and vocational retraining, moving allowances, and so on for "hard to place" unemployed persons.

The public sector's real draft on the resources and output of the economy is for collective consumption and investment. In Sweden in

1969, collective consumption amounted to 34.7 billion kr. or 23.6 percent of GNP, and the lion's share of this, 56 percent, was spent for public services related to education, health care under the national health insurance scheme, and social assistance or public welfare work. Only 16 percent of these billions, or 3.8 percent of GNP, was devoted to the national defense establishment.[12]

In 1969 the public sector investment of 16.1 billion kr. in Sweden corresponded to 10.9 percent of GNP. Nearly one-quarter (some 23.6 percent) of these investment expenditures was made for education, health care, and public welfare purposes. About 20 percent went for investments in roads, streets, and sewer and water systems, and another 19 percent was invested in housing (chiefly by the local communities). About two-thirds of the remainder (some 24.5 percent) was spent for investments in the government's public enterprises, such as the state railways, the telephone and telegraph network, the state and local governments' electric power plants, gas works, bus systems, and so on.

It is interesting to note how rapid has been the growth of the public sector expenditures (including social transfers). The ratio of public sector employment to total employment had grown to 18.3 percent in 1960 and is projected at 23 percent for 1975. In 1950 public sector expenditures came to 24.5 percent of GNP in Sweden; by 1960 this ratio had risen to 33.3, by 1969 to 44.9, and by 1974 to 52.0 percent inclusive of fairly modest amounts of deficit finance. This amounts to an expansion rate of the public sector and of the system of taxation of approximately 1.0 percent of GNP per year over the twenty-four-year span, 1950–74.

Evidently, if that rate of expansion were to continue (which is doubtful), the public sector would in not too long a time become coextensive with the economy as a whole. There has been no strong disposition, when Labor or Social Democratic governments have been in power in Denmark, Norway, and Sweden, for them to nationalize any of the major private industries. In essence, such nationalization is what would be called for, at least indirectly, if the public sector's GNP share went much beyond the 50 percent mark. That prospect is deemed to be unlikely, although it is difficult to see just where the line against the public sector's further expansion might be drawn.

---

[12] For Sweden, Norway, and Denmark respectively: Konjunkturinstitutet, *Konjunkturläget Hösten 1974* [The business situation, fall 1974] (Stockholm: Konjunkturinstitutet, 1974), pp. 9, 69, 135 and 136; Statistisk Sentralbyrå, *Økonomisk Utsyn over Året 1973* [Economic survey 1973] (Oslo: Statistisk Sentralbyrå, 1974), p. 94; *Perspektivplan-redegørelse 1972-1987* [Report of the perspective plan 1972-1987] (Copenhagen: Statens Tryckningskontor, 1973), pp. 395, 415.

However, there has already been a reaction to the growth of the public sector at the level of taxation. In recent years the Scandinavian governments, which used to rely primarily on the progressive income tax and tax on wealth for their revenues, have shifted to greater reliance on indirect taxes, most notably to value-added taxes, which are now levied at rates of 15 percent or higher. As more and steeper indirect taxes have been introduced, the progressivity of the income tax has been modified. It has been eased especially for those income brackets in which the great majority of taxpayers are organized wage-workers.

Moreover, several factors militate against any substantial further rise in social transfer payments from the public sector: not only do increases in such transfers have to be matched by increases in tax revenues, but also it is the case that the position of certain categories of passive recipients of increased transfers would improve faster than that of active tax-burdened participants in the labor force. To a considerable degree this is a consequence of the demographic situation in the Scandinavian countries considered here.

If we follow Swedish practice and define as "economically active" that part of the population from sixteen to sixty-four years of age and regard the remainder of the population as "economically passive" and "dependent," directly or indirectly (for instance, through social transfers such as pensions) on the former, by division we obtain a ratio between the "active" and the "dependent" population. Such a ratio is a good approximation to the prevailing reality. There is little question that children under sixteen years of age are dependents, and, although some 15 to 20 percent of all persons sixty-five years old or older remain in the labor market, their presence among the "actives" is approximately offset by the fact that a substantial proportion of the young "actives" between sixteen and twenty-four years old are out of the labor market most of the year in pursuit of further education—vocational or professional training.[13]

---

[13] Traditionally "working life" is defined in Scandinavian vital statistics, labor force, and manpower data as "sixteen through sixty-four years of age," even though the general "pension age" was sixty-seven years until recently (reduced to sixty-five in Sweden in 1975). In practice all national and local government employees have been pensionable at sixty-five all along and members of the armed services even earlier. In addition a large proportion of white-collar workers in private employment have been pensionable at 65. Hence it was chiefly the blue-collar workers who had to wait until they were sixty-seven in order to qualify for full pensions, although they could retire earlier at reduced pensions. Finally, in recent decades it has turned out to be increasingly difficult for "older workers" (fifty-five and over) once they have become unemployed, for example, when their plant has shut down either to liquidate or to move elsewhere, or in a recession, to obtain new employment. In practice many an

As long as the active/dependent population ratio is greater than a critical value of 2 to 1, then the greater it is (and for demographic reasons it can hardly rise above 3 to 1 in societies that do not permit children under sixteen to have full-time employment), the less costly it is for the actives to support the dependents directly or by social transfers. But once this ratio sinks below 2 to 1, then the smaller it is, the more costly it becomes for the actives to permit their political representatives to be generous in social transfers to the dependent population.[14]

In Sweden the active/dependent population ratio was greater than 2 to 1 (actually 2.18 to 1) for the last time during the early 1940s. As it happened, it was in 1947–48 that the very considerable expansion of Sweden's social security and welfare system began. But already by 1950 this ratio had declined to 1.87 to 1. By 1970 it had fallen to 1.76, and for 1980 it is projected to be 1.6 to 1. Much the

---

older worker is forced into early retirement after an extended spell of unemployment. Consequently the definition of adult working life as stretching from sixteen to sixty-five seems to coincide with the reality.

[14] The "critical value" of an active/dependent population ratio of 2 to 1 with respect to social transfer payments refers to or implies a tax ratio to net national product (NNP) which, though high at about 40 percent per capita among the active population, may be accepted as tolerable, while a higher tax ratio, say one of 50 percent, may prove intolerable, especially if the tax burden is distributed progressively.

To see what this means, let us assume that: (1) 10 percent of NNP must in any case go for taxes to pay for all government services and outlays except social transfers; (2) all social transfers are paid out of taxes to the dependent population (which population pays no or at best negligible taxes); (3) the dependent population is supported entirely by social transfers at a consumption standard per capita intended to equal half the per capita standard among the actives. We have, then, a situation where the actives generate all the NNP and pay all the taxes, a significant proportion of which must go to support the dependent population.

An active/dependent population ratio of 3 to 1 means that the people divide into 75 percent actives and 25 percent dependents. Since 10 percent of NNP goes for taxes for government services, another 12.5 percent of NNP must be taken to support the dependents at half the per capita standard of the actives. Thus taxes come to 22.5 percent of NNP, and since they are paid only by the 75 percent of the people who are actives, this makes the per capita tax rate among the actives $22.5/75.0 = 0.3$ or 30 percent.

Now let the active/dependent population ratio drop to 2 to 1: two-thirds of the people are actives and one-third dependents. Accordingly taxes will now be 10 percent of NNP for ordinary government services and 16.7 percent for social transfers, a total of 26.7 percent of NNP, which results in a per capita tax rate on the actives of $26.7/66.7 = 0.4$ or 40 percent.

Finally, let the active/dependent population ratio decline to 3 to 2: the actives are only 60 percent of the population. Then, besides taxes of 10 percent of NNP for government services, an additional 20 percent must be taken for social transfers. Total taxes will be 30 percent of NNP and the per capita tax rate on the actives will be $30/60 = 0.5$ or 50 percent.

244

same holds for the active/dependent population ratios for these same decades in Denmark and Norway.

What this implies in terms of public sector expansion in the social transfer dimension is poignantly indicated by the following statement from the Danish long-term or "perspective" economic plan for the years 1970–85. Among other things this plan visualizes that the expenditures of the Danish public sector, which amounted to 45 percent of GNP in 1970, will rise to 58 percent by 1987:

> Calculations show that the maximum margin for increase in private consumption in the 15-year period ahead averages 2.0–2.5 percent per annum. . . . Transfer payments now represent roughly one-sixth of total private consumption. While a total increase of 5 percent per year in pensioners' consumption may not appear large in comparison with increases recorded in the 1960s, this would require that increases in private consumption for the active classes of the population be kept below 2 percent per year. In other words the standard of living of the inactive groups would improve twice as fast as that of the active classes.[15]

Redistribution of Income. Whether or not public sector expenditures as a proportion of GNP may rise further, so long as they are supported by a tax system that is still progressive (even if less so now than it was some years ago), their effect ought to be a considerable redistribution of income, significantly reducing the degree of income inequality. After all, the social transfer payments are predominantly made to the low-income groups in the community.

It is generally conceded by way of inference that expansion of the public sector must have had income equalizing effects, but there is thus far surprisingly little firm evidence on the extent to which this has been the case. One reason for this is that the expansion of the public sector has occurred under inflationary conditions. Although most of the social transfer payments are periodically adjusted (by escalator clauses) for the rise in cost of living, such adjustments always occur with a certain lag. During the lag periods some erosion of the real value of the transfers takes place, which is not fully compensated for by the next cost-of-living adjustment. Moreover, pension benefits and the like, which (apart from cost-of-living adjust-

---

[15] *Problems of Long-Term Economic Planning in Denmark 1970-1985* (Copenhagen: H. J. Schultz Forlag, March 1971), p. 24. This is a summary in English translation of the much larger Danish economic planning report produced by a working party set up by the government in November 1968, *Perspektivplane-laegning 1970-1985* (Copenhagen: H. J. Schultz Forlag, March 1971).

ments) are altered in basic amounts only by statutory enactments, do not possess the flexibility and freedom of movement that characterize profit rates, collective wage bargains, and wage drift in inflationary periods. The income redistribution one expects to find is thus often washed away in part or in full by the movement of prices. Nevertheless, S. A. Hansen has found that in Denmark the combination of progressive taxes and social transfers to the low-income earners effected a 5.5 percent redistribution of aggregate income in favor of the latter in 1949, a 6 percent redistribution in 1955, and a 7 percent redistribution in 1963.[16]

For Norway I do not have any relevant data at hand on the redistribution of income. The Swedish long-term economic survey of 1970 presents an analysis of a number of factors that have contributed to a reduction in the dispersion of incomes in Sweden around the mean or median. Apart from qualitative inferences that progressive taxes have such a dispersion-reducing effect (as has an increase in labor-force participation by elements of the population distributed over the income deciles), the only concrete conclusions presented in quantitative terms were that:

> Basic pensions increase the uniformity of total income distribution by about 12 percent. . . . The period 1966–75 shows a strong rise in the effect on income distribution. Without the national supplementary pension benefits, the disparity of income distribution would have been 0.8 percent greater in 1966 compared with 2.1 percent in 1970 and 4.1 percent in 1975.[17]

These conclusions entitle one to believe that there are measurable income redistribution effects of the combination of progressive taxes and social transfers to low-income groups. But it is difficult to visualize just what an X percent reduction in income disparity means unless detailed data concerning the patterns of income disparity in successive years are available for a given economy. From such data it would be possible to determine statistically how these patterns have changed.

This description of the recent economic development of the three Scandinavian countries leaves the impression that events unfolded and structures evolved from one period to the next in a fairly harmonious, tranquil fashion—except during the years of the war. This has not been entirely true, but such disturbances as Scandinavia's

---

[16] Hansen, Økonomisk vaekst, p. 185.

[17] Sekretariat för Ekonomisk Planering, *The Swedish Economy 1971-1975 and the General Outlook up to 1990*, pp. 184-85.

economic development encountered and generated were overcome without breaking its trend or changing its direction.

Concluding Comments

It is clear that in recent decades the three Scandinavian countries discussed here have been remarkably successful in achieving one of the highest standards of living in the world. To an appreciable extent this has been due to a favorable concatenation of forces. Scandinavian business and labor have shown great adaptability to technological and institutional change. Organized labor has as a rule readily accepted automation, and the Scandinavian labor markets have been relatively tranquil, free from frequent and serious disturbances as they have hammered out a succession of collective bargaining agreements. Moreover, substantial stability in the political sphere has made it possible to enact economic policies and reforms on a piecemeal year-to-year basis without significant deviations and reversals of direction—thus, for instance, the gradual expansion of the social security and welfare programs in these countries.

These achievements are all the more impressive considering the fact that not so long ago, from the 1820s up to World War I, Denmark, Norway, and Sweden were regarded as poor countries that had reason to fear the progressive loss of their labor force by emigration, primarily to the United States. The economic success these countries have recorded has been accompanied by a thoroughgoing democratization of Scandinavian politics and by a considerable reduction of the income inequality that characterized the economic and social distance between managers and workers, between white-collar and blue.

Still, while abject poverty has been alleviated, it has not been eliminated. Fairly extensive pockets of poverty are still to be found among single mothers with young children, among older workers (fifty and older) in the ranks of semi-skilled and unskilled labor, and among adults of working age who are in poor health, weak but not entirely disabled.[18]

---

[18] Concerning the extent of poverty in Sweden's celebrated welfare state see: Lars Sandblom, "De extremt lågavlönade" [Workers with extremely low earnings] in *Låginkomstutredningen* [The investigation of low incomes, a set of reports of a parliamentary inquiry into the subject] (Stockholm: Allmänna Förlaget, 1970); Betänkande avgivet av Låginkomstutredningen, *Svenska folkets inkomster* [Report of the low incomes inquiry: incomes of the Swedish people] (Stockholm: Statens Offentliga Utredningar 1970:34, Esselte Tryck, 1970); and Per Holmberg and Holger Ström, *Välstånd med slagsida* [The listing welfare ship of state] (Stockholm: Publica and Allmänna Förlaget, 1970).

It now seems that the splendid economic achievement of the Scandinavian countries is threatened simultaneously from several directions. The continuous gradual decline in labor supply and man-hours of input in production that is anticipated may reduce or even eliminate the 4 to 5 percent annual economic growth rate to which Scandinavians have become accustomed ever since the end of World War II. Demands for tax reform and relief from very heavy tax burdens may block any further expansion of the public sector and of the welfare-state features of these economies. Moreover, if no tax relief is granted, a progressive flight of capital and investment from Scandinavia may occur, and economic initiative and work incentives might become seriously impaired. At the same time, from the ranks of labor on the factory floor, so to speak, come increasing demands for "economic democracy at the place of work" as well as concern over the "quality of life." Many thousands exhaust themselves doing monotonous piece-work at incentive rates of pay or for high earnings.

These problems call for operational solutions, yet none of them is simple or readily resolved. It is clear that their solution will call for far-reaching adjustments in working life. It may well be that a good part of the problem of declining man-hour input in production can be solved by expanding the practice of split-shift and part-time work. It may also be that some of the problems relating to tax relief might be solved by making more of the many public services (currently supplied free to users and financed by general taxes) subject to fees and charges approximating their costs of production. These are some of the easy if not very popular partial answers to two of the problems outlined. Much more imaginative solutions will be needed, however, to assuage the demand for "economic democracy" at places of work, not least because the concrete meaning of economic democracy on the factory floor has yet to be spelled out.

It is clear, then, that for all their achievements—indeed, because of them—the Scandinavians face a set of challenging new problems. For these they may, with luck, find feasible answers by the gradualist and pragmatic approaches that have served them so well in the past.

8

THE CHANGING ROLE OF PRIVATE ENTERPRISE IN SWEDEN

Göran Ohlin

The *modus operandi* of private enterprise in industrialized countries is everywhere undergoing significant change. The relationship between business and state is evolving in response to new objectives of public policy. Most of these new objectives have emerged at roughly the same time everywhere; there is a strong common tide in most industrial countries. Naturally, private enterprise in the Scandinavian countries is also working under new rules and restraints.

Especially outside of Scandinavia, it is often thought that the relatively strong position of Scandinavian Social Democratic parties has already produced socialist societies in which private enterprise is particularly circumscribed. After more than forty years of what is loosely described as socialist rule, Sweden is probably the country in which the impact of this development on economic organization can best be examined. When it comes to the terms and conditions of private enterprise, the Scandinavian economies are very similar, but more often than not its neighbors follow Sweden's lead in institutional reform.

Socialization of Income, Not Production

To those who believe that socialism is the antithesis of private ownership of the means of production, the dominance of private enterprise in Sweden comes as a surprise. The public sector includes health and education, railways and telecommunications, half the output of electric power, a small number of large industrial firms, and a larger number of small ones. All in all, some 25 percent of the Swedish GNP is produced in the public sector. However, in industry the public share is only some 5 percent, a considerably smaller proportion than in most European countries.

On the other hand, the public use of resources is rather more extensive in Sweden than in many other mixed economies, especially outside of Scandinavia. Taxes and other government revenue constitute about 60 percent of the country's GNP, roughly half of which goes into current expenditures or investment, while the other half is redistributed as transfers—pensions, family allowances, welfare payments, industrial subsidies, and so forth. A sizable portion also goes into the supplementary pensions system, of which more later. The tax bite has been steadily rising in most industrial countries, but Sweden has by most measures been at the top of the league for some time. As Assar Lindbeck has aptly said, instead of socializing the means of production, Sweden has socialized incomes.[1]

The thrust of Swedish policy has also been labeled functional socialism, which suggests a pragmatic rather than a doctrinaire conception of socialist ideology. In any case, Swedish Social Democrats have for decades used the powers of government to build up a welfare system based on generous social security, regional employment policy, and educational reform. The structure of production, on the other hand, has until recently been left untouched. The prevalence of private enterprise was one cornerstone of the triangular relationship between business, labor, and the state, that had already taken shape before World War II and did not change much after it. In the 1950s and 1960s, it almost seemed as if the mixed economy had reached a state of harmonious equilibrium that might last forever.

Not even restraint of trade and competition was subjected to public policy until the 1950s when relatively mild legislation was introduced, banning resale price maintenance and collusive tendering but tolerating many restrictive practices as long as they were not proved harmful.

The government was conspicuously absent from the scene of industrial relations. Virtually all wage earners were organized in the tightly centralized Federation of Labor, with the white-collar unions running far behind in strength. The employers too were closely organized, and in 1938 a basic agreement was concluded by the employers and the unions. It was for all intents and purposes a piece of private legislation, regulating industrial relations and collective bargaining more closely than they were regulated by the law.

---

[1] Assar Lindbeck, "Vart är vår ekonomi på väg? Nationella och internationella aspekter" [Where is the economy heading? National and international aspects], in Vårt ekonomiska läge 1972 [The position of the economy 1972] (Stockholm: Sparframjandet, 1972), p. 20.

In spite of the strong links between the Federation of Labor and the Social Democratic party, the unions shared the employers' desire to keep the state out of the labor market and rely on negotiation rather than legislation.

Social conflict in Sweden reached its peak toward the end of World War I, before the introduction of universal suffrage. The image of reasonableness and compromise projected by Marquis Childs's famous account of *Sweden, the Middle Way* was not without foundation.[2] Yet Swedish society remained status-ridden and rigidly formalistic. Industrial organization was almost military in its adherence to hierarchy, and the social distance between executives, engineers, foremen, and the rank and file was great.

The line of demarcation between the public and the private sector was sharp. Traditionally, government maintained a nondiscriminatory attitude toward business and kept its distance. In foreign affairs, informal cooperation occurred when prominent bankers and industrialists participated in negotiations during and after World War II or when the Foreign Office lent its discreet support to large Swedish exporters in their dealings with foreign governments. In domestic affairs, "Swedish pluralism" secured an active role for business and labor organizations in the preparation of new legislation, which was usually worked out in royal committees where representatives of those organizations participated along with politicians from the major parties.

One reason for the general satisfaction with this arrangement was that it seemed to work. At least in leading political circles, there was a consensus that the Swedish standard of living was largely a function of the performance of Swedish industry, which, in spite of a late start, had managed to give the country one of the highest per capita incomes in the world. This particular conception of the mixed economy now seems more precarious than it did a few years ago. It has been undermined by a great variety of political initiatives that tend to limit the rights of private enterprise in favor of other interested parties—the state, local government, employees, and consumers. If one interprets this change as a sudden return to socialist principles, one might ask why it was not undertaken earlier.

One explanation for the Fabian nature of Swedish socialism is that Swedish Social Democrats have always operated in a parliamentary system in which their possession of governmental power has

---

[2] Marquis W. Childs, *Sweden, the Middle Way* (New Haven: Yale University Press, 1936).

been far from secure. They have not had a mandate for the drastic and wholesale reform of Swedish society.

Professor Leif Lewin, who has written a magnum opus on "the planning controversy" in Sweden,[3] makes the rash assumption that all steps taken by the Swedish government since the 1930s, opposed as they were by liberals and conservatives alike, flowed from Social Democratic ideology. But in other countries many of the same measures were introduced by nonsocialist governments and opposed by socialists. It is, one might conclude, the business of governments to govern and that of oppositions to oppose. Historians will find, I believe, that Swedish Social Democratic thought was gradually purged of many specific propositions of the socialist tradition during a long period in which the Social Democratic party exercised government responsibility on an electoral and parliamentary base slender enough to preclude drastic social change. Whatever was actually done could be presented as a manifestation of socialist spirit, even when in fact it was primarily a response to new political situations. In some respects, however, the positions of the Social Democrats have been stable and consistent for quite some time, and many of their moves in the last few years have been in line with objectives already put forth thirty years ago.

The Postwar Program of Swedish Labor. In 1944 the Swedish Social Democrats presented a program for the postwar period, which was largely drafted by Gunnar Myrdal. They dropped a number of references to the class struggle from the party platform, leaving incendiary language to their opponents on the left. Instead, the 1944 program ratified the pragmatic approach to social change and economic organization that had been forced upon the party in the 1930s. It also fairly succinctly set out a number of general directions. The principal targets were full employment, a fairer income distribution, and industrial democracy. The nationalization of industry was not recommended except where private enterprise resulted in gross inefficiency or monopoly, but close attention to industrial structure and reorganization was counseled.

The Social Democrats' ambition was to extend government control and influence over the economy by whatever means might recommend themselves in each individual situation. Thus, in view of the critical importance of the capital market, the nationalization of the insurance companies was advocated, as was the creation of a body for

[3] Leif Lewin, *Planhushållningsdebatten* [The planning controversy] (Uppsala: Almqvist & Wiksell, 1967).

the control and coordination of private investment projects. The key-note of the document was a deep distrust of market forces. Impressed by the performance of wartime controls, the authors of the report proposed their prolongation.

"Planning" was a recurrent term in the 1944 Social Democratic platform as it had been in the 1930s, but its meaning was not that of Soviet planning or even so-called indicative (French) planning. Planning meant instead the government's exercise of control and influence over the economy, and any and all steps it might take to achieve the desired objective—for the most part a loosely conceived notion of economic efficiency. This slightly confusing attempt to exploit the prestige planning enjoyed on the left contributed to the heated reaction it provoked from the right. Although the program contained few specific proposals for immediate action, it was received as thoroughly controversial, and the references to planning were thought to point to the *Road to Serfdom*, Hayek's antisocialist tract that was widely quoted by conservative critics.

Beyond the Welfare State

In fact, little planning or major change in economic organization took place in the first postwar decades. The political agenda was taken up with reforms in the social field, mainly the establishment of exten-sive welfare machinery not unlike that in other European industrial countries. However, two developments in the 1950s were to prove highly important and to give a distinctive character to later economic policy. They provided new instruments for active intervention in two key areas: the labor market and the capital market.

Structural unemployment in the North and in part of the countryside elsewhere had proved impossible to fight by general fiscal and monetary expansion. The so-called Rehn-Meidner model, elaborated by the two leading economists of the Federation of Labor around 1950, assumed that the general level of demand had to be restrained to avoid inflationary excess demand.[4] Where local struc-tural unemployment emerged, this policy provided that it should be met primarily by measures enhancing the mobility of labor and its transfer to growth sectors. The private cost of moving or changing occupation was thought to exceed the social cost so greatly that no cost-benefit calculations were even necessary to justify the financing

---

[4] The Rehn-Meidner model is described in Rehn's and Meidner's contributions to Erik Lundberg et al., *Wages Policy under Full Employment* (London: William Hodge, 1952).

of extensive retraining schemes and the subsidization of mobility. This manpower policy rested on a network of government employment agencies and a manpower board that soon became a locus of power in the Swedish economy. Its activities were popular in all quarters and aroused international attention. The policy seemed to work with the market rather than against it, aiming as it did to remove rigidities and make structural change less painful.

In 1959, supplementary old-age pensions (ATP) were introduced, after a stormy battle over their compulsory character. Fewer objections were raised against the overall design of the scheme, which (unlike the existing universal pensions system) was not carried in the regular government budget but provided for a fund to be built up on the basis of payroll fees submitted by employers. This ATP fund grew rapidly and became a principal supplier of long-term capital. These collective savings, often referred to as wage-earners' money, were endowed with an ideological mystique; above all they put most of the capital market safely under government control. The Central Bank retained its control of bond issues, and the ATP picked up more than two-thirds of the authorized issues in the 1960s, dividing its purchases about evenly among state, municipal, and industrial bonds.

These two institutions—the manpower board and the ATP fund—were to play a prominent part when the government moved toward more active intervention in the industrial field.

Industrial Location and Regional Policy. In 1961 a working party set up by the Federation of Labor submitted an extensive and thoughtful report on coordinated industrial policy, which resurrected and articulated many of the ideas in the half-forgotten party program of 1944.[5] Market forces were criticized once more, but chiefly for being too weak to be relied on. Along with active measures to maintain and strengthen competition, the report called for central control of important private investment decisions. It recommended the creation of a new ministry and the promotion of energetic regional policies to restrain the growth of the metropolitan regions around Stockholm, Göteborg, and Malmö and to promote the development of the North. The document was a few years ahead of its time but was eventually to prove highly influential.

The immediate cause of new government action in the early 1960s was the increasing political pressure from the north. The

---

[5] Strukturutredningen, *Samordnad näringspolitik* [Coordinated industrial policy] (Stockholm: Landsorganisationen, 1961).

manpower policy, with its efforts to move people out, had not brought much relief and was increasingly unpopular. Suasion and programs of information to induce firms to move into labor-surplus regions had been relatively fruitless. The manpower board was therefore given large sums for so-called location grants and concessional loans.

Another financial incentive for investment in the development or labor-surplus areas was found in the so-called investment funds, which were pressed into use for purposes of regional policy. These tax-deductible funds can be accumulated out of company profits by each company's depositing a sum corresponding to the corporate income tax normally due in an interest-free account with the Bank of Sweden. When the government wishes to stimulate investment, it authorizes the utilization of these investment funds. There is then no outstanding tax liability—the company has avoided paying the corporate income tax—but on the other hand no depreciation is allowed on such investments. The net tax incentive is of the order of 10 to 15 percent of the investment cost. If the deposits are withdrawn without authorization, the funds are taxed at normal rates. Unlike ordinary tax credits, these are meant to restrain investment in the booms as well as stimulate it in times of slack.

In 1963, investment funds were "released" for general use in the development areas, but soon thereafter a different practice evolved. Under "joint releases," the use of the funds was authorized for major investments in the industrial regions of the country, provided that the company receiving funds undertook a minor investment project in the development areas for which it would receive additional subsidies. This created an interesting trade-off and bargaining situation, but it amounted to a break with the tradition of essentially nondiscriminatory and arms-length treatment of business by government authorities. Companies found the grants and credits too large to pass up, especially in years when capital was scarce.

Today those engaged in the financing of business activity in Sweden must make an extensive study of the subsidy options. Big projects tend to float up from the administrative level to the political, and knowing one's way in the corridors of power is far more important to business executives than it was in the past.

The new practice of direct deals between business and government could be fitted into the rejection of "general" policies on the Rehn-Meidner model. The more piecemeal and local style of intervention, termed "selective" policy, did not have to be blatantly discriminatory. General rules specifying more or less automatic levels of support by region could have been used, but the authorities preferred a more discretionary system. Criticism of the new policies has largely focused on this significant element of discretion and bargaining. Critics in the business community or in the Conservative and Liberal parties have objected to the discriminatory effects, while criticism from the left has charged a sellout to capitalist interests. A broad spectrum of opinion has shown considerable concern about the fact that it may become more profitable for business executives to court politicians than to run their companies. Similarly, it is feared that the government's ambition to be a partner in a number of private companies undermines its role as an impartial arbiter.[6]

One strong reason for preferring selective to general measures was the balance-of-payments situation. The government feared that an attempt to stimulate employers by general fiscal or monetary policy would spill over into a larger deficit. Almost miraculously, Sweden had escaped balance-of-payments troubles since 1949, but in 1965 there was a serious deficit and concomitant loss of reserves. To the fear of demand inflation was now added the spectre of the "English disease" and the prospect of falling into the hands of the gnomes of Zürich. This reinforced the policy makers' reluctance to expand and explains why a slowly rising trend of unemployment was tolerated. Selective measures have not been able to counter this trend. Many economists and some civil servants have also been critical of the increasing reliance on ad hoc subsidies, but the handing out of government favors has great attractions from a political point of view.

What started as an attempt to influence the location of industrial companies by a system of incentives soon grew into a full-fledged regional development program. Decentralized machinery for physical planning was created, and one of its first tasks in planning for 1980 was to allocate the 1980 population among the country's regions. Since all ambitions could not be satisfied with the number of Swedes and immigrants that central planners projected as available by 1980, some trade-offs had to be made. This turned out to be too politically sensitive a matter to leave to the planners, and in 1972 a regional pattern for the distribution of population was somewhat hesitantly approved by the parliament. The targets for the various regions were described as provisional planning tools. Soon enough, however, they graduated to the status of objectives.

[6] On the shift toward selective policy, see Anne Wibble, "Selektiv och generall politik" [Selective and general economic policy], in Erik Lundberg et al., *Svensk finanspolitik i teori och praktik* [Swedish fiscal policy in theory and practice] (Stockholm: Bonniers, 1971).

Until now, regional policy has relied mostly on incentives. This can be difficult enough if competition is arbitrarily tampered with, as when a heavily subsidized firm merely replaces a competitor who was doing quite well before. The temptation to resort to more powerful instruments of intervention is therefore strong. A commission appointed to look into regional policy reported in the fall of 1974 that it would be necessary to resort to licensing and permits if companies and employment were to be forced into the population pattern that the statisticians, the planners, and parliament had established. Not only the business community but also local governments that stand to lose from such practices will oppose the idea, and probably it will not be adopted. Nonetheless, it is interesting to note how closely the ambitions of the public agencies skirt the border between incentives and controls.

Industrial Policy. By the middle of the 1960s, European governments were everywhere devoting themselves to structural and regional problems of industry and to the mysteries of science and technology. In many of those countries, industrial policy had a long tradition of service to the business community, as did the Department of Commerce in the United States. The Organization for Economic Cooperation and Development (OECD) was a forum where top Swedish civil servants and ministers participated in an exchange of views on these subjects. However, in Sweden the government's attitude toward private enterprise and industry was more ambivalent than in most other countries, and the private sector tended to be seen as an adversary.

It was not until 1967 that a specific industrial policy emerged. In the fall of 1966, the Social Democrats had done badly in the local elections and were in a weak position that required the taking of some forceful initiatives. At the opening of parliament in January 1967, the government made a dramatic but vague announcement in the budget that a substantial fund would be set up for the financing of urgent industrial projects. Only a few weeks later, the fund turned into a bank to channel ATP funds into medium- and long-term finance for industrial reorganization, for large and risky projects, and for purposes of "great social benefit." The bill introducing the new bank was so perfunctory and its language so strident that it was bound to alarm the business community. But the Swedish Investment Bank, to which this episode gave birth, took a long time to get under way and then turned into a welcome addition to the thin medium-term market—if anything, an addition slightly too conservative by many estimates.

The bank bill was only the first in a sequence of ambitious initiatives that seemed designed to satisfy the impatient critics to the left of center, whether inside or outside the government party. These initiatives presented industrial policy as an opportunity to continue the transformation of society in a socialist spirit, reaching beyond welfare objectives. The Rehn-Meidner principles had offered productivity and wages as the reward of mobility, at the expense of local unemployment. This conception of things was gradually rejected as more emphasis came to be placed on the employees' influence inside the firm and less on the important option to move—to other firms, other industries, and other regions. In Hirschman's terminology, exit yielded to voice, both in the reformers' view of the labor market and in actuality.[7]

As business closures multiplied under the impact of structural change and of mergers and increasing industrial concentration, the reluctance of workers to move seemed to grow. Jobs available in other parts of the country were turned down. In the North, which was most severely hit by structural unemployment, the new slogan was "we ain't quitting." In such circumstances, unemployment figures were bound to rise. The hopes for a magic cure fastened on industrial policy. For a few years at the end of the 1960s it held the center court in Swedish politics. A Ministry of Industry was created in 1968 and assumed responsibility for the management of state-owned industries, the semipublic nuclear program, research and development in general, and industrial reorganization. A council for industrial policy, with business and labor representation, was to advise on policy and supervise numerous studies of ailing industries. A technological development board (STU) was set up to supervise and promote research and development. One public development corporation was created to engage in product innovation (SUAB), and another for the launching of industries in depressed areas (SVETAB). A powerful agency for the protection of the environment scored relatively quick results, and a new agency for consumer protection was established.

The new moves threw government agencies into frenzied activity, but their administrators were lacking in business experience. A number of embarrassing incidents were to haunt the publicly owned industries. The Ministry of Industry was anxious to show

---

[7] Albert O. Hirschman, *Exit, Voice and Loyalty* (Cambridge, Mass.: Harvard University Press, 1970).

that the state could run business firms as well as anyone else, but this turned out not to be true. In some cases, government intervention was justified as a way of contributing to workable competition, but sustained losses occurred too often for comfort. In the Durox case, for example, the government ventured into the manufacture of building materials but had to close down in 1969 after four unhappy years and much publicized bungling. Much was also made of a new delivery truck, the manufacture of which was to bring employment and prosperity to a declining industrial community, but this project had to be ignominiously abandoned.

A few years later, most of the state industries were incorporated in a central holding company, Statsföretag AB, which turned into the seventh largest corporate group in Sweden (after the cooperatives, Volvo, the Johnson group, SKF, Saab-Scania, and ASEA). After a groping start, Statsföretag was eventually given efficient leadership and gained a solid reputation in the business community in spite of the handicaps of some of its companies. The creation of Statsföretag kept the humdrum problems of everyday management out of the ministry and the cabinet. It may even have performed too well. In 1974 and 1975, there were rumors that the ministry was finding the group too businesslike and not sufficiently mindful of the desire for a social profile. When industrial policy became a liability, it disappeared from the political agenda almost as fast as it had appeared, but the substantive problems and the new agencies remained.

Old Business and New

The makers of industrial policy in the 1960s were anxious to cope with the exciting challenges in new and dynamic sectors, to lead the way in atomic energy, aerospace, and computers, but they were constantly dragged down by the need to attend to the losers at the other end of the spectrum. There are basic asymmetries in economic life, as we all know, and by and large the problems of contraction are much worse than those of expansion.

In Sweden, as elsewhere in Europe, a merger wave began in the 1960s and is still increasing industrial concentration. For many communities this has meant a steady pressure of stagnation and a besetting concern with survival. Industrial reorganization has in many cases reduced the number of firms to a small fraction of what it was a decade ago. Even in industries that are still expanding, smaller and closely held companies are often up for sale. Inheritance taxes have hit this category of business hardest. Corporate taxation is fairly soft in Sweden, where depreciation allowances are generous, but the transfer of a family business from one generation to another is difficult. The migration of industrialists who have sold their companies and retired to the outskirts of Geneva or some other tax haven has become familiar. Related to this is an "hour-glass" size distribution of industrial firms, which has resulted from the attrition of medium-sized firms. New large firms used to arise from among those of medium-size, but this middle category is now decimated by purchases and mergers with larger companies.

In about 1970 the thrust of political controversy shifted. Since then, the internal organization and policies of private enterprise have been scrutinized and modified by legislation or control in order to promote industrial democracy and job security.

"Codetermination" in the sense of labor participation in management had traditionally been opposed by the unions, who objected to the blurring of the lines of demarcation between employers and employees. In accordance with the 1938 agreement already referred to, most issues in industrial relations had been settled by negotiation between the organizations of the employers and the unions. Both sides were anxious to minimize government intervention and legislation. In the 1960s, agreement was reached on the creation of company committees to provide channels of information and consultation. In the early 1970s, the government suggested the appointment of representatives of the state to the boards of all private companies. Such representatives had already been put on the boards of the banks and insurance companies, and the suggestion that the practice be extended to industry was in line with the avowed objective of shifting the "power" over private companies to the public sector. Neither the companies nor the unions saw this proposal as a contribution to industrial democracy. They accepted, however, legislation providing for employee representation on boards of companies with more than 100 employees.

The opposition of the business community was automatic and instinctive, but in the end businessmen accepted the measure in stride. New questions have been raised, however, by a proposal to create a body of publicly employed consultants to assist inexperienced employee representatives on the boards. Critics such as the Federation of Industries and the employers' organizations see this as a measure more apt to enhance public control than to promote industrial democracy.

In 1974, controversial job-security legislation was passed, making it more difficult for employees to be fired and increasing the employers' liabilities toward employees. Inevitably, some companies will seek to avoid regular employment contracts. However, big companies tended to see the law as a ratification of existing personnel policies, and apprehensions were at first expressed mostly by small firms and academic economists. By late 1975, the Federation of Labor was worrying about the prospect that employees would convert themselves into firms, signing ordinary contracts for services rather than employment contracts.

New legislation also obliges companies receiving development grants and subsidies to hire a certain proportion of their employees from categories of labor not easily placed—in the first place, women, but also older and physically handicapped people. In practice this entails close cooperation between the companies and the local branches of the manpower board that have discretion in enforcing the rule. The rule must be seen in relation to the attempt by the unions and the government to reduce wage disparities and incentives both by taxation and before tax. In the name of equality, predictable employment problems have thus been created for the groups that the legislation intended to favor.

Heated arguments are currently being exchanged over the latest issue in the field of industrial relations—no less than the right of employers to organize work and to hire and fire. This right has already been circumscribed considerably and is now being directly contested. At present, controversies arising from decisions of this kind are referred to labor courts, but until they have been resolved the employers' decisions are respected. It is now proposed to reverse this privilege—that is, to accept the union's position until the matter is resolved, and to make all aspects of work organization subject to negotiation. Both the practical and the symbolic importance of this proposal is considerable, and its possible extension to the public sector raises basic issues about the conflict between employee influence and political democracy.

The International Nexus. One-half of Swedish industrial output is exported, and in the technologically advanced sectors the share is closer to two-thirds. Moreover, most of the large Swedish companies are multinationals, and in recent decades their operations abroad have grown much faster than their operations in Sweden. This international dependence has constrained Swedish economic policy in more ways than one. The traditional free-trade policy has kept international competition vigorous in domestic markets, which may explain the relative lack of political interest in legislation against restraint of trade and competition. Monetary policy labors under heavy influence from international credit markets. In fiscal matters, the international nexus has become increasingly important. Already the high level of taxation in Sweden has occasioned a steady trickle of funds and labor out of the country at the very time when a shortage of unskilled labor has attracted a growing number of immigrants from Southern Europe.

The suspicions recently aroused, in Sweden as in all other countries, against multinational companies have so far resulted in a tightening of the supervision of Swedish investments abroad. Companies wishing to finance overseas operations from Sweden are subject to control by the Bank of Sweden, and when they operate in less developed countries their wage policies and industrial relations are supposed to be examined by a special body. How far the Swedish economy can step out of line with other mixed economies is difficult to say, but international dependence clearly sets some limits.

A New Industrial Society?

The list of restrictions that have recently been imposed on private enterprise could have been made much longer. The result is that one of the serious problems that management now faces is the need to keep track of all the regulations and to supply, at its own expense, the information that the regulatory agencies demand.

The climate of opinion and public policy in Sweden in the last decade confirms Schumpeter's prediction, in *Capitalism, Socialism and Democracy*, that private enterprise would provoke distrust in democratic societies.[8] It is too early to say how private enterprise will perform under the new conditions. The loss of flexibility and freedom of maneuvering may seem ominous, and it is of course possible that the outcome will be costly. So far, however, there has been no noticeable weakening of Swedish industrial performance. The Swedish wage level is the second highest in the world, but industrial productivity has been steadily rising. It is true that there has been some slowdown in the 1970s, but it would be rash to ascribe this to the new policies.

The chief assets of Swedish industry are no longer the natural resources on which it once was founded. Management, technology, and industrial relations are the important assets today. The task of

---

[8] Joseph A. Schumpeter, *Capitalism, Socialism and Democracy* (New York: Harper, 1942).

reconciling the many and conflicting interests that converge on a company is becoming an increasingly difficult managerial function—but there is no reason to think that it cannot be mastered. No one could really contemplate the indefinite continuation of the traditional pattern of industrial organization, with its strict hierarchies, its status distinctions, and its communications barriers. In an increasingly egalitarian society, the old pattern was bound to become an anomaly.

It could well be argued that legislation is not the best instrument in the search for new patterns of organization. The most significant changes in the style and conduct of Swedish enterprise in the postwar period have come about spontaneously, such as the switch to a near-universal use of informal rather than formal modes of address in speech, regardless of status and function. Sweden has simply become a consensus society where no organization, be it in industry or even in the military, can be operated without broad participation.

A disruptive note in Swedish industrial policy has been the persistent hounding of private business by the governing party and the mass media. Industrialists, who not long ago were considered the founders of Swedish prosperity, are now often seen as robber barons, exploiters of labor, purveyors of shoddy wares, and despoilers of the environment. The press, television, and many politicians, including an occasional cabinet minister, inveigh against companies, big or small, as enemies of the public interest. There has been much talk about a crisis of confidence in the relationship between the state and business, and one member of the *Riksdag* even felt impelled to remind his colleagues that "businessmen are human beings too, especially small and medium-sized ones." [9]

But the mood among young executives is not one of despondency. On the contrary, one often encounters an almost exuberant pride among managers who feel capable of meeting their new responsibilities toward all interested parties—employees, customers, stockholders, and community—without renouncing their competitive strength. Such men tend to be impatient with the perennial grumbling about the new rules of the game on the part of the trade associations and other business organizations, which seem to many of the young to be fighting a sterile rearguard action against the course of history.

The Political Response. If the business community is ambivalent, the same is true of the politicians. Although the Social Democratic party has initiated a new phase of socioeconomic reform that aims at

---

[9] *Dagens Nyheter*, December 19, 1971.

a profound reorganization of economic life, it has not met a concerted opposition. In the 1950s and 1960s, the great increases in welfare spending and tax levies were rarely wholeheartedly opposed by other political parties, who seemed to suspect that it would be politically unpopular to block reforms and immoral to suggest tax cuts without indicating any expenditure cuts. In the 1970s, tax fatigue had certainly set in, but there has been no Swedish counterpart to Glistrup's tax revolt in Denmark or to similar manifestations in Norway. The most common explanation for the lack of such a revolt is that, never having been in power, the traditional opposition parties have not yet been discredited by any failure to live up to their own claims. They have thus retained their credibility and their ability to channel discontent into the current political machinery. It may be equally important that the Common Market issue was never allowed to fragment political life in Sweden, so that the old parties emerged unscathed from a period that left Danish and, to a lesser extent, Norwegian politics in shambles.

Tax fatigue is undoubtedly a principal reason why the Swedish Social Democrats have turned to the issue of industrial democracy, where reforms have the great advantage of not costing any money, at any rate not to the treasury. And in this area, too, the torrent of new laws and regulations has in the end been accepted by the other political parties, including those that originally opposed them. There is practically no talk of revoking the innovations of recent years in the event of a change in government.

Interestingly enough, opinion polls have shown politicians in all parties to be consistently to the left of their electors, and every party seems to concentrate its efforts most heavily on the battle on its left front. The conservatives—in Sweden appropriately called the Moderate party—have been the most outspoken critics of recent policy trends and are the only ones to praise the virtues of private enterprise with much conviction. The Center party, which in the 1970s has emerged as the chief opposition, has an electoral base that overlaps with that of the Social Democrats and is deeply committed to decentralization and regional development. In spite of its role as champion of small business, it is not hampered by any economic philosophy that would oppose it to market regulation or extensive subsidization. The Liberal party, which has long been based on a precarious alliance of intellectuals, religious dissenters, teetotallers, and other minorities, has dwindled in recent years. Approached by the Social Democrats in 1974, it lent its support to the government's stabilization policy in return for various concessions in the fiscal field. The impression that the party has moved to the left of its traditional voters was confirmed by the secretary of the party when he remarked that the party was in the course of "changing its base of support." The change has created some doubt as to whether the three nonsocialist parties could ever form a government, even if they were in 1976 to gain slightly more than the 50 percent of the vote that they won in the election of 1973.[10]

The Communists have supported all measures that seemed directed against business and its owners, only lamenting that they did not go far enough. They have carefully refrained from joining the opposition on the right of the Social Democrats in order to bring the government down.

Thus, even the new policies of industrial regulation that were opposed at the time of their introduction tend to appear irreversible. This is not to say that, if the long period of Social Democratic rule were to end before it had lasted half a century, there would not be significant change. The spirit and style of government policy would undoubtedly become less aggressive toward business than it has been under the Social Democrats, and attempts would be made to improve the terms on which small and medium-sized enterprise is carried on. But there would be no real turning back toward laissez-faire.

---

[10] For more recent developments in the changing fortunes of the Social Democrats and the three nonsocialist parties, see pp. 115-29 in this volume.

9

CURRENT PROBLEMS OF SCANDINAVIAN TRADE UNIONISM

Walter Galenson

The Setting

It is difficult to deal with the problems of trade unionism in Denmark, Norway, and Sweden within the confines of a single brief paper. There are very substantial political and economic differences among these countries and the differences inevitably affect the trade unions. While some common themes, attributable in considerable measure to intra-Scandinavian cooperation and borrowing, unite them, other problems and interests are specific to the individual countries.[1]

The Economic Context. The economic developments against which the current situation in the Scandinavian labor market must be viewed have been quite favorable, on the whole. A few salient indicators are presented in Table 9–1. West Germany, which, according to the Organization for Economic Cooperation and Development (OECD), grew faster than any other European country in the period 1963–72, and the United Kingdom, which grew more slowly than any other, are included for purposes of comparison. Denmark and Norway enjoyed relatively high rates of GDP growth for the period 1963–72, even in comparison with West Germany, while Sweden lagged somewhat behind. The relatively low Swedish rate of growth for the

[1] This paper is based upon interviews conducted in Scandinavia during the fall of 1974, and a reading of the relevant literature. I am greatly indebted to the American-Scandinavian Foundation for financial assistance that made a visit to Scandinavia possible and to my host organization, the Research Section on Postwar History at the University of Göteborg. I owe a particular debt of gratitude to the director of the Research Section, Dr. Bernt Schiller, who helped make my stay pleasant as well as intellectually stimulating. Those who were kind enough to answer my questions are too numerous to name individually. I would like to thank them collectively for their time and their hospitality.

Table 9–1
GROWTH RATES OF SELECTED ECONOMIC INDICATORS FOR SCANDINAVIA, WEST GERMANY, AND UNITED KINGDOM, 1963–72
(in average annual percentage increases)

	Denmark	Norway	Sweden	West Germany	United Kingdom
Real GDP [a]	4.99	4.69	3.64	4.61	2.60
Consumer prices [b]	6.07	5.36	4.45	3.31	5.21
Money wages [c]	11.39	8.93	9.32	8.36	8.54
Real wages [d]	4.99	3.39	4.69	4.84	3.13

[a] The original data are in fixed prices at purchasers' values.

[b] Includes all consumer commodities.

[c] For Denmark, hourly earnings in industry; for Norway and Sweden, hourly earnings in manufacturing and mining; for West Germany, hourly earnings in manufacturing; for the United Kingdom, weekly earnings in manufacturing.

[d] Money wages deflated by the consumer price index.

Source: Calculated from OECD, *Main Economic Indicators*, Paris, *passim;* United Nations, *Yearbook of National Account Statistics, 1972*, New York, *passim;* United Nations, *Statistical Yearbook, 1973*, New York, *passim.*

decade was due in considerable measure to the experience of 1971 and 1972, when real national product rose at an average annual rate of little over 1 percent; for the rest of the decade, Sweden did as well as its Scandinavian neighbors.

Denmark had a high rate of consumer price increases during the period, which contributed to its persistent balance-of-payments weakness. Whether the correlative increase in money wages was cause or effect is difficult to determine. Suffice it to say that repeated efforts to develop an incomes policy did not prove particularly effective.[2] Real wages rose at a satisfactory rate, but since the tax burden was increasing, higher wages did not automatically produce an improvement in the standard of living. The Norwegian performance, while better than the Danish, nevertheless necessitated several instances of ad hoc government intervention in the collective bargaining process.[3] The Swedish price record was the best of the three. Money wages

[2] See Lloyd Ulman and Robert J. Flanagan, *Wage Restraint* (Berkeley: University of California Press, 1971), pp. 116-46.

[3] There is no good description in English of the Norwegian experience for the entire decade. In Norwegian, see the so-called Skåneland Report: *Norges Offentlige Utredningar*, 1973:36, June 22, 1973.

Table 9–2

GROWTH RATES OF SELECTED ECONOMIC INDICATORS
FOR DENMARK, NORWAY, AND SWEDEN, 1973 AND 1974
(in annual percentage increases)

	Denmark	Norway	Sweden
Real GDP			
1973	3.9	3.7	3.3
1974	1.5	4.0	3.0
Consumer Prices			
1973	9.3	7.0	6.1
1974	15.0	10.0	13.8
Money Wages			
1973	18.7[a]	10.7[b]	8.4[a]
1974	22.8[a]	17.7[b]	11.0[a]

[a] Hourly earnings of wage earners in mining and manufacturing.

[b] Hourly earnings of males in manufacturing.

Source: OECD, *Main Economic Indicators*, Paris, March 1975; the 1974 real GDP figures are estimates of the OECD Secretariat.

rose quite rapidly, but substantial productivity gains prevented rising unit labor costs from exerting undue pressure on prices.[4]

The Scandinavian nations, heavily involved in international trade, could hardly escape the inflation that began in 1973. As Table 9–2 indicates, Denmark had the worst price record in both 1973 and 1974, although Sweden was not far behind in 1974. Both Norway and Sweden did fairly well in real national product growth in these two years, but the Danish growth rate dropped sharply in 1974. These data clearly reflect the increasing economic difficulties that the Danes have had to contend with in the last few years.

Inflation has presented some major problems for the Scandinavian trade unions, particularly those in Denmark. The unions are under government pressure to accept formal incomes policies but have not been prepared to limit their freedom of action. The pressure comes not only from the Social Democratic parties with which the unions are closely allied, but to some extent from the labor

---

[4] See Ulman and Flanagan, *Wage Restraint*, pp. 88-115, and Erik Lundberg, "Income Policy Issues in Sweden," in Walter Galenson (editor), *Incomes Policy: What Can We Learn from Europe* (Ithaca: Cornell University Press, 1973), pp. 41-58.

market as well. Throughout the 1960s Denmark had a level of unemployment that was relatively high by European standards. It began to rise in 1971, shot up to almost 5 percent in the summer of 1974, and may well have gone higher in 1975. This was the major factor behind the March 1975 decision of the Social Democratic government to break a deadlock in collective bargaining simply by extending the previous agreement through legislation. One of the complicating factors for the Danish labor movement is that unemployment is concentrated among the unskilled and semiskilled, who belong to a single general workers' union that includes 28 percent of total union membership. Unemployment, in general, is low among the skilled workers, which leads to disagreement on appropriate policy within the labor movement.

Sweden's unemployment rate has been lower than Denmark's, but it did become a political issue in 1972 and 1973, when it reached 2 percent. Although it fell to 1.6 percent in 1975, white-collar employees have had greater difficulty finding jobs recently than blue-collar workers, and the employment outlook for university graduates is the worst of all.

The Norwegian unemployment rate has been low for many years, rarely exceeding 1 percent. Nevertheless, problems might well have developed by now were it not for an unexpected external event—the oil boom. The implications of the North Sea oil discoveries are not yet entirely clear, but they have aroused intense interest. The Norwegian Federation of Labor has established an oil secretariat to represent trade union interests in this matter. Norway is expected to have a surplus of oil and natural gas for export in 1975, and 1981 production is projected at 50 million tons of oil and 45 to 50 billion cubic meters of gas, most of which will be exported. It is estimated that government revenue from taxes and royalties may rise to an annual level of N. kr. 10 to 15 billion annually by 1980 (at 1974 prices). The Norwegian government is currently running a substantial deficit in the balance of payments in anticipation of future oil exports.

At the close of 1974, only about 15,000 Norwegian workers, some 1 percent of the labor force, were engaged in directly petroleum-related activities, mainly in the fabrication of oil platforms. This figure may double by 1980. It is difficult to estimate the employment effects of the greater availability of oil, inasmuch as they depend in large measure on whether the oil is exported or used domestically in new industries. In any event, the outlook is for a continuing high demand for labor.

Up to the end of the present decade, it may be concluded, barring a further deterioration in international trade, the supply of labor will probably be in balance with the demand in Norway and Sweden, and perhaps in continuing surplus in Denmark. But there is not likely to be a surplus of *skilled* blue-collar workers even in Denmark, so that, even if the unions were to agree to pursue policies of wage restraint, these might not be easy to effectuate.

Specific manpower shortages, if there are any, could be eased by importing labor, but the unions are opposed to any increase in the number of foreign workers. There were 20,000 foreign workers in Norway in 1972, 8,000 of them from other Scandinavian countries, and while the number may have increased since then, now only specialists in oil platform construction are admitted, and these only for limited periods of time. Sweden has many more foreign workers, 222,000 in 1973, some 5.6 percent of the labor force (141,000 from the rest of Scandinavia, including 110,000 Finns). As a result of legislation demanded by the unions, the number of foreign workers is declining. There were 36,000 non-Scandinavian foreigners working in Denmark in 1973, though current unemployment may tend to reduce this number.

Trade Union Organization. Before the major issues that confront Scandinavian unions can be examined, a brief look at their strength is in order. Table 9–3 contains some relevant membership data. Scandinavian employees are among the most highly organized in the world. Not only are virtually all blue-collar workers in unions, but a large proportion of white-collar and professional employees are organized as well. Top civil servants, military officers, and physicians, among others, engage in collective bargaining.

Swedish labor organization is legendary. The Swedish Federation of Labor has within its ranks 45 percent of the labor force. The Salaried Employees' Federation (TCO) represents white-collar personnel, while the Swedish Federation of Professional Associations (SACO) speaks for a variety of professional groups. There are no equivalents of TCO and SACO in Norway, and to the extent that white-collar groups there are organized, they are mainly organized within the Norwegian Federation of Labor. Denmark holds an intermediate position: the Danish Federation of Labor has a good many white-collar members, but there is also an independent Civil Service and Salaried Employees' Organization (FTF) and a smaller central union of professionals.

Table 9–3
MEMBERSHIP IN SCANDINAVIAN TRADE UNIONS

	Membership (in thousands)	Percentage of Labor Force[a]
Denmark		
Danish Federation of Labor, January 1974	930	39
Civil Service and Salaried Employees' Organization, 1974	230	10
Other, 1974	140	6
Total	1,300	55
Norway		
Norwegian Federation of Labor, December 1972	604	37
Other, 1972	193	11
Total	797	48
Sweden		
Swedish Federation of Labor, December 1972	1,772	45
Salaried Employees' Federation, December 1972	805	20
Swedish Federation of Professional Associations, December 1972	122	3
Other, December 1972	42	1
Total	2,741	69

[a] The base of the percentage calculation is the civilian labor force, derived from OECD publications.

Source: For Denmark, *Danish Labour News,* June 1974, and Det Danske Selskab, *Employers and Workers in Denmark,* 1974, pp. 11-13; for Norway, *Statistisk Årbok* [Statistical yearbook], 1973, p. 53; for Sweden, *Statistisk Årsbok* [Statistical yearbook], 1973, p. 239.

Simply on the basis of their size, Scandinavian trade unions should be of great political importance. However, divided loyalties complicate the picture. The blue-collar unions in all three countries have been aligned exclusively with Social Democratic parties and indeed used to be the main source of political funding for these parties. (Recent legislation providing for campaign funding by the state has reduced their importance in this respect.) While the blue-collar socialist alliance is still firm, there may be trouble ahead because of the growing strength of the various leftist groups that reject moderate social democracy. It may be a straw in the wind that the large Danish General Workers' Union voted in 1974, for the first time in its history, to support all the "labor parties," including the Communist party, in proportion to their parliamentary strength.[5] The Norwegian Federation of Labor continues to support the Labor (Socialist) party, but there is within it a bloc that favors assistance to the far left and an even stronger one, consisting mainly of civil servants and white-collar workers, that would prefer political neutrality.

In Sweden, where the Social Democratic party is in a stronger relative position than its Danish and Norwegian counterparts, there has apparently been no break in the solidarity of the Federation of Labor and the Social Democrats. One of the reasons is that those who might tend to oppose continuation of this arrangement are organized in other unions. TCO and SACO are politically neutral, as are similar but smaller bodies in the other Scandinavian countries.

A debate at the last congress of the Norwegian Federation of Labor, held in 1973, suggests that the political stance of the trade unions is a lively issue in Norway. A left-inspired resolution was introduced, proposing the insertion in the Federation of Labor constitution of a specific obligation to work for "the development of a socialist society." This was opposed by the national leadership on the ground that "we have all political views represented in LO [the Federation of Labor]. If we want to gain members in trade and in offices, we should not approve a purpose that would drive many away from us." A representative of the civil servants pointed out, "we are not only trying to organize socialists and communists. The labor movement is open to all. . . . The Norwegian Civil Service Union is a young organization, but it has 30,000 members. Many of these are people who in the past were more or less opposed to unionism. Many of them have important functions in our society, and we should not alienate them."[6] The resolution was voted down in deference to the substantial bloc of nonsocialists within the Norwegian Federation of Labor, but it will undoubtedly come up again.

It would be premature to predict any imminent collapse of the coalition between the Federations of Labor and the Social Democrats that has prevailed in Denmark, Norway, and Sweden since the beginning of the century. Nevertheless, various forces are working toward

---

[5] The Danish Federation of Labor, however, would have to amend its constitution to support parties other than the Social Democrats, and this does not seem likely for the present.

[6] Landsorganisasjonen i Norge, Protokoll fra den 23. ordinaere kongress [Proceedings of the 23rd regular congress], 1973, pp. 56-60.

a possible realignment, not least the political decline of social democracy. Now that the Danish Social Democratic party has only about one-quarter of the seats in parliament, while the Norwegian and Swedish parties have had to rely on the support of an assortment of left-wing extremists, some unions may begin to find exclusive reliance on the Social Democrats less attractive. After World War II, the late Harold Laski and other Europeans predicted confidently that American unionism, in its political orientation, would inevitably move toward the European model. It is not inconceivable that, at least in Scandinavia, the trend will be in the opposite direction.

Wages and Taxes

Scandinavian trade unions are still concerned primarily with the traditional union subjects of wages, hours, and other conditions of labor, but some new problems have emerged as a consequence of inflation, and these are tending to modify well-established practices. In particular, the high degree of organization among all social groups is tending to transform wage bargaining into income determination for the entire nation.

Scandinavian tax policies are an important part of the problem. The Scandinavian countries stand out among the noncommunist nations of the world as those in which the government takes the largest share of national income. OECD data show that in 1971, current public sector revenue as a percentage of GDP was 44.6 in Denmark, 47.3 in Norway, and 49.1 in Sweden. The corresponding figures for major OECD nations were: West Germany, 38.4 percent; United Kingdom, 38.6 percent; and United States, 30.5 percent.[7]

The rapidly growing government share of total income has led to a taxpayers' revolt in Denmark and Norway, with serious political repercussions. In Sweden the voters have not yet manifested concern about this problem at the polls. Indeed, though the Swedish nonsocialist parties favor tax reduction, the municipalities they control tend to raise taxes along with the municipalities controlled by the socialists. However, high marginal income tax rates have affected collective bargaining in Sweden as elsewhere.

The precise nature of the problem can best be clarified by a few examples. The average Swedish blue-collar worker earned about Sw. kr. 35,000 per annum in 1974, while the average white-collar income was Sw. kr. 45,000. Let us assume that the rate of inflation

---

[7] OECD, *Economic Surveys, Norway*, March 1974, Appendix.

Table 9–4
AVERAGE AND MARGINAL INCOME TAX RATES
IN SWEDEN, 1974

Taxable Income (in Swedish kroner)	Average Tax Rate (in percentages)	Marginal Tax Rate (in percentages)
1– 15,000	7	32.5
15– 20,000	12	32.5
20– 25,000	17	37.5
25– 30,000	22	42.5
30– 40,000	28	47.5 [a]
40– 45,000	33	53.5 [a]
45– 50,000	38	58.5
50– 60,000	38	63.5
60– 65,000	38	63.5
65– 70,000	43	63.5
70–100,000	48	73.5 [b]
100–150,000	52	77.5
150,000 and over	56	81.5 [c]

[a] The marginal tax rate is 47.5 percent from Sw. kr. 30-35,000, and 53.5 percent from Sw. kr. 35-45,000.

[b] The marginal tax rate is 65.5 percent from Sw. kr. 70-75,000.

[c] The marginal tax rate is 77.5 percent up to Sw. kr. 155,000.

Source: Information supplied courtesy of the Salaried Employees' Federation.

is 10 percent and that the union target is to raise real *disposable* income by 5 percent. Given the prevailing (1974) marginal tax rate of 53.5 percent for the average blue-collar employee (see Table 9–4), money wages for blue-collar workers would have had to rise by 32 percent if the union were to achieve its goal.[8]

In fact, the settlement reached in April 1975 between the Swedish Federation of Labor and the Swedish Employers' Association (SAF) provided for a basic wage rise of 25.3 percent during the two-year period of 1975–76. The government reduced 1975 income taxes, and the Federation of Labor expected that with the anticipated

[8] The average tax rates in Table 9-4 are to be interpreted as meaning, for example, that if an employee earned between 40,000 and 45,000 kroner in 1974, he would pay 33 percent of it in income taxes. If the rates were unchanged in 1975, any *additional* earnings that put him in the 45-50,000 kroner bracket would be taxed at 58.5 percent, leaving him only 41.5 percent of the additional earnings after taxes.

rate of inflation, real disposable wages would rise by 3 percent in 1975. SAF pointed out, however, that the money wage increase plus fringe benefits would increase labor costs over the two-year period by between 31 and 35 percent and that real wages might not rise at all because of the higher rate of inflation produced by the increase in labor costs. This agreement provides a good illustration of the uncertainties in collective bargaining when prices and taxes are added to the money wage variable.

The average Norwegian industrial worker earning N. kr. 35,000 in 1972 had the following experience: his money wages rose by 9 percent but his real disposable income fell by 1 percent. However, he had the satisfaction of knowing that his employer paid an additional tax of 3.2 percent on his earnings.[9] Denmark has similarly high tax rates and an even higher rate of price inflation.

There is an obvious answer to the problem: adjust marginal tax rates so that disposable income can be raised without imposing money wage increases of a magnitude that threatens export possibilities. But implementation of this answer will not be an easy matter, especially inasmuch as socialist governments have welcomed the rise of the state's share in the national income and are reluctant to accept its remaining static, let alone its declining.

The Danish Social Democrats were the first to be forced to come to grips with the problem as a result of a major taxpayers' revolt. Indeed, many of their constituents were among the revolutionaries. The party's 1973 program contained the following statement on taxes:

> Enlargement of the contribution to the state should increase, also taking into consideration the fact that there is a place for a reasonable increase in private consumption. . . . The income of the state sector has reached about half the national income, with personal income taxation contributing approximately 55 percent of total taxation. Our income tax system has gradually become overloaded. Unloading can be secured, within limits, through a change from income taxes to other forms of taxation. It must therefore be a principal aim of our tax policy to reform the income tax, which falls too heavily on average incomes, and which taxes marginal income too heavily as well. Unloading should take the form, *inter alia*, of stretching the tax brackets so that most taxpayers would have lower marginal rates on overtime work, for example.[10]

---

[9] Skåneland Report, p. 55.

[10] *Social Demokraterne Former Fremtiden* [The Social Democrats shape the future], pamphlet, 1973, p. 42.

In its 1975 budget, the Norwegian government proposed a reduction of between 5 and 10 percent in income taxes, which, it was estimated, would yield an increase of about 6 percent in private consumption. However, government expenditures were to increase as well, and the deficit was to be covered by foreign loans.[11] This sharp break with previous socialist policy was made easier by the expectation that oil revenues would soon be coming in. The Swedish government gave equal money rebates to all taxpayers in 1974 but raised payroll taxes to compensate for the loss of revenue.

Even if the socialists were persuaded that private consumption should increase relative to government expenditures, the precise manner in which the necessary tax adjustment should be made would provide a further complication. Let me take the case of Sweden: The Swedish Federation of Labor advocates an income tax adjustment that yields greatest relief to people in the low income brackets. SACO argues for the reverse, on the ground that marginal tax rates are oppressive at the top.[12] TCO is somewhere in between. The Federation of Labor and TCO engage in discussions, and if they can reach agreement, in all probability the government will accept their solution. SACO may be consulted, but its influence is not great. Collective bargaining has thus become an integral part of fiscal policy.

The Norwegian Federation of Labor is also increasingly aware of the problem. In 1973, for the first time in its history, it urged a reduction in marginal tax rates. The vice-chairman rationalized the new policy as follows:

We face difficult alternatives in our national economy. The future perspective is such that plans for increasing the share of the state sector in the coming years will mean that there is room for an increase of real private consumption by active producers of about 1 percent per annum during the 1970's. This is substantially less than what we were getting in the 1960's. . . . This will necessitate a critical review of the programs that are proposed for raising the government share in various areas in the years ahead, so that the plans are brought into conformity with the economic means of the country.[13]

---

[11] *Dagens Nyheter* [Daily news] (Stockholm), October 8, 1974, p. 7.

[12] A Swedish professor—and there are very few of them, since most university teachers are in lower grades—earned Sw. kr. 95,000 in 1974, of which he retained about Sw. kr. 45,000 after taxes. His marginal tax was 73.5 percent on the first additional Sw. kr. 5,000 of earnings, and 77.5 percent thereafter. He did not have much incentive to moonlight.

[13] LO i Norge, *Protokoll, Kongress 1973* [Proceedings, 1973 congress], pp. 163-64.

Income Equalization. All of this ties in with another important theme in union circles, one that in Sweden goes under the name of the "solidaristic" wage policy. It was first enunciated there in 1936, and what it means is the reduction of income differentials—between agriculture and industry, between industry and services, among industries, within individual industries, between the sexes—in order to bring about a more egalitarian society.[14]

Until the early 1960s, the leveling process was frustrated by a variety of factors, but for the past decade a good deal of wage compression has occurred. The hourly earnings of women in manufacturing as a percentage of male earnings rose from 69 percent in 1960 to 80 percent in 1970.[15] The general index used in Sweden is the so-called maximum equalization coefficient, which is the ratio of (1) the amount of income that must be transferred from the better- to the worse-off for everyone within a particular sector to have the same income to (2) the total sum of sector income, multiplied by 100. The coefficient index (1951 = 100) for the Federation of Labor-SAF sector was 101 in 1960, 74 in 1966, and 49 in 1972.[16] Similar changes occurred within the TCO and SACO sectors as well; TCO has adopted the same policy in principle, but in the case of SACO, external forces, including the loss of a strike in which the maintenance of pre-existing income advantages was a major factor, appear responsible for the change.

Much the same thing has occurred in Denmark and Norway. Some recent calculations of estimated lifetime earnings of various occupational groups in Denmark, before and after taxes, are shown in Table 9–5. The premium for skill declined from 16.6 percent in 1958 to 11.5 percent in 1972, before taxes. The corresponding after-tax figures were 13.3 and 6.0 percent.

The Norwegians claim that their wage differentials are even smaller, in general, than those in Denmark and Sweden. For example, in the first quarter of 1974, the average wage of skilled metal workers was N. kr. 21.40 per hour; that of semiskilled workers in the same industry, N. kr. 19.94; and that of unskilled workers, N. kr. 19.08.[17] When asked why anyone bothers to learn a skilled trade for a wage premium of 12 percent (before taxes), a union official replied that

---

[14] For a good review of the history of this policy by one of its principal architects, see Rudolf Meidner, *Co-Ordination and Solidarity: An Approach to Wage Policy* (Stockholm: Prisma, 1974).

[15] Ibid., p. 55.

[16] Ibid., p. 59.

[17] Data from the Norwegian Metal Workers' Union.

Table 9–5

ESTIMATES OF LIFETIME EARNINGS IN DENMARK,
BY OCCUPATION, 1958 AND 1972

(in thousands of Danish kroner)

	1958	1972
Before Taxes		
Unskilled workers	675	2,418
Machine operatives	776	2,609
Skilled workers	787	2,697
Lawyers and economists in government service	1,263	4,305
Secondary school teachers	1,225	4,604
After Taxes		
Unskilled workers	555	1,671
Machine operatives	621	1,736
Skilled workers	629	1,773
Lawyers and economists in government service	906	2,385
Secondary school teachers	883	2,493

Source: Danish General Workers' Union.

skilled work was more interesting and rewarding to the individual. He asserted that the narrowing of the differential created no internal problems for the union.

It could be argued that market forces, rather than union policy, were responsible for the reduction of differentials. To determine this would require a careful econometric study over time, and it would be difficult to keep other factors constant. Scandinavians, however, are of the view that union policy was the major force contributing to this reduction, though they do not deny that the condition of the labor market influenced the ease with which the policy could be effectuated.

Income equalization has not always been achieved without protests from groups in the upper income brackets. SACO mounted a strike in 1971 in an attempt to arrest a decline in the relative real income of its members. After the state bargaining agency had announced its intention of locking out 3,000 officers in the armed services, the parliament stepped in with a compulsory settlement that gave the strikers considerably less than their demands. As a consequence of its losing the strike, SACO has also lost some of its influence, and it does not appear that professional men and women will be able to use the strike weapon again in the near future.

Scandinavia appears to have gone as far as any part of the world, communist or noncommunist, in equalizing incomes. This should be of great interest to those concerned with motivational psychology. It is not at all clear what sort of a utility function Scandinavians who undergo long periods of training are trying to maximize, unless one broadens the function to include aspects of life style that cannot be quantified. Serious skill shortages may eventually develop, but except in extraordinary cases, like that of the Norwegian shipyards where oil platforms are being built, businesses are managing well at present.

In fact, a major problem currently facing the labor market is the placement of university graduates in jobs appropriate to their training. Many graduates, particularly in Denmark, go directly onto the unemployment insurance rolls, on which they can remain for several years, receiving benefits equal to almost 90 percent of the average industrial wage. There has been a drop in university enrollment, particularly in Sweden, but simple scarcity of jobs rather than relative income decline appears to be the major cause.

Wage Drift. Wage and income equalization produces problems of its own. One of the most difficult is what Erik Lundberg has aptly termed the "compensation devil," the complex of forces that seeks to nullify equality.[18] Wage drift has been occurring in Scandinavia for many years, but it is particularly difficult to control under inflationary conditions. In some industries, national collective agreements merely determine minimum wage rates, in contrast with the U.S. practice of specifying the actual rates paid. Further bargaining by the local union and even by the individual employee determines effective wage rates. In addition, there is a substantial amount of incentive work in Scandinavian industry, a fact that also facilitates the upward drift.

Meidner argues that it would be "erroneous to interpret wage drift simply as the expression of the correction by market forces of wage agreements which do not conform to the market."[19] Income structure involves many elements of custom and tradition that are independent of immediate market forces; drift can represent an attempt to restore long-established norms.

There has scarcely been a year since World War II in which Swedish industrial wage drift fell below 3 percent.[20] Since 1953,

[18] Erik Lundberg, "Incomes Policy Issues in Sweden," in Galenson, *Incomes Policy*, p. 51.

[19] Meidner, *Co-Ordination and Solidarity*, p. 53.

[20] Ibid., p. 52.

wage drift has provided more than 50 percent of total wage increases for skilled workers in Copenhagen and somewhere between 45 and 50 percent for the unskilled.[21] In Norway, for the twenty-year period 1953–72, wage drift exceeded contract wage increases in thirteen years and fell below 3 percent in only four years.[22]

Wage drift adds greatly to the difficulty of effectuating incomes policies. In periods of stable prices it can be handled through the bargaining mechanism by allowing for it when new contracts are negotiated, but when prices are rising rapidly, it gives an added push to the wage-price spiral.

It might be argued that wage drift has some logic in Sweden during periods of inflation, inasmuch as wage indexing is not practiced there, but Denmark and Norway have had some form of indexed wages for many years. At the present time, Danish workers automatically receive two-thirds compensation for increases in living costs. The Norwegians accepted a 45 percent compensation agreement in 1973, but they have become somewhat chary about the entire concept of indexing. The following statement by Tor Aspengren, chairman of the Norwegian Federation of Labor, might be of interest to partisans of indexing:

> Full compensation for price increases is a common demand. The arguments in favor are fully understandable and acceptable viewed in isolation; nevertheless, it can be to our disadvantage taking into account the consequences of total wage increases upon the economy that we are part of. We do not have to look beyond the boundaries of the Nordic countries to find examples of the results of frequent wage compensation for price increases. . . . In a situation in which we are all interested in securing a lower ceiling on price increases, it does not seem that frequent compensation for price increases will solve our price problem. . . . The Secretariat believes that index regulation of wages must be subordinated to the main goals of the labor movement: securing real wage increases and social goods in line with production increases.[23]

A "solidaristic" wage policy with wage drift and price inflation is an ideal formula for stepping up the wage-price spiral. Even Meidner concedes that this combination constitutes "a severe limita-

---

[21] Dansk Arbejdsmandsforbund [Danish General Workers' Union], *Betaenkning fra Lavtlønsudvalget* [Report of the Low Wage Committee] (Copenhagen: The Union, 1971), p. 47.

[22] Skåneland Report, p. 34.

[23] LO i Norge, *Protokoll, Kongress 1973* [Proceedings, 1973 congress], pp. 103-4.

tion on the prospects for co-ordinated wage policies."[24] Moreover, there have been other (presumably unforeseen) labor market consequences of wage solidarity. Marginal firms that depend upon relatively low wages for their continued existence are being eliminated. The originators of the "solidaristic" policy have viewed this as a favorable development, on the ground that it leads to desirable change in industrial structure and higher productivity. The "active labor market policy," for which Sweden is famous, was designed to ensure prompt and painless reemployment for the displaced workers. But in practice ensuring reemployment has not proved to be simple. About 50,000 persons a year have been losing their jobs because of enterprise failures, of whom 7,000 to 8,000 disappear from the labor market, creating a hard core of unemployed. Moreover, a policy that puts the burden of mobility upon the weaker elements of society is beginning to lose favor.[25]

Proponents of wage and income solidarity are not discouraged, although they concede that the rough guidelines used in the past are no longer appropriate. As Arne Geijer, the chairman of the Swedish Federation of Labor, has put it, "there is no absolutely clear definition of those who should be considered low paid. One might simply define all employees whose wages are below the average for adult wage earners as low paid. But this would be an altogether too simplistic concept and would also reduce the possibility of making any strong efforts on behalf of the worst situated wage groups."[26]

The way out of this dilemma is to find criteria for further income equalization more precise and capable of gaining general acceptance. The Federation of Labor and TCO have set up a task force to develop a national job evaluation scheme. This is, of course, not a novel idea, nor is it peculiarly Swedish. Job evaluation originated in the United States; the Netherlands operated such a scheme on a national basis for some years, though it was eventually abandoned; and it has been the basis for Soviet industrial wage structure since 1960. What the Swedes have in mind, however, is something much more ambitious than what has been tried so far: nothing less than appraisal and evaluation of every job in society.

This will be an interesting experiment, if it materializes. Despite the claims of its proponents, job evaluation is an art rather than a science. Job qualities must be defined, weights assigned to them, and

---

[24] Meidner, *Co-Ordination and Solidarity*, p. 53.

[25] See, for example, Anders Leion, *Den Svenska Modellen* [The Swedish model] (Stockholm: Raben and Sjögren, 1974), p. 132.

[26] LO i Sverige, *Kongressprotokoll 1971* [Proceedings of the 1971 congress], p. 739.

each individual job rated accordingly. It is difficult to fit labor demand into the appraisal, and impossible without periodic review of the job classifications. The problem is complex even for fairly closely related jobs, such as those in a steel mill. Comparing the great numbers of different occupations beyond the confines of the factory is a task of breathtaking magnitude.

In the meantime, the propensity for wage drift is increasing. More than half the total wage increase in Scandinavia came in this form in 1974. One method of curbing it might be to reform the wage system itself. There has been a general trend toward the reduction of individual piece work, but often it has merely been replaced by group-incentive systems. In the Norwegian metal trades, for example, the proportion of workers on piece rates declined from 75 percent in 1965 to 30 percent in 1974. In their place, local agreements have been reached providing for semiannual wage bargaining on the basis of productivity change. Local unions have productivity secretaries with the right to examine company records in the event of disputes. The history of productivity bargaining in Great Britain would hardly lead one to the conclusion that this form of wage adjustment is less inflationary than ordinary piece work.

The so-called minimum wage trades in Scandinavia show no inclination to accept standard wages. In fact, the concept of local bargaining to supplement nationally determined minimum wages is reinforced by the anticentralization ideology currently in vogue. Drastic reform of the wage system does not seem to be a practical possibility at the present time.

Collective Bargaining

The Danes are by now thoroughly habituated to a system of national collective bargaining in which the government is an active partner. In 1973 there was a three-week strike involving 260,000 workers, the largest number involved in a strike since 1936. Government commitments on taxes and rents were central to the eventual solution. The Danish Federation of Labor and the Social Democratic party are agreed upon a "socially just" incomes policy, "which would involve all forms of income, equal absolute cost of living allowances to all groups, a reduction of income taxes with a compensating increase in indirect taxes, and an allocation to workers of a share in capital growth." [27] The Federation of Labor has taken the position, however,

---

[27] *Social demokratiets helhedsplan* [The Social Democratic plan], election pamphlet, August 1974.

that it will not become a party to a formal incomes policy agreement on any other basis.

The 1975 wage settlement in Denmark, reached against a background of substantial unemployment and a difficult balance-of-payments situation, exemplifies the dilemma faced by the unions and the government. The Federation of Labor either could not or would not sign an agreement consistent with the economic realities, whereupon a minority Social Democratic government, as its first act upon assuming power, imposed a wage settlement limiting increases to 2 percent a year in 1975 and 1976, though with cost-of-living allowances. As a concession to the unions, the method of calculating the cost-of-living adjustment, which is expected to constitute most of the 1975 wage increase, is to become more egalitarian than the method used in the past; as a result the real income of the higher paid is almost certain to drop. Collective bargaining in Denmark has thus become an integral part of macroeconomic policy, union reluctance notwithstanding.

Norway, too, has become accustomed to national bargaining with government participation. The 1973 wage reopening provides a good example of recent practice. An ad hoc committee, consisting of representatives of the government, the Federation of Labor, the Employers' Association, and organizations of fishermen and farmers, was established to see what could be done about wage restraint. The final agreement included (1) an increase of government subsidies by N. kr. 250 million a year to prevent public utility rate increases; (2) reduction of government budgetary expenditures by N. kr. 100 million for 1973; (3) increased government subsidies for consumer goods equal to N. kr. 175 million per consumer price index point increase if the index exceeded a specified amount by September 15, 1973. As a quid pro quo, the Federation of Labor agreed to accept only 45 percent compensation for the cost-of-living increase since the previous agreement. This solution was by no means universally liked by workers; the contract was accepted by the Metal Workers' Union, for example, by a majority of only 50.8 percent of those voting.

In 1972 the Norwegian *Storting* appointed a committee to look into the possibility of a permanent system of national group bargaining. The committee proposed the establishment of a Council for Price and Incomes Policy on which all the main interest groups would be represented in order "to reach agreement on mutually consistent goals and mutually acceptable employment of the *modus operandi* within the capabilities of each group." The real import of the proposal was to establish a mechanism that would facilitate advance commitment by government and the Federation of Labor on economic stabilization policies.

This was not an easy matter for the Federation of Labor. With the best will in the world, the enforcement of agreements in the presence of wage drift is difficult to accomplish. Although the Federation of Labor representative on the parliamentary committee agreed to the proposal, no formal action has been taken, and the outlook for acceptance is not good. In a recent interview, the vice-chairman of the Federation of Labor, Odd Höjdahl, agreed that the country needed a comprehensive stabilization policy, but concluded:

> The trade union movement must never give up its freedom of action in such an operation. It has not been my experience that cooperation went in the same way from one settlement to another—and it will certainly not be the same in the future. The forms of cooperation must be determined on the basis of the actual situation—and not through binding, long term rules. . . . The Committee proposed that many groups shall participate in the Council, and others have demanded representation. This implies a corresponding weakening of trade union influence on incomes and price policy.[28]

Sweden, unlike Denmark and Norway, has had a long tradition of collective bargaining without government intervention. The Swedish unions have always prided themselves on their willingness to accept a good deal of responsibility for the national economy. The following remarks of Arne Geijer, made when he was chairman of the Swedish Federation of Labor, exemplify this attitude:

> It is no trick for us to stand society on its head. It is easy, in a ticklish contract situation, to act so that society can no longer function. But such a conflict is no longer a conflict against employers, but rather against society and ourselves. At present, a serious labor market conflict affects all citizens and our own members to a greater extent than employers. LO alone now organizes every fifth Swede, between half and a third of all persons of working age. We are no longer a small social minority, society is to a large extent ourselves and our families. . . . I believe that however we act in the future we must, willingly or not, take the national economy into consideration. It will never happen in this country that there will be more to distribute than what is produced.[29]

However, future Swedish collective bargaining will have to involve the government if only because of the fiscal problems dis-

[28] *Arbeiderbladet* [Workers' daily] (Oslo), October 3, 1974, p. 1.
[29] LO i Sverige, *Kongressprotokoll 1971*, p. 745.

cussed above. What seems to be emerging is a system whereby the major bargaining partners, the Federation of Labor, the Salaried Employees' Federation, and the Swedish Employers' Association, will operate within a fiscal framework determined in advance of wage negotiations. On its side, the government, even under the present rules of the game, does not have complete freedom to determine tax policy. The Federation of Labor, if it wanted to frustrate government action with which it did not agree, could drive money wages up and endanger Sweden's export position. This is so obvious to all that the prospects for mutual accommodation are favorable. The Swedish Federation of Professional Associations may be the odd man out, but it is not in a position to do much.

In general, for the time being, Scandinavian trade unions are attempting to continue their drive for greater income equality without completely discarding their established collective bargaining systems. To do this, they are prepared to enter into comprehensive agreements with employers and government on an ad hoc basis. However, there are challenges on the horizon that may force change. The more affluent union members may not be willing to sacrifice their relative income advantage any longer and are already indicating at the polls that income redistribution through higher taxation does not meet with their approval. The radical left, which has been gaining strength among the younger workers, wants to move more rapidly toward utopian egalitarianism and is prepared to foment wildcat strikes at the local level to achieve its goals.

Scandinavian unions in the past have had at least as good a record as U.S. unions in honoring collective agreements. A representative of union leadership warned the Swedish Federation of Labor congress:

> How can the trade union movement operate and keep together if we do not accept signed agreements as legally binding and if there are no guarantees of peace during the contract term? . . . The difficulties that arise during the term of the agreement must in the first instance be solved through negotiations.[30]

But there are those on the left, not only in Sweden, who do not agree.

Non-Wage Issues

The Working Milieu. The Scandinavian trade unions have become interested in a number of nonwage issues of considerable impor-

[30] Ibid., p. 663.

tance to future job conditions. There has been growing concern with health and safety regulations, partly in response to the rapidity of technological change. The experiments with small group production, which have aroused a great deal of interest outside the borders of Scandinavia, owe more to employer than to union initiative, but the unions are actively involved in them.

A Workers' Protection Act, adopted in Sweden in 1973, contains detailed regulations governing all aspects of job conditions. Every firm with fifty or more employees must have a safety committee with broad powers to plan and supervise safety work in the enterprise. In addition, where there are five or more employees in an enterprise, the local union may appoint a safety delegate. If it is alleged that particular processes involve an immediate or serious danger to the life or health of an employee and if no remedy can be obtained through negotiation with the employer, the safety delegate may order suspension of the work on his own authority until a final decision by the Labor Inspectorate is secured. He is exempt from any damages resulting from the suspension order. The legislation came after complaints by the Swedish Federation of Labor that new materials and products, as well as production methods, were subjecting its members to excessive health risks and physical stress. The Swedish law goes further than protective legislation elsewhere in permitting employees to regulate their working environment.

Recent experiments with the rearrangement of production had their origin a decade ago at the Work Psychology Institute near Oslo and have since been conducted extensively in Scandinavia. Management tends to regard them as a means of reducing absenteeism and raising productivity by improving labor morale. Various factors are involved: autonomous working groups, job rotation, and rearrangement of work flow, among others. Replacement of individual with group incentive rates is often part of the schemes.

There are many anecdotal reports of the results, but thus far conclusive analyses are lacking. A recent report made by the Swedish Employers' Association on the experience of a Saab plant manufacturing trucks and auto engines is one of the more careful attempts at evaluation available.[31] The investigators found, on the positive side, that labor turnover dropped, particularly on chassis assembly work. Interest in job rotation increased if rotation resulted in higher pay. Rotation tended to reduce the incidence of physical ailments, par-

[31] Jan-Peder Norstedt and Stefan Aguren, *The Saab-Scania Report* (Stockholm: Swedish Employers' Association, 1973).

ticularly back complaints. Down time was reduced, productivity and quality rose. On the other hand, not all workers wanted to rotate their jobs, and problems arose within groups when individual members were not conforming to the group activity level. Saab plans to expand the scope of the new methods, having concluded that the additional costs in terms of transportation equipment and space were outweighed by the higher productivity.

The trade unions have been fairly cautious in their approach to these experiments. There is some concern that small working groups may become too isolated from other workers; that groups may become reluctant to retain or admit workers with reduced working capacity because of age or physical infirmity. However, the unions are by no means attempting to block the experiments. A representative of the Norwegian Federation of Labor recently stated that his organization was "convinced that cooperative projects and partly autonomous groups will be the right way to go to make the employees more interested in their own enterprises by giving them a greater influence over their own work situation." [32]

It is still too soon to predict the outcome of this effort to change the working milieu. One of the key questions, as yet unanswered, is whether small group production can be made economically competitive with traditional mass production. There will be more conclusive answers when some of the larger projects, such as the Volvo plant at Kalmar, come into full operation.

Industrial Democracy. For the past twenty-five years, there has been great interest in Scandinavia in the development of institutions affording employees increased authority over decision making in their enterprises. A good deal has already been done, and the movement has recently taken some new turns.

Various kinds of works councils are to be found in most Scandinavian enterprises. In Sweden a 1972 inquiry revealed that 34 percent of a sample of 1,662 enterprises had works councils and that the percentage rose to 82 percent for firms with over 1,000 employees. The rise in the incidence of councils was particularly rapid between 1968 and 1972. Many enterprise councils had subcommittees dealing with recreational facilities, food, education, problems of the aged and handicapped, personnel policy, and repair of plant facilities. [33]

---

[32] Statement of Ragnar Røberg Larsen, August 22, 1974 (mimeographed).

[33] Utvecklingsrådet for Samarbetsfrågor SAF. LO. TCO. [Committee for Problems of Cooperation, SAF, LO, TCO.], *Foretagsanpassning på samarbetsområdet* [En-

Under an agreement between SAF, the Federation of Labor, and TCO, works councils can be given the right to make final decisions in matters of worker welfare. The councils normally do not have jurisdiction over individual personnel questions, though they participate in determining general policy norms. They must be given advance notice of projected layoffs. Council members are compensated by the employer for time spent on council business.

The right of works councils to secure economic and financial information from the firm was extended by an agreement between SAF and the trade union federations reached in 1975. There is no limit, in principle, to the range of information that must be made available to employee representatives on the works council at their request, though there are three alternative methods through which the information may be transmitted. The works council can appoint a bipartite committee to study the information, or it can appoint a consultant from within the company; the most controversial provision gives the employee members of the works council the right to appoint an outside expert to assist them. Sensitive information must be kept secret, and both works council members and expert consultants may be held liable if outside disclosure results in financial loss to the enterprise. Swedish employers were not entirely happy with the agreement, particularly the provision regarding outside consultants, but the threat of legislation forced them to accept the union demands for additional information.

Several years ago, the Scandinavian trade unions decided that the consultative right of the works councils did not go far enough and that there should be greater worker participation in making decisions. As a consequence, in Denmark, beginning January 1, 1974, all companies with more than fifty employees were required to give their employees the right to elect two members to the corporate board of directors, under a plan similar to the system of general codetermination in Germany. A recent survey in the Danish metal trades indicates that 80 percent of all workers eligible to vote in board member elections have done so, which suggests a high degree of interest.[34]

A Norwegian law that went into effect on January 1, 1973, goes somewhat further. In firms with over fifty employees, the employees have the right to elect one-third, or at least two, of the members of the board of directors. Where there are more than two hundred employees, a new body, the corporate assembly, must be established.

terprise adaptation in cooperation] (Stockholm: Personnel Administration Council Press, 1972).

34 Statement to author by a Danish trade union official.

The assembly consists of at least twelve members, one-third elected by the employees and two-thirds by the stockholders. In turn, it elects the board of directors on the basis of proportional representation. It may examine all company books and records; it is the final authority in investment decisions of substantial size and in any projected change in operations that involves a reallocation of the labor force; it may stipulate the maximum amount of dividend distributions. The assembly is typically a larger body than the board of directors, and its purpose is to bring decision-making authority closer to the shop floor.

Experience with this law is still limited, but a few observations may be made. The fear that left-wing groups would be able to control board and assembly member selection has proved to be unfounded. Workers on occasion elect leftists as shop stewards, but not as board members. Employers report that employee board members have been cooperative and helpful. However, the corporate assembly has its drawbacks from their point of view, not because of any undue impact on policy, but rather because the assembly tends to delay vital decisions and to waste management time.[35]

Thus far, corporate assemblies have not attempted to control managerial salaries, though some worker members have tried to make them public. In only one reported case has there been an objection to planned dividends, but there is a belief in management circles that this is one of a number of issues on which there are likely to be clashes in the future. Shareholders still have the majority on both boards of directors and assemblies, but the demand for equal representation may not be far off.

The Swedish trade unions have been rather cautious about codetermination, for fear of blurring the functional line between management and unions. However, legislation came into force on April 1, 1973, affording employees (in companies with 100 or more employees) the right to appoint two members to boards of directors. Where more than 80 percent of the employees under collective agreement belong to the same local union, the union selects both board members. Otherwise, the two local unions with the highest number of employees appoint one each. Employee board members participate in all corporate decisions except those involving collective bargaining. The reaction of Swedish employers to this form of codetermination has been favorable thus far. According to SAF, which had refused to grant codetermination through collective bargaining, there

---

[35] Statement to author by an officer of the Norwegian Employers' Association.

has not been any major controversy as a consequence of employee representation.[36]

Although the Swedish codetermination law does not go as far as the law in Norway, another recent piece of Swedish legislation goes further. On July 1, 1974, an act concerning employment security came into effect. The basic rule now is that all dismissals must be based upon objective cause. There must be minimum notice of one month for younger employees, rising by specified steps to a minimum of six months for those over forty-five years of age, provided the employee worked the preceding six months or a total of twelve months during the preceding two years. During the notice period, the employee is entitled to full pay, less any earnings from other jobs, even if the employer has no work for him. Seasonal workers are entitled to a month's notice of intent not to reemploy for the next season.

An employer may discharge an employee for just cause, but if there is a dispute about the validity of the discharge, the employee is entitled to full pay until at least the end of the required notice period, and longer if the labor court which makes the final adjudication of the dispute so decides.

The notice period applies equally to dismissals and to layoffs due to lack of work. In such cases, moreover, a strict seniority rule has been imposed. An employee is entitled to an extra month of seniority for each month of employment beyond the age of forty-five, up to a maximum of sixty such months. There is a right to reemployment for one year after employment has ceased, also based on seniority. The trade union is entitled to advance notice of intended discharges or layoffs of between two weeks and one month, depending on the nature of the action.

At one fell swoop, Swedish employees gained the job security that U.S. workers achieved gradually through a quarter of a century of collective bargaining—and the Swedish legislation goes beyond customary U.S. practice in the notice requirement and the protection accorded older employees.

The law has just come into effect, and many problems of administration are certain to arise. Determination of the seniority unit, suitability of alternative work that the employer may offer, measurement of seniority, are just some of the issues that have been the subject of many controversies in the United States. There is also the potential payroll liability facing employers in case of sharp cyclical downturns. Employers may be reluctant to expand employ-

---

[36] Statement to author by an official of the Swedish Employers' Association.

ment and may attempt to substitute temporary for permanent workers to avoid the notice liability.

The Swedish Employers' Association had conceded the necessity of specifying just cause for individual discharges in 1964, but it opposed the new legislation as going too far too quickly. However, SAF and the Swedish Federation of Labor have established a joint committee to study the problems that may arise in applying the law.

Another piece of legislation is in the offing, the outcome of a 950-page report, *Democracy at the Workplace*, published early in 1975 by a state commission on which both employers and unions were represented. This huge document recommends, essentially, a reversal of the traditional right of the employer to direct and allocate work, subject to union challenge. Before making any final decisions on the organization of work, the choice or operation of machinery, or output norms, employers would be required to secure union approval. In the event of disagreement that cannot be resolved, the *union interpretation* would have to be adopted, with the employer having the right of appeal to the labor courts.

Appropriate legislation to this effect has not yet been drawn up, but it is expected that bills will be submitted to the legislature in the spring of 1976. Elections are scheduled for September of that year, and this reform could become a matter of political controversy, particularly if the Social Democratic government proposes some provisions favored by the union members of the commission but opposed by the employer representatives. If all were to go according to plan, the legislation would become effective in January 1977, and the Swedish trade unions would have achieved a degree of authority at the shop floor level unparalleled in contemporary systems of industrial relations.[37]

All of this legislation on industrial democracy, coming rapidly within the past few years, is bound to have a great impact on Scandinavian industrial practices. It marks a sharp break with the past, when the unions tended to secure their demands through collective bargaining rather than legislation, particularly in Sweden. The unions justify the new policy on the ground that employers are unwilling to bargain over managerial authority, and that they must thus resort to political means. Whatever the ultimate outcome for the conduct of labor relations, political power is being employed to a much greater degree than in the past to bring about change in the institutions of the labor market—and political action is a two-edged sword.

---

[37] Developments since this paper was written are discussed on pp. 115-29 of this volume.

Economic Democracy. As a general proposition, the Scandinavian labor movement does not favor direct nationalization of industry on the British model, where the state simply takes over enterprises by legislative fiat. But there are schemes already in effect and on the horizon that may achieve the same result indirectly.

Sweden has a generous national pension scheme financed by a tax on payrolls. The National Pension Insurance Fund, into which these contributions are paid, had an asset value of Sw. kr. 66.3 billion (about $15 billion) in January 1974 and is now a major source of industrial credit. The fund is administered in four separate units, three of which have invested their assets mainly in housing and in loans to industry and municipalities. The fourth fund, however, has been allocated Sw. kr. 500 million that can be used to buy corporate equities. This was done following a resolution at the 1971 Federation of Labor congress calling upon the government "to put before the parliament a proposal for changing the placement rules of the pension fund which would make it possible to invest in risk capital. . . ." [38]

Pursuant to this authority, the fund has recently purchased a 4.5 percent interest in Volvo for Sw. kr. 100 million. This is its largest single investment thus far. The present allotment will not buy a substantial share of Swedish industry, but parliament can always increase the limit. The chances are that it will do so. The pension fund is viewed, however, as somewhat remote from the worker's view of what constitutes an individual share in the progress of the economy. There is also some concern that expansion of the fund's holdings may lead to state capitalism. The Federation of Labor, therefore, has established a study committee with a mandate to bring a new scheme before its 1976 congress, and this is currently in preparation.

As a model, the Swedes are using a proposal that the Danish Social Democrats introduced into the Danish parliament in 1973, but which is in limbo because of the decline of Social Democratic political strength. It contains the following elements:

(1) An employees' investment and dividend fund would be set up, financed by a payroll tax that would begin at 0.5 percent per year and would increase by the same amount each year until it reached 5 percent, at which level it would remain. The fund's resources were to be invested in risk capital.

---

[38] LO i Sverige, *Kongressprotokoll 1971*, p. 877. For more detail on the LO position, see LO i Sverige, *Yttranden til Offentlig Myndighet* [Statement to the public authorities], 1971, p. 861.

(2) Every employee regardless of income would receive an equal share in the fund. Shares would be nonnegotiable, but after seven years an employee might draw on the value of his shares, plus interest and dividends. The share value could be withdrawn by the employee when he reached the age of sixty-seven, or by his heirs after his death; otherwise, it would be frozen for seven years.

(3) The enterprise would pay no taxes on its contribution. The employee would be taxed at a maximum of 35 percent if he withdrew his share after seven years, or 25 percent after twelve years.

(4) Two-thirds of the contribution made by each corporate enterprise would be invested in its own stock, while the rest would be used to purchase stock in other corporations.

(5) The investment fund would be governed by a council of sixty members, thirty-six appointed by unions and twenty-four by the ministry of labor. A parliamentary committee would exercise supervisory authority.

(6) The right to vote the corporate shares held by the fund would be exercised for each corporation by its own employees.

(7) It was estimated that if the scheme had gone into effect in 1974, fund holdings in 1981 would amount to 10 percent of all Danish share capital and, by 1988, to 35 percent. However, the fund was not to purchase more than 50 percent of the share capital of any company.[39]

The concept of employee stock ownership is by no means a new one. It had considerable vogue in the United States in the 1920s, it was De Gaulle's plan for France, and it interests the German Social Democrats. Trade unions have been concerned lest employees identify too closely with the employer. The Danish scheme is an ingenious attempt to combine economic democracy—that is, control of share voting by the employees of each company—with a national fund in which risk is diversified so that no employee need fear that setbacks suffered by his own company would impair the value of his holdings. The employee would not have to choose between the value of his shares and his wages. There is also an egalitarian appeal in the proposal of equal shares for all.

This scheme has been controversial, even within the labor movement. A trade union leader, in the course of an interview with the author, expressed the belief that the unpopularity of the proposal among workers contributed to the political decline of the Social Democratic party, since many interpreted it as just another tax. However,

[39] Ministry of Labor, Denmark, *Economic Democracy: Introduction and Bill,* pamphlet (Copenhagen: 1973).

the Danish Federation of Labor seems to be committed to the program, which will probably be reintroduced if the Social Democrats are in a position to promote it. In all likelihood, Sweden will pioneer this variety of economic democracy. Norwegian labor has nothing comparable in the planning stage as yet.

Conclusions

(1) The most immediate problems currently facing the Scandinavian labor unions are those arising from inflation. The high marginal tax rates that confront the average worker necessitate close integration of fiscal policy and collective bargaining. An incomes policy, formal or informal, seems inescapable. The longstanding problem of wage drift has been exacerbated by inflation.

(2) There seems to be a growing conviction on the part of union leaders that a greater share of the national income must be paid to currently productive members of society in the form of personally disposable income. Egalitarianism can no longer be promoted through expansion of the government sector. This does not mean that the welfare state must come to an end, only that it may have to stop growing.

(3) Concern with health and safety on the job is increasing. However, whether the much publicized experiments with new job arrangements will lead to economically viable solutions is still an open question.

(4) Codetermination is of recent origin in Scandinavia, and it is too soon to predict its impact on decision making within enterprises. Employer reaction has thus far been generally favorable.

(5) The schemes for economic democracy that are in the offing have great potential for bringing about fundamental change in the control of enterprises. The recent Swedish pension fund investment in corporate equities may be the opening wedge for this movement.

(6) The Scandinavian collective bargaining systems have been justly famous for their efficiency and stability. There has been a growing tendency, however, to resort to legislative action through allied political parties when bargaining fails to yield the desired results. It remains to be seen whether the flexibility of employers and the responsibility of trade union leadership will be sufficient to preserve a set of institutions that has served Scandinavia so well for half a century or more.

Twenty-five years ago in a study of Scandinavian unionism, I wrote, "the small nations that comprise the Scandinavian area constitute a social laboratory for the Western world." [40] This is even more true today than it was then.

---

[40] Walter Galenson, *Labor in Norway* (Cambridge: Harvard University Press, 1949), p. 1.

CONTRIBUTORS

ERIK ALLARDT is research professor at the Academy of Finland and has taught sociology at several major universities in the United States. He is chief editor of *Scandinavian Political Studies* and has written several books in Swedish and Finnish, as well as coediting *Mass Politics: Studies of Comparative Political Sociology.*

OLE BORRE is professor of political sociology at the Institute of Political Science, Århus University, Denmark. In 1970–71 he visited the Survey Research Center at the University of Michigan. A specialist in survey research dealing with voting behavior, he is the coauthor of two books on the ecology of electoral behavior in Denmark and has contributed to *Scandinavian Political Studies.*

WALTER GALENSON is professor of economics and industrial relations at Cornell University. His published work investigates labor issues in the United States, the Soviet Union, and the People's Republic of China as well as Scandinavia. He is the author of *Labor in Norway, The Danish System of Labor Relations,* and *Trade Union Democracy in Western Europe.*

WILLY MARTINUSSEN is professor of sociology at the University of Trondheim, Norway. During 1967–68 he was associated with the Survey Research Center at the University of Michigan, and in 1972 he became research director of the Institute for Social Research, Oslo. He is an editor of the *Norwegian Journal of Social Research* and author and coauthor of several books in Norwegian.

GÖRAN OHLIN is professor of economics at the University of Uppsala, Sweden. He has taught at Stanford and Columbia Universities, and from 1966 to 1969 he was a senior economist for the Federation of

Swedish Industries. His publications have focused on development economics, economic policy, and economic history.

Bo Särlvik is professor of government at the University of Essex. Formerly a research associate in political science at the University of Göteborg, Sweden, he has also been a visiting fellow at the Institute for Social Research of the University of Michigan. His major publications include *Electoral Behavior in the Swedish Multiparty System*. Recently his research and writing have focused on British electoral behavior.

Steen Sauerberg is associate professor at the Institute of Political Studies of the University of Copenhagen. He has worked in media research both in universities and outside them and has published on subjects such as political apathy, the impact and history of research in Danish radio, voting behavior and mass communication, and Scandinavian political broadcasting policies.

Daniel Tarschys is a research associate in political science at the University of Stockholm. He holds a law degree and a Ph.D. from the University of Stockholm as well as a Ph.D. from Princeton University. He is a frequent contributor to Swedish newspapers and author of a number of books including *Beyond the State: The Future Polity in Classical and Soviet Marxism*.

Niels Thomsen is professor of modern history at the University of Copenhagen. He is the editor of *Pressens Årbog* [Yearbook of the press] and author of books and articles on the history and the political and economic structure of the Danish press. He has also served on the Danish Press Commission and the media committees of the Council of Europe.

Carl G. Uhr has been professor of economics at the University of California, Riverside, since 1954. Formerly an economist for various state and federal agencies, he has taught and conducted research in Australia, Finland, and Sweden. His published works include *Economic Doctrines of Knut Wicksell*, *Sweden's Social Security System*, and *Economic Doctrines of David Davidson*.

Henry Valen is professor of political science at the University of Oslo. He has spent several years at the Survey Research Center of the University of Michigan and other universities in the United States and England. With Professor Stein Rokkan, he launched a large-scale program of electoral research in 1956 which is still underway. He is the coauthor of *Political Parties in Norway*.

INDEX

Abortion: 54–60, 66–70
Access to media: *see* Equal time rule
Aftonbladet (Stockholm): 201–202, 206
Age of voters:
  and party affiliation: 16, 48–50, 53, 95–96
  and radical socialist parties: 134–135, 138–148
Agrarian Center party (Norway): *see* Center (Agrarian) party (Norway)
Agrarian Liberal party (Denmark): 3n, 6, 7, 28
  bases of support: 4, 16–17
  comparative tables: 5, 13, 15, 24
  since 1973: 9–11, 12–14
Agriculture: 221–222, 224, 231–232, 235–236
  subsidies: 222, 236
Ahlmark, Per: 127
Alienation (Political): *see* Distrust of government
Alienation (Psychological): 155–161
Anders Lange's party (Norway): 40
  election results, 1973: 42 (table), 43, 44n
  issue positions: 56, 58, 60, 64–71 (tables p. 55, 59, 65, 69–70)
Arbeiderpartiet: see Labor party (Norway)
Aspengren, Tor (cited): 281

B.T. (Copenhagen): 201, 208
Baunsgaard, Hilmar: 7, 23
Berlingske Tidende (Copenhagen): 203
Bohman, Gösta: 127

Boards of directors (Employee representation): 289–290
Bourgeois parties: *see* Nonsocialist parties

Cabinet formation (Sweden): 126–128
Center (Agrarian) party (Norway): 39n, 41, 46, 52
  election results (1973): 42 (table), 43, 44n
  issue positions: 56, 58, 61, 63–71 (tables p. 55, 59, 65, 69–70)
Center Democratic party (Denmark): 3n, 9, 10, 11, 22, 197
Center party (Sweden): 73n, 124–126, 264
  and nonsocialist bloc: 75–76, 87, 115–119
  and Social Democratic party: 75, 76, 82, 84–87
  comparative tables: 83, 86, 96, 100–101, 102–103, 104, 106, 108–109, 114
  election returns: 74 (table), 75, 90, 116 (table)
  in governing coalition: 127–129
  voter preferences, social bases: 84–85, 86, 87, 89, 90, 96
Centerpartiet: see Center party (Sweden)
Centrumdemokraterne: see Center Democratic party (Denmark)
Christian People's party (Denmark): 3n, 9, 10, 12
Christian People's party (Norway): 39n, 41, 46, 52
  election results: 42 (table), 43, 44n

issue positions: 56, 58, 60, 62, 63–71 (tables p. 55, 59, 65, 69–70)
Civil Service and Salaried Employees Organization (FTF) (Denmark): 271, 272 (table)
Class conflict: 163–167, 166 (table), 251
Codetermination: 288–292, 295
Collective bargaining: 283–286
Comintern:
and Scandinavian socialist parties: 133, 135
Communist parties: 133–134, 148
and New Left: 139, 142–145
and U.S.S.R.: 136, 141, 152
newspapers: 184
Communist party (Denmark): 4, 9, 11, 134, 143, 273
Communist party (Norway): 40, 41, 134
Communist party (Sweden): 73n, 137–138
and radical youth: 96, 143, 147–148
and Social Democratic government: 78–80, 147–148, 265
comparative tables: 83, 86, 96, 100–101, 102–103, 104, 106, 108–109, 114
election returns: 74 (table), 75, 77, 115, 116 (table), 133
voter preferences, social base: 84, 88, 93, 95–96, 125
Concentration of industry (Sweden): 258–259
Conservative party (Denmark): 3n, 4, 7, 10, 11, 23, 28
Conservative party (Norway): 39n, 41
election results: 42 (table), 43, 44n
issue positions: 56, 57, 58, 60, 61, 62–65, 67–71 (tables p. 55, 59, 65, 69–70)
Corporate income tax (Sweden): 255, 259–260

Dagbladet (Oslo): 201, 203, 206
Dagens Nyheter (Stockholm): 203
Danish Federation of Labor: 271, 272 (table), 284
Danmarks Radio: 194, 196, 197, 198
Democratic League for the People of Finland: 134n
Danmarks Retsforbund: see Justice (Single-Tax) party (Denmark)
De Uafhaengige: see Independent party (Denmark)

Denmarks Kommunistiske Parti: see Communist party (Denmark)
Det Nye Folkepartiet: see New People's party (Norway)
Deviant behavior: 26, 155
Distrust of government: 30–37, 113, 114 (table)

Economic development and structural change (1919–1973): 219–237
Economic growth rates: 219, 225–233, 237, 238–239, 240, 248, 267–268
tables: 227, 230, 268, 269
Education of voters: 16–17, 46–50, 53, 146–147
"Eisenhower hypothesis": 155–156, 157
Ekstrabladet (Copenhagen): 201, 207, 208
Election of 1975 (Denmark): 11
Election of 1976 (Sweden): 115–129
Election returns (tables):
Denmark (1953–1975): 5
Norway (1945–1973): 42
Sweden (1952–1973): 74; (1976): 116
Elections of 1973: 39, 73, 81, 82
Denmark: 3, 9, 208–215
Norway: 39, 41–44, 45–71 passim
Sweden: 73, 75–76, 78
Employers' organizations: 189–190, 192, 193
Employment policies: see Manpower policies
Energy policy (Sweden): 123–124, 128
Equal time rule: 194, 198–200
European Economic Community: 153, 193
in Danish politics: 7, 8, 21–22, 27–29, 35–36
in Norwegian politics: 40, 44, 54–55, 60–71, 143–145
in Swedish politics: 105, 107, 110–111, 112
European Free Trade Association (EFTA): 110
Expressen (Stockholm): 201–202, 203

Fälldin, Törbjorn: 115–116, 123–124, 127
Farmers: 51–52, 63, 90, 161, 182
Farmers' organizations: 193, 284
Federation of Labor (Sweden): 251, 261
Finland: 134n, 196–197

Finnish minority (Sweden): 126, 136
Fishermen: 51–52, 63
Fishermen's organizations: 284
Fishing: 231–232
Folket i Bild/Kulturfront: 144
Folkpartiet: see People's party (Liberals) (Sweden)
Foreign policy:
    in Danish politics: 24–29
    in Norwegian politics: 61–67
    in Swedish politics: 105–111
Foreign workers: 271
    political participation: 126
Forestry: 231–232
Fremskridtspartiet: see Progress party (Denmark)

Geijer, Arne (cited): 282, 285
German occupation: 222–223
Gilstrup, Mogens: 8, 11–12, 26, 145, 168
    and mass media: 198, 209
Government and business (Sweden): 251, 255–256
Government expenditures: *see* Public sector consumption
Gross domestic product: tables p. 226, 227, 223–229, 230
    see also Economic growth rates
Gustavsen, Finn: 138

Hagberg, Hilding: 137, 147
Hartling, Poul: 9–11
Health insurance: 233
Health of workers: 287, 295
Hermansson, C. H.: 137, 138, 141, 148
Höjdahl, Odd (cited): 285
Housing: 22, 25, 233–234
Hoyre: see Conservative party (Norway)

Income
    per capita: 237, 251
    distribution: 245–247, 252
    equalization policy: 278–280, 286
Income tax: *see* Taxation
Incomes policies: 268–269, 283–285
Indexing (wages): 281
Industrial democracy: 25–26, 248, 252, 260–261, 264, 288–292, 295

Industrialization: 221–222
Inflation: 120, 224, 268–269, 274–275, 295
Inheritance taxes (Sweden): 259–260
"Insubstitutability" (Psychology): 156–157

Jacobsen, Erhard: 9, 145
    and mass media: 197, 198, 209
Job evaluation: 282–283
Job security: 291–292
Jorgensen, Anker: 8, 12
Justice (Single-Tax) party (Denmark): 4–5, 9, 27

Kommunistiska förbundet marxist-leninisterna, revolutionärerna: 142
Konservative Folkeparti: see Conservative party (Denmark)
Krag, Jens Otto: 7, 8, 23
Kristelig Folkeparti: see Christian People's party (Norway)
Kristeligt Folkeparti: see Christian People's party (Denmark)
Kristen Demokratisk Samling: see Christian Democratic party (Sweden)

Labor legislation (Sweden): 260–261
Labor-management relations (Sweden): 260–261, 263
Labor organizations: *see* Trade unions
Labor party (Norway): 39–40, 41–43, 44, 50–54, 133, 137
    issue positions: 57, 58, 61, 63–71 (tables p. 55, 59, 65, 69–70)
Labor supply: 239–241, 271
Lange, Anders: 40
    see also Anders Lange's party (Norway)
Language movement (Norway): 61, 66
Larsen, Aksel: 136–137, 138, 143, 148
Lay religious movement (Norway): 61, 66
Left Socialist party (Denmark): 7, 134, 148
Left-wing parties: *see* Radical socialist parties
Lewin, Leif (cited): 252
Liberal party (Norway): 40, 41, 43, 56, 62–65

comparative tables: 42, 55, 59, 65, 69–70
Liberalt Centrum: see Liberal Center party (Denmark)
Libraries: 185
Lindbeck, Assar (cited): 250
Local elections (Sweden): 125–126
Location of industry (Sweden): 254–257
Lundberg, Eric (cited): 280

Magazines: 183, 185, 187, 189
Manpower policies: 250, 253–254
    see also Regional economic development
Martinussen, Willy (cited): 156n
Marxist-Leninist Communist League Revolutionaries: 142
Mass media: 181–216
Middle classes: 52–53, 90–95
    and alienation: 159–161, 175–176
Moderata Samlingspartiet: see Moderate party (Conservatives) (Sweden)
Moderate party (Sweden): 73n, 75, 87, 89, 264
    comparative tables: 83, 86, 96, 100–101, 102–103, 104, 106, 108–109, 114, 116
Multinational corporations (Sweden): 261–262
Myrdal, Gunnar: 252

NATO: *see* North Atlantic Treaty Organization
National accounts statistics: 225, 234
National Central Bureau of Statistics (Sweden): 120–121, 125
National Pension Insurance Fund: 293
Nationalization of industry: 242, 252, 293
New Left: 138–143
    cultural influence: 140–141, 150–152
New parties: 30–31, 33, 209, 211
    and equal time rule: 198–200
New People's party (Norway): 40, 43, 56, 57, 62–65
Newspapers:
    finance and concentration: 200, 206–207, 215
    political affiliations: 181–183, 202–208 (204–205 table)

readership and influence: 184–189, 209, 211–215
Nonsocialist parties:
    Norway, 1973, shifts in voting: 44–50, 52–54
    Norway: 41
Nonsocialist parties (Scandinavian countries): 111–115
Nonsocialist party bloc (Sweden): 75–76, 81–82, 87, 122 (table)
    governing coalition: 115–119, 126–128
Norbotten (Province): 136, 138, 143, 146, 148
Norges Kommunistiske Parti: see Communist party (Norway)
Norrskensflamman: 135
Norsk Rikskringkasting (NRK): 195, 198
North (Sweden): 254–257
    see also Norbotten (Province)
North Atlantic Treaty Organization: 28, 35, 60–63, 137, 139
North Sea oil discoveries: 270
Norwegian Federation of Labor: 270, 271, 272 (table), 273, 277
Norwegian Radio Council: 195
Nuclear power plants: 123–124, 128

Occupations of voters: 16, 45–46, 50–54
Ombudsman: 199
Opinion surveys: 3–4n, 43n, 73n, 97, 120–121, 155
Organizations: 181, 182, 185, 189–194

Palme, Olof:
    as prime minister: 79, 107, 124, 152
    resignation and future role: 115, 126, 152
Party attachment and party switching: 29–34, 44–50, 81–85, 181, 210–212
Pensions: 234, 243–246, 293, 295
    Sweden: 98, 100–102 (tables), 250
People's Campaign Against the Common Market (Norway): 144
People's party (Liberals) (Sweden): 73–76, 79, 81, 86–89, 90, 264
    and Social Democratic party: 79–80, 82, 85, 87
People's Socialists: *see* Socialist People's party (Denmark); Socialist People's party (Norway)

Planning (Sweden): 253
Political parties: 111–115, 170–174, 190, 191, 192
   and newspapers: 181–182, 183, 202–208
   see also chapters on individual countries
Political participation: 30, 32–36, 156–159
   see also Voter participation
Politiken (Copenhagen): 203, 207
Population trends: 239–241
Populist movements: 144–145, 161, 168
Pospelov, Pyotr: 136
Press: see Magazines, Newspapers
Privilege (Perceived): 164–167
Progress party (Denmark): 3n, 8, 10, 11, 12–14, 16, 22, 36, 208–209
Proportional representation: 9, 76–78
Public development corporations (Sweden): 259–260
Public opinion polls: see Opinion polls
Public sector consumption: 231, 233–234, 240–248, 249–250, 274, 277

Radical Liberal party (Denmark): 3n, 4, 6, 7, 10, 11, 23, 28, 212
Radical socialist parties: 111–112, 115, 133–153
   and social democratic parties: 78, 148–150
   in Denmark: 6, 12–16, 133–134, 145
   in Norway: 39, 41, 44–50
Radikale Venstre: see Radical Liberal party (Denmark)
Radio broadcasting: 183–184, 186–187
   public control: 194–196
Radio Council (Denmark): 194–195, 196
Radio newscasts: 187, 196–198
Regional economic development: 126, 250, 254–257
   as election issue: 98, 99, 100–104 (tables), 254–257
Rehn-Meidner model: 253, 255, 258
Riksdag (Sweden): 76–77, 115, 126–127
Rural-urban migration: 223, 232, 236

Saab-Scania Report: 287–288
Safety of workers: 287, 295

Salaried Employees' Federation (TCP) (Sweden): 123, 271, 272 (table), 277, 278, 282, 286
Satisfaction and dissatisfaction: 161–174
   and political affiliation: 167–174, tables pp. 166, 169, 171, 172–173
   comparison of countries: 161–167, 175, 176
Saving and investment: 233, 234, 248, 252–253
   public sector: 242
Self-employed:
   political behavior (Norway): 53–54
Senterpartiet: see Center (Agrarian party (Norway)
Service and related industries: 232–233, 240–245
Skytte, Karl: 11
Social democratic parties: 40, 219, 111–115, 133, 134
   and trade unions: 193, 272–273, 274
   and radical socialists: 138, 130, 138–150
Social Democratic party (Denmark): 3n, 23
   and European Economic Community: 27, 28, 29
   comparative tables: 5, 13, 15, 24
   election history: 3, 9, 11, 12
   membership and support: 4, 14–16
Social Democratic party (Sweden):
   and mass media: 197, 199, 206
   and nonsocialist parties: 79–80, 82, 85–88
   and private enterprise: 250–251, 252, 263–265
   comparative tables: 83, 86, 96, 100–101, 102–103, 104, 106, 108–109, 114
   election history: 73, 74 (table), 75–78, 81ff, 90, 111–115, 116 (table)
   voter preferences, social bases: 83 (table), 84–85, 86, 90–97, 99–105
Social mobility: 17–21
Social security: 237–238, 243–245, 250
Social welfare: see Welfare policies
Socialdemokratiet: see Social Democratic party (Denmark)
Socialdemokratiska Arbetarepartiet: see Social Democratic party (Sweden)
Socialist Election Alliance (Norway): 40, 41, 144, 145
   election results, 1973: 41–44, 46, 47, 48, 50, 134

issue positions: 58–60, 61, 63–71 (tables p. 55, 59, 65, 69–70)
Socialist People's party (Denmark): 3n, 23, 28, 134, 148, 212
origin and development: 6, 7, 136–137
Socialist People's party (Norway): 39n, 40, 41, 134, 137, 149
Socialistisk Folkeparti: see Socialist People's party (Denmark)
Socioeconomic classes: 90–95, 159–161
Söder, Karin: 127
Sosialistisk Folkeparti: see Socialist People's party (Norway)
Sosialistisk Venstreparti (Socialist Left party) (Norway): 41n, 134n
Sosialistisk Valgallianse: see Socialist Election Alliance (Norway)
Standard of living: 162, 174, 177, 247–248
Statsföretag AB: 259
Stock ownership by employees: 293–295
Students: 95–96, 141–142, 145, 146–147, 151
Subsidies: 222, 235–236, 255–256
Sveriges Radio (SR): 195–196
Sveriges kommunistiska parti (Swedish Communist party): 142
Swedish Employers' Association (SAF): 275, 286, 237, 292
Swedish Federation of Labor: 123, 272
Swedish Federation of Professional Associations (SACO): 271, 272 (table), 277, 278, 279
Swedish Investment Bank: 257–258
Swedish Public Opinion Research Institute (SIFO): 121, 122, 125, 143
Sydsvenska Dagbladet (Malmö): 203

Tabloid newspapers: 181, 187, 201–202, 207, 208
Taxation: 220, 248, 250, 286
and wage levels: 245–246, 275–277
as election issue: Denmark: 22, 25, 26, 40; Norway: 54–60, 66–70; Sweden: 98–99, 100–102
Television broadcasting: 185–186, 215
and other media: 181, 206, 208, 209, 211
newscasting: 188–189, 196–198
public control: 194–196
Temperance movement (Norway): 61, 66

Trade press: 187, 192
Trade unions: 129, 251, 267–296
membership: 271, 272 (table)
political affiliations: 140, 148, 193, 273–274
political communication: 182, 189–190
Tumin, Melvin (cited): 155n

U.S.S.R.:
and Scandinavian Communist parties: 133, 136, 141, 147, 152
Unemployment and employment: 105, 120, 121–122, 270
see also Manpower policies; Regional economic development
United States:
foreign policy as political issue: 105–107, 152
Universities: *see* Students

Value-added tax: 7
Vänsterpartiet Kommunisterna: see Communist party (Sweden)
Venstre: see Agrarian Liberal party (Denmark), Liberal party (Norway)
Venstresocialisterne: see Left Socialist party (Denmark)
Verdens Gang (Oslo): 201
Vietnam War: 105, 107, 139, 152
Voter participation: 81, 125, 182

Wage drift: 280–283
Wages: 262, 268–269, 274–276
Welfare (Concept): 177–180
Welfare policies: 220, 237ff, 248, 250
as political issues: 3, 26, 40–41, 57, 70, 98, 100–102, 105
Women: 126, 182, 261, 278
Working classes: 90–95, 135–136
and alienation: 159–160, 176
and student radicals: 141–142, 145–147
Working conditions: 287–288
Workers' Information Committee (Norway): 40
Works councils: 288–289
World War II and recovery: 222–224

Youth and politics: *see* Age of voters